Valuation

The Market Approach

For other titles in the Wiley Finance Series
please see www.wiley.com/finance

Valuation

The Market Approach

Seth Bernström

Library of Congress Cataloging-in-Publication Data is available.

A catalogue record for this book is available from the British Library.

ISBN 9781118903926 (hardback)   ISBN 9781118903902 (ebk)
ISBN 9781118903896 (ebk)   ISBN 9781118903889 (obk)

Set in 10/12 pt Times by Sparks – www.sparkspublishing.com
Printed in Great Britain by TJ International Ltd, Padstow, Cornwall, UK

Contents

Acknowledgments

Acknowledgments are due to:

My colleague Rickard Wilhelmsson, who has been an invaluable source of help since the inception of this book. Rickard has not only reviewed the manuscript many times, but has also been my constant source for testing the book's reasoning, logic and structure throughout the process. Our discussions on how to handle various valuation issues over the years we have worked together, not only in the context of this book, have contributed immensely to the emergence of this text.

I'm also deeply indebted to all my other PwC colleagues, both in my own office as well as abroad, who over the years have contributed with both vivid discussions and great insights that have had a great impact on me.

I would moreover like to extend thanks to Tomas Sörensson at KTH Royal Institute of Technology in Stockholm. Tomas' comments on the manuscript have brought great value. Additionally, I would like to thank Tomas for persuading me to teach at KTH. Tomas was keen to respond to the students' continuous requests to supplement the teachings of the DCF with an in-depth attention and review of the market approach. The great interest and dedication shown by the students for this topic over the years has influenced me greatly.

I'd also like to thank the outstanding team at Wiley. Werner Coetzee, my acquisition editor, was always accessible and the consummate professional. He never wavered in his support for my vision, and provided strong leadership throughout the process. To Jennie Kitchin, Carly Hounsome, Lori Laker, Wendy Alexander and the rest of the team at John Wiley & Sons, who have done an outstanding job to shepherd the book through its production process. Also, Richard Walshe (of Prufrock) and Tom Fryer (of Sparks Publishing Services) for working wonders with the text and the structure of the book. I owe you all great thanks.

Introduction

The market approach is in practice, i.e. in the "real world," by far the most widespread valuation methodology. In spite of this, the methodology has been and continues to be more or less neglected in the present body of literature. The reason that the methodology is, from a literary perspective, overlooked by academics as well as practitioners is most likely because it is generally considered, in relation to the very well-considered discounted cash flow methodology, to be a bit too simple.

The fact that the methodology is generally considered, compared with the discounted cash flow methodology, as simple should also be the reason for its popularity. Who among us has not taken the average or median value multiple, e.g. the average or median P/E or P/S ratio, from a peer group of listed companies, applied it to the relevant base metric of the valuation subject in question and taken the result to be its market value of equity? Moreover, it is not uncommon in different contexts to be told that a certain type of company, or a certain kind of business enterprise, in a given industry should be valued at, say, ten times its operating earnings (EV/EBIT 10x), 1.5 times its book value of equity (P/BV 1.5x), $0.5 million per consultant, etc. We can illustrate this problem further using the following created example:

XYZ Corporate Finance has estimated the fair market value of 100 percent of the common shares, i.e. the fair market value of equity, in the retail company ABC Corp. In order to minimize the risk of erroneous conclusions due to extreme values and other types of "anomalies," we have used a variety of generally accepted valuation methods and models. Based on these methods and models we assess the fair market value of 100 percent of the shares in ABC Corp at $507 million. The results of our analysis are summarized in Figure I.1.

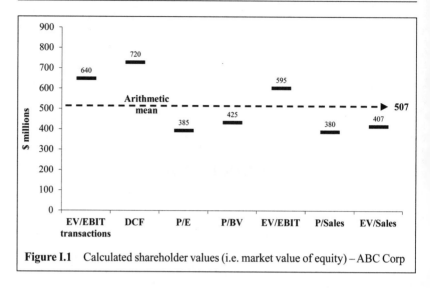

Figure I.1   Calculated shareholder values (i.e. market value of equity) – ABC Corp

So what is the problem? Does this valuation not appear to be straightforward as well as thorough? The problem is that the fair market value of ABC Corp is likely to be more or less anything *but* $507 million. Certainly, the market approach can at first glance be perceived as simple. However, as we shall see later in this book, unfortunately it is deceptively simple. The rest of this book will, in one form or another, take apart the XYZ valuation of ABC Corp piece by piece.

The chief purpose of this book is that of practice, i.e. to provide a hands-on tool for valuation using the market approach. Notwithstanding this, the value of that taught practice is rendered useless if not accompanied by a substantiated, clear-cut explanation or rationalization (giving you as a reader enough information to let you make up your own mind about the subject matter(s) at hand). Arbitrary adjustments and statements like "that's just theory, this is how you do it in real life" will not fly either in this book or real life (just try that in a negotiation or in a court of law!). Hence, if you cannot explain *exactly* how and why you have reached your conclusion (that is, if your reasoning and conclusions are neither transparent nor commonsensical), the value of such conclusion(s) is zero. To put it in even simpler terms: if I don't understand it, I won't buy it. Consequently, although the purpose of this book is not theory, no adjustment and no conclusion will be allowed without the support of thorough theoretical and commonsensical reasoning.

Chapters 1–2 provide an introduction and overview of business valuation methodologies, standards of value and the issue of marketability and control. Chapters 3–4 deal with the peer group composition. Chapter 5 addresses the relationship between enterprise value and equity value. The relationship is straightforward yet very important in order to appreciate the subsequent chapters. Chapters 6–7 provide a description of some common value multiples and their accompanying value drivers. In Chapters 8–10 we use a case study to follow the valuation of a fictitious engineering company, Engineering Corp. These chapters are at the heart of the matter and summarize in a concrete and practical manner the technical and theoretical review that we carry out in Chapters 1–7.

I suggest that the reader first reads this book from cover to cover in order to get an overview of the individual parts as well as their relationship to each other, and then goes back to those sections in which they wish to immerse themselves.

I would also like to draw it to the reader's attention that financial terms and ratios are not in any way protected by design rights. Hence there are myriad different concepts and definitions describing basically the exact same variables and parameters. Consequently, terms and key ratios of the same name may represent different things to different players. For that reason, I will try my utmost to define exactly what I mean when I build or refer to a specific term or ratio.

1
Corporate Valuation

In essence, there are three generally accepted methods of valuation: the discounted cash flow approach, the market approach, and the net asset approach. This book deals with the market approach. However, a common misconception is that these three concepts represent three fundamentally disparate or independent methodologies that, applied to the same subject of interest by the same analyst under the same valuation purpose, should or may generate three fundamentally different outcomes. *This is not the case.* Carried out correctly, a business valuation (under an assumption of continued pursuit of activities, i.e. under a going concern assumption), given a single well-defined subject and valuation purpose, shall in theory *as well as in practice* produce *exactly* the same output (i.e. value) irrespective of the model(s) utilized. To put it another way, *company value is driven by company fundamentals, not by the choice of valuation model(s).*

From a strictly theoretical perspective, the value of a company (or any other cash flow generating asset for that matter) will equal its projected future returns discounted to a present value by a risk-adjusted rate of return. This relationship will hold regardless of the methodology or methodologies used to derive that value. Hence the three methodologies presented above express exactly the same thing, but in three totally different ways. In order to fully appreciate the concept and structure of the market approach it is vital to recognize the fundamentals of the other two methodologies in isolation as well as in conjunction with each other. Set out below is a brief introduction to these three methodologies.

1.1 THE DISCOUNTED CASH FLOW APPROACH

The discounted cash flow approach (DCF) aims to establish the net present value of a cash flow generating asset (e.g. a company) by discounting its future expected returns with an appropriate required rate of return.

Performing business valuations, the cash flow which forms the basis of the net present value calculation is usually the "free cash flow to firm" (FCFF), explicitly the expected cash flow of the business independent of its financing (i.e. cash flow accruing to the company's shareholders and lenders). Consequently, the cash flow in question should not be affected by such things as interest or dividends; however, it will be burdened by tax. Hence, the discount rate must reflect a weighted cost of capital for debt and equity financing after tax. A discounting (i.e. a net present value calculation) of the expected cash flow at the appropriate weighted average cost of capital will give the value of the business enterprise (i.e. the market value of operating capital or, alternatively, the market value of invested capital).

To obtain the value of the shares, i.e. the value of the equity, the business enterprise value needs to be adjusted by the net debt position at the valuation date, i.e. subtracting financial liabilities, and including excess cash and non-operating assets.

It is also possible to compute the equity value, i.e. the market value of all shares, via a direct approach, that is, by projecting future cash flow specifically attributable to the shareholders of the company, free cash flow to equity (FCFE). Such cash flow has already been charged with financial items (interest and suchlike) and should accordingly be discounted by a matching rate of return (specifically a required return on equity). Hence, discounting this cash flow at the appropriate capital cost of equity therefore gives the equity value directly.

1.2   THE MARKET APPROACH

The market approach aims to derive the value of a company based on how similar firms are priced on the stock exchange or through company transactions.

Using the market approach, price-related indicators such as price in relation to sales, earnings, number of employees, etc. are utilized. Consequently, the pricing of the valuation subject will implicitly be dependent upon other actors' assessment of future growth potential, profitability, risk profile (cost of capital), etc. for the valuation subject in question, which may or may not be appropriate.

The task is therefore to find comparables with as similar a structure and operations as possible to the company in question. Differences between the comparator group of companies and the valuation subject at issue as regards the size and nature of their operations, among other things, will justify correspondingly different levels of business risk, growth potential, margins, etc. These differences must therefore be considered when justifying different levels of value, i.e. when justifying the relevant or appropriate value multiple to be applied to the subject company.

1.3   THE NET ASSET APPROACH

The net asset approach implies an adjustment of the balance sheet with regard to the market value of assets and liabilities. The net asset approach is often cited as an independent valuation method, but given an assumption of ongoing business operations, i.e. a going concern assumption, a proper implementation will, in order to properly capture the value of the subject company's intangible assets, and synergies among assets, normally require the use of several DCF calculations. Consequently, fully executed, the concluding value derived from the net asset approach under a going concern assumption will, to the dollar, match that derived by the DCF approach.

Often a simplified form of the net asset approach, where only book tangible and intangible assets and liabilities are adjusted to their market value equivalents, is applied. The net asset value thus calculated can then be used as a basis for comparison and reconciliation of the DCF value. The difference between the simplified net asset value above and the DCF value may then be deemed to represent the value of non-book intangible assets including goodwill.

2

What Value?

A common misconception is that, in the world of business valuation, only one single universal value exists. Unfortunately that is not the case. There is a whole variety of different types of values available as well as definitions of value. For this reason, before even working on any spreadsheets, it is very important to clearly define what value we are looking for and why.

2.1 STANDARD OF VALUES

As indicated above, there is a vast number of generally accepted standards of value. The most common when working with unlisted companies are:

- fair value[1]
- fair market value[2]
- investment value.

Fair value and fair market value may, in a broad context, be categorized under the umbrella term "market value."

The market value aims to define or describe the subject interest from a "neutral" value perspective; in other words, the value shall reflect a well-informed financial investor's point of view. This implies a value equivalent to a transfer of the shares, or the business enterprise entity should that be the case, in an open and unregulated market between a rational seller and a prudent buyer with no coercion and when both parties have access to equivalent and relevant information. The value remains free from any type of extra or additional synergistic values or premiums (strategy, economies of scale, acquisition of market shares, etc.) which are likely to benefit only one, or a certain group of, specific investor(s).

---

[1] For legal purposes, the fair value definition varies from jurisdiction to jurisdiction. In International Financial Reporting Standards (IFRS), fair value is defined as "The amount for which an asset could be exchanged, or a liability settled, between knowledgeable, willing parties in an arm's length transaction" (IFRS 3, Business Combinations, Appendix A, Defined terms).

[2] Fair market value is defined by The American Society of Appraisers as "The price, expressed in terms of cash equivalents, at which property would change hands between a hypothetical willing and able buyer and a hypothetical willing and able seller, acting at arm's length in an open and unrestricted market, when neither is under compulsion to buy or sell and when both have reasonable knowledge of the relevant facts." (American Society of Appraisers, Business Valuation Standards, Definitions).

Investment value represents the value for an explicit investor and therefore includes premiums that can be realized by only one, or maybe a small class of, specific investor(s) through various types of synergy. The values of synergies hence make the difference between the estimated market value as defined above and the investment value.

The market approach, based on quotes derived from publicly traded shares, is particularly handy when making use of the fair value or the fair market value standard of value.

On the other hand, should the valuation be based on multiples derived from transactions (listed as well as unlisted companies) rather than publicly traded shares as above, one should be aware that these multiples may include a variety of premiums and discounts of different nature and size (see the "Transactions" section for information on the factors that can give rise to these premiums and discounts).

The actual price paid for acquired companies may thus be based on factors and synergies that only those specific purchasers were able to identify and/or assimilate. Consequently, financial investors, who cannot assimilate these kinds of synergies, cannot pay such premiums either. The value of the subject interest as derived from a transaction-related multiple may thus run the risk of reflecting the value of (i.e. the prevailing conditions for) that particular peer during that particular transaction rather than the more "neutral" market value set by a well-informed financial investor (in other words, the valuation subject will be given the investment value of that particular peer as acquired by that particular purchaser at that specific point in time rather than the market value as defined above).

On the flip side of the coin, value multiples derived from normal stock trading in public companies are accordingly not appropriate for the valuation of synergy-fueled acquisitions. As these investors may be able to realize synergies that financial investors cannot take advantage of, they may also have the opportunity to realize values that a financial investor cannot take advantage of.

Logically, then, should not multiples derived from company transactions be appropriate for value derivation when considering an acquisition or disposal of a majority stake (in which it can be considered to be scope for synergies)? Although multiples derived from transactions often involve the value of synergies, these are unlikely to be identical to that of your specific position/acquisition. Hence caution needs to be exercised when using value multiples derived from company transactions data (more on this later).

Consequently, if one wants a valuation from a specific investor's point of view (i.e. a valuation including various kinds of synergies), a DCF approach is recommended instead. In this case, the DCF valuation can be tailored to the specific circumstances and conditions of the specific company or acquisition.

2.2 MARKETABILITY AND CONTROL

We move on to what is, within the framework of valuation, an extraordinarily complex issue that can have a significant impact in terms of value if handled incorrectly:

1. What level of marketability and ownership interest does the equity stake at issue embody? The identical share, in a given company, may hold different values depending on the ownership interest and level of marketability associated with just that particular share.
2. What adjustments are required to recalculate the resultant value, based on its present given ownership interest and marketability, to the level of ownership interest and marketability that one de facto wants it to represent?

2.2.1 Marketability (liquidity)

The value of an individual share, in the form of a minority interest stake, in a given unlisted company (i.e. a non-marketable minority interest) is lower than that of an equivalent single share of a publicly listed company (i.e. a marketable minority interest), all else being equal. This is because a minority stake in an unlisted company may be very difficult to divest – in many cases perhaps even unsaleable – as interest in the share among stakeholders other than the company's current (often very limited) group of shareholders may be close to non-existent (i.e. there is no public market for the shares in question, and so the individual owner must himself find a buyer and negotiate an appropriate selling price for the share/equity stake in question). Equivalent listed shares can, on the other hand, normally be sold and transformed into cash more or less instantaneously (assuming, of course, that the shares in question trade fairly frequently).

2.2.2 Control

The lower value per share as indicated above applies only to a single share in the form of a non-marketable minority interest (i.e. a minority shareholding in an unlisted company) vis-à-vis an equivalent share in the form of a marketable minority interest (i.e. a minority shareholding in a *listed* company). The imaginary value of this individual unlisted share, in the form of a non-marketable minority interest, multiplied by the number of outstanding shares, does *not,* however, give the value of the company if you are that company's sole proprietor (i.e. if you are sitting on a non-marketable *majority* interest).

Just as a rational investor is willing to pay more for a stock that is liquid, compared with a corresponding illiquid one, all else being equal, the same rational investor is willing to pay more for a stock that provides control vis-à-vis a corresponding one that does not, all else being equal. The right or option to influence the strategy, management policy, capital structure, salaries, and allowances of senior executives, dividend policy, listing policy, etc. of the company in question in general represents considerable value. This is evident if not in context with buy-out acquisitions where acquirers often pay a significant premium for the right of control.[3] It is rare to find premiums being offered for listed minority interests (and should someone do that, it would most likely be a minority interest that, together with the bidder's other possessions, would give rise to some form of controlling interest). Hence, the value of the one and the same type of share in a given unlisted company is therefore higher if it is part of a larger controlling stake as compared to that exact same share as part of a stake containing only one or a few shares.

In its most basic form there are four different combinations of ownership interest and marketability:

1. a marketable majority interest
2. a marketable minority interest
3. a non-marketable majority interest
4. a non-marketable minority interest.

The connection between these four positions is illustrated in Figure 2.1.

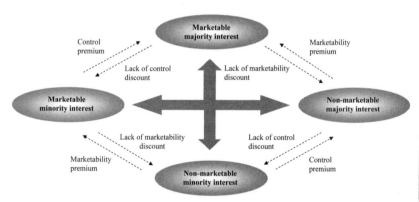

Figure 2.1   Different levels/combinations of ownership and marketability

---

[3] Note though that these premiums often contain, in addition to that of the right to control, extensive expected synergy gains.

2.2.3   Adjusting for marketability and control

In addition to a strict classification of each position, in accordance with the description above, it is also important to emphasize that utilization of different valuation methods and models, and different assumptions regarding input data of these methods and models, can result in different characteristics in terms of ownership and marketability. This may in turn cause the exact same share to be assigned different values depending on no more than the choice of valuation methodology and/or input data. An analyst/appraiser under a well-defined assignment must therefore keep track of his or her actions when he or she derives the value of a company based on a mixture of methods and models.

That a 100 percent ownership of a company's shares represents a majority or a controlling interest, and that a 1 percent ownership of a company's shares represents a minority interest is, of course, obvious in the same way that an exchange-listed stock is more liquid than an equivalent unlisted one. However, should we face a situation in which adjustments would be considered necessary, i.e. if we are forced to adjust the given value(s) in order to move from a set to a desired position/definition, then how do we go about this and, if action should be necessary or is taken, at what premium/discount size/sizes, and, finally, from what basis of value(s) are we starting?

For example, an individual share in the form of a majority stake in an unlisted company (i.e. a non-marketable majority interest) is not liquid in the same way as an equivalent quoted minority share (i.e. a marketable minority interest), but it is not as illiquid as an individual share in the form of a minority stake in an unlisted company (i.e. a non-marketable minority interest). A majority owner may, of course, on his or her own initiative launch a divestment scheme. This option is usually not available to shareholders of minority interests since the majority holder, as indicated above, holds the privilege to decide upon divestment initiatives, if any. However, if the company in question is not already courted by a vast number of potential buyers, this process will take a minimum of several months to complete. The delineation as to how liquid or illiquid the non-marketable controlling interest really is may thus be discussed (i.e. subject to careful analysis). The interest in question is not as liquid as a stock market share, which can be transformed into cash in a few days, but neither is it as illiquid as an unlisted minority interest, which in turn, in its worst-case scenario, can be virtually unsaleable. The complexity of the appropriate or relevant premiums and discounts due to control and minority issues are analogous.

Normally, the chief difficulty is not to classify the category in which to position the value in question, but which adjustments and how large these need to be in order to transform a given definition of value to a desired one. The area is challenging and can bring about large premiums and discounts from the initially calculated/derived value. The direction and impact will depend upon the valuation methodology and data utilized for the initial value derivation, as well as the magnitude of any rights or restrictions associated with the interest in question (the discounts/premiums may in extreme cases be 50 percent or more in any direction). Furthermore, the size of these prospective premiums and discounts cannot normally be set by precise mathematical accuracy, but is instead subject to individual case-by-case analysis.[4]

Should the value of the subject interest be derived by way of publicly traded minority shares, typically the result is a marketable minority interest value (or, put another way, a value to which a minority share in the valuation subject would be traded if listed on a public market under going concern), i.e. a valuation in line with the left oval of Figure 2.1. The exchange-traded shares, from which the multiples of the comparables have been derived, do after all represent trading of marketable minority shares.

- Therefore, if you are about to value a listed share (i.e. a marketable minority interest) by means of multiples derived from listed comparables, e.g. if your objective is to seek over- or under-valued shares on the stock exchange using the market approach, the valuation subject and its peers will normally be on comparable basis (that is, the subject interest as well as the publicly traded comparables all represent, under normal circumstances, marketable minority interests). In other words, we will find ourselves in the same oval of Figure 2.1 at all times (that is, the oval on the left-hand side). In such contexts you normally need not make any adjustments in terms of either ownership or marketability.[5]
- If, on the other hand, you aspire to value a corresponding share in an unlisted company (i.e. a *non-marketable* minority interest), by way of value multiples derived from normal stock trading of comparables (i.e. marketable minority interests), a discount for loss of liquidity may very well be justified (i.e. we move, in Figure 2.1, from a value corresponding to the oval on the left-hand side to a value corresponding to the oval at the bottom). The discount (if any) needs to be based on a careful analysis of the variables that affect the possibility of future liquidity (whether the company in question pays dividends or not, is considering an initial public offering (IPO), is active within a transaction-intensive industry, etc.). The deduction may be

---

[4] There are, however, a number of studies to rely on when assessing appropriate discounts/premiums. For a summary of relevant studies, including various techniques for practical application, see Business Valuation Resources (2013), *BVR's Guide to Discounts for Lack of Marketability*, 5th ed., Business Valuation Resources, LLC., and Pratt, Shannon P. (2009), *Business Valuation Discounts and Premiums*, 2nd ed., John Wiley & Sons, Inc.

[5] This is, of course, given that the subject company as well as its peers trade with satisfactory liquidity.

substantial, and the range of possible outcomes might be as wide as a few percent to 50+ percent.

• Should your intention, however, be to value not a minority interest but an interest that represents a majority ownership (i.e. should you, for example, as the sole proprietor of an unlisted company, wish to get an understanding of your company's value on the basis of a non-marketable *majority* interest), certain adjustments may, if the company's value is based on value multiples derived from exchange-traded minority shares, be required. In order to move from a classification equivalent to a marketable minority interest, i.e. the value definition given by the market approach under the conditions and assumptions referred to above, to a classification equivalent to a non-marketable majority interest (note: non-marketable in relation to a publicly traded minority share), a premium for control (you gain control of the company in relation to a publicly traded minority share) and a discount for lack of marketability (you lose liquidity in relation to a publicly traded minority share) is justified. As indicated previously, the appropriate level(s) of such adjustment(s) is/are difficult to estimate and would typically require a comprehensive analysis. However, it may be the case, but does not in any way have to be so, that the discount charged for illiquidity proves equal to the premium applied for control, i.e. the justified discount for illiquidity will be cancelled out by the analogous justified premium for control. Should this be the case, the net effect will be zero, and the resultant net value adjustment will consequently be none, i.e. the value definition for non-marketable majority interest will then equal the value definition for marketable minority interest (see Figure 2.2).

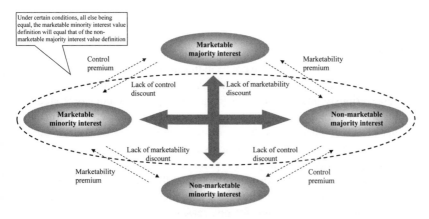

Figure 2.2   Different levels/combinations of ownership interest and marketability – marketable minority interest vs. non-marketable majority interest

What definition of value can then be assumed if instead of the above-referenced publicly traded minority shares we derive our value based on transactions of whole companies (i.e. the purchase/sale of majority stakes)? Well, this is a far tougher nut to crack. It should at least be fairly uncontroversial to assume that the resultant value should typically represent a controlling interest (although there might be several situations where even this cannot be taken for granted, see below for a more developed argument on the matter).

Notwithstanding the above, what about liquidity? It is usually not possible, over the stock exchange, to trade controlling stakes with the same liquidity as equivalent minority stakes. An at all times fully marketable majority interest will therefore exist only in theory.

However, if we are a little less rigorous and assume that a controlling stake in an unlisted company has changed hands through a structured bid or auction process, then the shareholding might be, if adding a good portion of goodwill, deemed as traded with at least a fragment of liquidity, if not in any way complete. Specifically, if a controlling interest in an unlisted company has changed hands via a structured bid process, some kind of functional liquid market may for that majority interest in question be said to have existed at least for a very short period of time. However, this "market" is by no means, as regards access to buyers and sellers acting on free will, on a par with that of exchange-traded minority shares (i.e. there was, for example, in the above-referred bid process, only one seller).

Moreover, were we to derive the value of a given company on the above basis, i.e. were we to value the subject interest based on multiples derived from the above-mentioned transaction, all else being equal, we must be aware that the resultant value will reflect conditions and circumstances of that specific transaction, i.e. we will transfer those exact premises/conditions of that exact transaction to our valuation subject in question. Specifically, all else being equal, the resultant value will represent a value at a point in time when all of the above-mentioned terms and conditions are present as well as in play. Should we at the valuation date not be in this position, i.e. should our valuation subject at that time not be in the final phase of a structured bid process with several seriously interested bidders in the running, we cannot use or credit the value multiple in question (in this case we would evidently overestimate the value of our company as we have, by using the applied transaction-derived value multiple, provided our valuation subject with features and benefits they cannot be considered to enjoy at this point in time).

We encounter the same kind of difficulty at the other end of this spectrum. Should the transaction in question have been preceded by a coercive situation, i.e. had the seller in question for one reason or another, to only one single buyer, been forced at short notice to divest, the existing transaction could not be considered representative of a marketable interest (note: when referring to "marketable" in this context, I mean as per the above section, not marketable as in regularly traded minority shares). In other words, if one derives the value of a company based on fundamentals of that particular transaction, i.e. on multiples resultant from that particular transaction, the resulting value would not be representative of a marketable interest. Additionally, referring to the aforementioned situation, it might also be relevant to question whether the transaction even reflects value of control, even though a controlling interest was transferred. As the vendor in question could not govern the transaction (i.e. he or she was at a negotiating disadvantage), he or she might thus not even have received payment for value of control.

The same type of reasoning applies to public buy-outs, i.e. when acquiring a controlling interest in a listed company. If such an offer is to stand a chance of success, one generally needs to offer a premium (to the current stock exchange price). Since stock exchange prices usually represent marketable minority interests, the bid premium (if any) would consequently represent (i.e. be embodied in the transaction-derived value multiples) the net value of control (and, possibly, potential synergies and/or streamlining opportunities as well) and the subsequent loss of liquidity (i.e. when unlisted, the shares in question would no longer carry full liquidity).

No matter what position you take (or whatever circumstances prompted the trade), multiples derived from transactions of whole companies must be handled with great care, as owing to control/marketability issues they are often associated with significant uncertainties as an effect of the more often than not undisclosed underlying terms and conditions of the sale. In addition, as indicated above, recognized synergies (e.g. cost efficiencies, a more effective use of sales channels, expansion into new markets, buy-out of competitors, etc.), might have played a noteworthy role when the transaction was priced. These factors fit well under control but have a tangible value that can be regarded as being beyond that normally meant by the term.

Finally, it should also be noted that the purchase price may have been higher or lower than the actual underlying value, depending on the bargaining power of the involved parties. In addition, the purchase price might have been driven by purely personal or emotional reasons. The desire of owner-managers to own or manage a large corporation might be so great that they consciously or unconsciously ignore basic economic relationships (who among us has not been lured into bidding out of pure prestige or devotion?) Such "black box" effects can sometimes be substantial (for further information regarding transaction-derived multiples, see the "Transactions" section below).

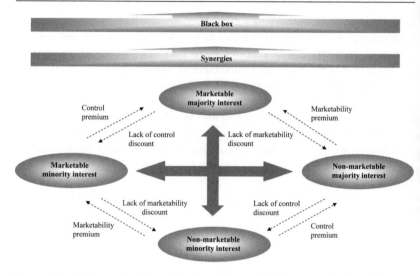

Figure 2.3   Different levels/combinations of ownership interest and marketability – synergies and "black box" effects[6]

Now it may, as a closing point of this chapter, be appropriate to link back to the initial discussion regarding fair value/fair market value vs. investment value. The four ovals above – the marketable majority interest, the marketable minority interest, the non-marketable majority interest, and the non-marketable minority interest – all generally represent/reflect different types of fair value/fair market value positions. Introducing synergies and "black box" effects into the equation would undoubtedly bring a migration to investment value territory. Fair value/fair market value represents/reflects asset value on a stand-alone basis, i.e. the benefits the asset in question can bear on its own, regardless of ownership (however – which is important to point out – different categories/classes of owners), whereas investment value represents/reflects asset value for an explicit unique owner (i.e. including additional gains, in the form of various well-defined synergies, attainable or realizable by only the particular owner in question).

---

[6] To realize synergies, operational as well as financial, some kind of control stake is typically required. However, under certain conditions companies may, on strategic/synergistic grounds, also acquire minority stakes. Hence, should a minority interest transaction take place in agreement (and in purpose initiate a future co-operation), synergistic values may be achieved even though the stake in question does not, in itself, bring control.

3

Exchange-traded Shares vs. Transactions

Generally, the peer group is composed on the basis of either exchange-traded minority shares or business entity transactions. The choice of data source is, as indicated in previous chapters, important as regards the resulting definition of output or value. Discussions regarding use of publicly traded shares or transactions in order to derive the value of a given company are therefore to a great extent associated with the foregoing discussion regarding control, liquidity, and synergies.

3.1 EXCHANGE-TRADED SHARES

When compiling a relevant peer group, exchange-listed stocks (i.e. marketable minority interests) are the most common starting point. Some points on publicly traded minority shares:

- Data is easily accessible in the form of public company reports, newspapers, television, the internet, etc. Accordingly, it is easy for anyone to access high-quality financial data, forecasts, business descriptions, etc. for the company/companies in question.
- Data is up to date at all times (stock prices are continuously updated). This provides the possibility to derive the value of the subject company or interest at any point in time.
- The market for public companies can be considered effective. Therefore observed prices may be considered to reflect all currently available public information.
- Stock market participants act on free will, i.e. in general, with no compulsion to either buy or sell shares.
- Stock market prices reflect a well-informed financial investor's point of view, i.e. the share price (that is, the value) reflects the benefits that a financial investor (in this case, a minority investor with access to a liquid market) expects to gain from the asset in question. Therefore the price is not "affected" by synergies, black box effects, etc., realizable by no other than a few very specific buyers or owners.
- Listed shares are normally fully liquid, in other words, an investor may realize his or her shareholding as cash whenever he or she wishes. The listed shares are in general therefore unaffected by marketability discounts.

- There is a wealth of listed companies in most industries and countries. As the value drivers of public and private companies do not differ (i.e. the external factors and risks in a given industry that are expected to affect the listed companies will accordingly affect the corresponding unlisted companies to the same extent), they may be valued on an equal footing. Consequently, there is always a good possibility to find a suitable reference subject.

3.2 TRANSACTIONS

Another approach when composing an appropriate peer group is to use multiples derived from company transactions. However, this is more complicated for a number of reasons. By and large, the problems are the reverse of the positive aspects of publicly traded minority shares mentioned above. Some points on transactions:

- It is difficult to access the data. Transactions mainly concern unlisted companies and since there is normally no requirement to publish data on private transactions, the consideration paid is often kept private. Moreover, it is difficult to gain a decent overview of completed transactions, i.e. they are rarely compiled and published freely in the same way as publicly traded shares.
- Independent analysts do not follow non-listed companies, meaning that forecasts of their future expected earnings are not available.
- Public disclosure is normally lower for non-listed companies than for comparable public companies (since they do not act under exactly the same set of rules and regulations); even though you should have access to the relevant transaction price, it is not certain that you can gain access to related company data (for example, annual reports, interim reports, business activity descriptions, etc.).
- Business valuation is perishable and acquisitions are stochastic. Finding corporate transactions in a particular industry at a particular point in time is often difficult. To rely on price data that may be several years out of date can lead to the risk of significant miscalculation. Should relevant value multiples of publicly traded companies in a given industry have changed in recent years, almost certainly the corresponding unlisted peers will have experienced a parallel change (all else being equal). Note that, in accordance with previous reasoning, privately held companies are subject to the same value drivers and risks as public companies.
- The size of the transaction may vary between acquisitions. Small stakes as well as 100 percent of the company may have changed hands. As discussed above, the concerned interest may have premiums applied as well as discounts. To mathematically recalculate a given value definition, e.g. to recalculate the value of a subject interest as provided by a transaction comprising

a privately held minority block of shares to a 100 percent ownership (or vice versa), can bring considerable difficulties (especially when the background of the transaction is often kept secret by the parties involved).

- There may be unknown arrangements and agreements between buyers and sellers in the share purchase agreement, making it difficult for an outsider to know whether the transaction price in question was based on agreements, warranties, and limitations that might have influenced the price in one way or another. Any additional consideration (e.g. "earn-outs") would complicate the calculations even more. In addition, unlike with liquid listed stocks, you cannot know whether the seller acted entirely with free will or not. In the case of a controlling interest transaction, there is always the possibility that a specific factor or circumstance forced the seller to sell his or her company (and maybe at a different price than if he or she could have chosen the timing and the purchaser at their leisure).

- It might be difficult to know exactly the type of assets transferred. Parts of the company's asset base may have been broken up in connection with or shortly before the acquisition in question. In the case of privately held companies, such information is often difficult to get hold of.

- The transaction may have been conducted with compensation other than cash. The selling party, for example, may have been paid in full or in part with shares or some other kind of financial instrument. Typically, investors prefer cash. The value of a transaction where the seller had been paid in cash may therefore be different from that of the seller receiving his claims in shares, for example. Moreover, should these shares be subject to some sales restriction (e.g. a lock-in clause) it is reasonable to assume that the corresponding value would be even lower.

- The transaction price may have included synergies which only that particular buyer in that specific situation and at that specific time could appreciate or assimilate. Synergies may be diverse, e.g. operational, financial, strategic, etc., and the resultant value effects may be substantial (and consequently also beyond what would normally be considered just "control"). Accordingly, the transaction price in question may hence be regarded as reflecting "investment value" (i.e. the value for a particular investor) rather than "market value" (i.e. the value for a well-informed financial investor, which would, in this case, be a controlling interest investor). Therefore, the calculated value, as derived from these transactions (i.e. the calculated value of the subject company as derived by multiples based on these transactions), will not be directly comparable with the corresponding value derived from exchange-traded stocks (i.e. the value of the subject company derived from multiples based on exchange-traded stocks).

- Finally, in accordance with the previous statement, one cannot ignore the potential presence of "black box" effects either.

An analysis of transaction-derived value multiples may, of course, also bring certain advantages; for example, listed companies are often larger and more diversified than similar private companies. As an owner (or an acquirer) of a very small, unlisted company it can therefore be interesting to take note of actual purchase prices for equally comparable unlisted small companies.[1] In addition, certain types of companies or industries may not be listed on the stock exchange, in which case the best alternative (or the only alternative in the worst case) might then be to seek relevant transaction data.

In addition, a controlling interest stakeholder in a large privately held company with the intention of divesting (and maybe even facing a concrete offer) could, by analyzing recent transactions involving comparable listed companies, gain interesting information for use in the subsequent negotiations. Any surplus value paid by industry players for a controlling interest, rather than the equivalent value of the just traded minority share, might indicate a latent additional strategic premium. If we can identify the origin of this premium (note: the net value of the premium should mainly relate to various types of synergies[2]), we may have the opportunity, even as a seller, to negotiate parts of these values.

In conclusion, it is important to carefully analyze the background of the input data in question before drawing conclusions from it. We must investigate (and adjust for) any differences between the valuation subject and the peers in a rigorous and consistent manner. You should also not mix ratios derived from business transactions with those derived from exchange-traded minority shares. Should you have access to key ratios originating from transactions as well as listed minority shares, it is advisable to separate them into two groups and conduct two separate analyses. Finally, if you are looking for the investment value (i.e. should you seek the value for a particular investor, or in other words, should you possess the opportunity to realize synergies) rather than the market value (i.e. the value for a well-informed financial investor), it is advisable to explore the discounted cash flow approach.

---

[1] It is, for example, not feasible or appropriate to derive the value of small shops, restaurants, etc. from value multiples of listed comparables. To derive the value of a small, local, privately held fast food restaurant or sports equipment producer outright from value multiples derived from large international stock market giants such as McDonald's and Nike is obviously unrealistic.

[2] Note, however, that the issue, as presented in this chapter, is highly complex. Alongside the obvious question of whether fundamentals exist at all, in the concerned valuation relative to that implicitly given by the utilized value multiple, that support an assumption of similar realizable synergies, the potential bid premium will most likely also accommodate a mixture or basket of other premiums and discounts (in essence, the previously referred to control and liquidity premiums and discounts, but it could also be black box effects, for example) that may, in relation to the conditions and assumptions applicable to the subject company, act in either direction.

4

How to Put the Peer Group Together

Selecting relevant peers is one of the most important steps in a market approach valuation. If the comparable companies are significantly different in structure and operations to that of the valuation subject, then the conclusions, of course, run the risk of being flawed.

4.1 THE SELECTION PROCESS

In most cases, it is natural to seek peers within the same geographical area and the same sector or industry as the valuation subject. If, for example, we are valuing a European car manufacturer, it would be natural to seek peers within that current pool of companies.

4.1.1 Geography

If suitable peers of immediate geographical proximity are limited, you might be forced to broaden your horizons. In such a case, the recommended approach is to seek peers in an area with general economic value drivers (and risks) that are in line with those of the area in which the valuation subject operates; for example, if valuing a Swedish service company that does not have domestic peers that are appropriate for reference, it would be better to seek supplementary peers in the rest of the Nordic region, Europe or possibly the United States rather than in India or China, for example. The variables or factors that are most relevant for China and India at any given time (e.g. the level of risk profile, maturity, interest rates, inflation, economic growth, etc.) are probably not the same, or at least not in the same phase, as the corresponding most relevant variables in Europe or the United States at the same time. As a consequence, the derived value multiples, and therefore also the resulting value conclusions, could prove inaccurate or flawed.

4.1.2 Business model

The above is, of course, not only true for geography but also for products and services offered. Two companies, however alike at a first glance (i.e. appearing to produce a more or less identical product or service in the same geographical area), may not necessarily be comparable from a market approach valuation perspective.

Let us illustrate this problem using a simple concrete example made up for the purpose (and accordingly also all too obvious!) that need not in any way correspond with reality. Let us suppose that we have been asked to value a privately held French company that manufactures propellers for boats and that we have identified a publicly traded French peer that manufactures propellers for aircraft. These two companies may appear to be a perfect match as both seem to produce pretty much the same product in the same geographical area (to a layman, a propeller is a propeller, isn't it?). However, if we reason in terms of value drivers rather than product and geography, we may identify some possible obscurities requiring a deeper analysis before moving on:

- In what specific market do these companies operate? The company producing boat propellers might specialize in recreational boats, whereas the company producing aircraft propellers might operate in commercial aviation. Maybe the business cycle for commercial aviation differs, in structure as well as in strength, from that of pleasure boats. This implies that the value multiples and value drivers derived from the peer in question might reflect a higher or lower risk exposure (as well as possibly also the top or bottom of an economic boom/recession), whereas the reverse may be the case for the valuation subject.
- What about the product mix? When searching for comparables in various databases, a brief description of the company in question can normally be found. This may state that the company in question manufactures propellers for the commercial aircraft industry. On closer investigation, however, it may prove that the company's product portfolio comprises other business areas and also perhaps even a large real estate portfolio. As a consequence, derived multiples and key ratios may reflect operations and assets of different industries and value drivers than that of the valuation subject.
- What about suppliers? Maybe the raw material used for these propellers differs between the two products. If the stress is higher and the reliability consequently has to be greater for commercial aircraft propellers than for pleasure boat propellers, the producers of the former may be more dependent on a potentially scarce resource or commodity. Moreover, a monopolistic supplier might control this scarce resource, leaving the producer in a very poor bargaining position (assuming, of course, that the supplier has alternative sales options other than to the industry or company concerned). Boat propeller manufacturers, on the other hand, may potentially produce their propellers from steel, for which there are typically a greater number of suppliers. The bargaining power and the consequent price of raw materials may then differ (or at least could potentially evolve differently) between these two industries/companies.
- What about the customers? Maybe there are, numerically, either more or fewer aircraft manufacturers than boat builders in need of propellers. This may, as in the case above, affect the producer's bargaining position either

positively or negatively. For example, if the number of propeller aircraft manufacturers has fallen in recent years and the corresponding range of aircraft propeller manufacturers has remained unchanged, while the reverse is simultaneously assumed in the pleasure boat industry, one may assume that these two industries have, at this time, quite different prospects for expected margins, growth, etc. A direct comparison between these companies (i.e. without making the proper adjustments) could therefore lead to erroneous conclusions.

- What about competitiveness in general? Are the companies fighting for market share or have a few companies established some type of monopoly or oligopoly? What about barriers to entry? For example, if the production of airplane propellers requires long and costly product development compared with the corresponding boat propeller industry, new entrants may not be such a great threat. As an result, expected growth, margins, risk, etc. between these industries may differ significantly.

- Are any of the respective industries subject to structural change? Maybe the aircraft propeller industry is experiencing the threat of substitutes. Consequently, suppose small aircraft manufacturers have begun to phase out propellers in favor of jet engines. It may be that the jet engine is faster, quieter, cleaner, and cheaper than propellers (or perhaps the reverse is true). If the boat propeller industry does not experience exactly the same pressure to change (or exactly the same threat of substitutes), a direct comparison between these two companies could again give rise to erroneous conclusions.

- What about geography? In what countries does the company in question operate? Manufacturers of aircraft propellers may operate globally, whereas boat propeller manufacturers may operate locally. This could bring advantages as well as disadvantages. A global company might benefit from positive risk diversification effects (i.e. an economic downturn in one part of the world may be offset by a corresponding upturn in another region). Local businesses, which may only operate in one or perhaps two countries, could conversely be more vulnerable to sudden local changes. However, local companies may also, as a consequence, have more or less infinite growth opportunities as they have not yet expanded internationally.

In the case of such a conflict, whether one should give priority to geographical proximity or similar business model is a trade-off. There is no 100 percent right or wrong answer to these questions; instead it is up to the analyst concerned to assess and justify on a case-by-case basis.

It should also be clarified that geography and business model as relevant selection criteria do not need to be universally prevailing in any way. It is up to the analyst to decide and justify relevant appropriate selection criteria, which can be more or less anything under the sun (size and risk profile, category of customers, addressable market, maturity, etc.), provided that the criteria can be explained and justified in a transparent and credible manner.

Finally, if the subject company's operations or, alternatively, its offered products or services are perceived as unique and no listed companies can be deemed as comparable, one may be forced to search for comparables outside the company's prevailing sector or industry. In such a case, one would preferably seek peers in a different sector or industry, but one subject to the same value drivers and external factors as the valuation subject; which, as indicated by the case of the French propeller manufacturers, thus also applies when considering peers of the same industry affiliation. Therefore, when selecting appropriate peers it is always paramount to reason in terms of value drivers rather than in terms of products and services.

4.2   HOW MANY COMPARABLES?

In general, it is clearly better to have more companies than fewer. However, one might need, when composing a peer group, to consider a few factors and circumstances that can have great impact on the outcome.

The number of companies needed is, in essence, a product of comparability. If you can find decent enough peers (not only in terms of structure and operations, but also as regards the quality of data that can be derived from them) then you can make do with just a few, but if you only come across less good ones then you would typically require more.

If good peers can be identified, a group of 5–10 companies might be a good starting point. There is no lower limit, but the sample should generally not be too narrow. Basing an analysis on only one or a few comparable companies is risky because some very company-specific factor(s) of the individual peer(s) could disproportionately affect the derived value of the valuation target.

In those rare cases where you can identify a great number of comparables, you can narrow the peer group down based on comparability. If you can identify more than 15 peers, there may be reason to eliminate the least comparable companies based on business offering, size, category of customer, suppliers, etc.

4.3   ANALYZING THE HISTORY

Historical analysis aims to present and explain a company's historical operating and financial performance as a basis for forecasting.

The most common time period for analysis of historical data is generally about 3–5 years. However, this is not universal – an individual assessment should be made on a case-by-case basis. The analyzed period should match the time series for which representative and relevant data are available. For companies sensitive to economic fluctuations, data on growth, margins, capital expenditure, etc. should cover a full business cycle. In such cases it may therefore be justified to increase the analyzed period. In contrast, should the industry or the concerned company/companies have recently undergone extensive structural changes, it may instead be relevant to shorten the analyzed period to cover only the subsequent period. What matters is not the actual length per se but that the period in question represents that company's or industry's future growth and earnings potential.

At times you may also need to make adjustments for items affecting comparability. If the data of the valuation subject, or any of the reference companies for that matter, have varied significantly in a given year for one reason or another (that may, additionally, be deemed as one-off or non-recurring effects) it may be appropriate to exclude these items from the analysis. However, this does not necessarily mean you should generally exclude all of the bad years and all of the great losses from the time series. Any normal business operation will, from time to time, suffer from various unforeseen costs and restructuring. Consistent exclusion of all historically bad decisions and temporary cost items could lead to a significant overstatement of the company's or the industry's future growth and earnings potential. What is extraordinary and what is part of a company's or an industry's normal business activities is debatable, but whatever route you choose to take, you should report the items identified and state the way in which you have chosen to deal with them.

In general, the type of adjustments carried out on the valuation subject should also be applied to the peers. Common adjustments include:

- adjusting for non-recurring items
- adjusting for non-operating items
- adjusting for income or expense items not in tune with market conditions
- putting the valuation subject and its peers on an equal footing as regards accounting principles (for example, adjusting for differences in the amortization of tangible and intangible assets and the handling of goodwill)
- adjusting for differences between the valuation subject and its peers in terms of the handling of leases (operational leasing vs. financial leasing)
- adjusting for acquired, divested or terminated businesses.

5

Market Value of Equity vs. Market Value of Operating/Invested Capital

What is to be valued: the equity capital or the operating/invested capital?

5.1 MARKET VALUE OF EQUITY

The equity market value or, alternatively, the market value of all outstanding shares (the market capitalization for companies listed on a stock exchange) is generally represented by the letter P (Price).

5.2 MARKET VALUE OF OPERATING/INVESTED CAPITAL

The market value of operating capital or, alternatively, the market value of invested capital, refers to the market value of the business operations as a whole (i.e. the entire capital structure, not just the market value of the equity as above), and so represents the value of the business enterprise in its entirety.

When applying the market approach, the market value of operating/invested capital is usually expressed using one of the following three terms: EV (enterprise value), MVIC (market value of invested capital) or PA (price assets). Consequently, when the enterprise value (i.e. the EV) of a company is referred to here, it refers to the market value of its operating/invested capital. Figure 5.1 illustrates the link between the market value of operating/invested capital, i.e. the enterprise value, on the asset side and the market value of operating/invested capital, i.e. the enterprise value, on the liability side (note: from now on, the terms "operating capital" and "invested capital" are interchangeable).[1]

---

[1] Note, however, that the operating/invested capital term can mean different things to different people depending on which definition is currently deemed appropriate. The difference in chosen definition is not arbitrary though; it is subject to instead relatively constrained boundaries. Thus, regardless of the chosen definition, the term "operating capital" or alternatively "invested capital" refers to the value of the company's operations or, alternatively, the company's capital structure. What falls within the concept of financial debt (total financial debt – less cash – net of cash and financial assets – net of only excess cash, etc.) may be discussed, however. As the terms EV, MVIC, and PA mirror those of the above-mentioned operating/invested capital expression, the definition issues as stated above stand, i.e. these terms can, within certain predetermined boundaries, mean different things to different people. In this book, the definition of interest-bearing net debt equals that of short- and long-term interest-bearing debt less cash, cash equivalents, and financial assets. At times a company may, for various reasons, keep more cash and cash equivalents than its business operations require. To eliminate any effects of such latent decisions, it may be advisable to use net financial debt as a point of reference.

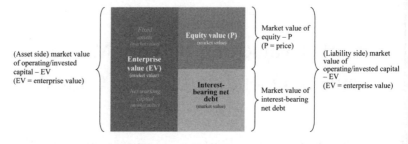

Figure 5.1   Enterprise value (i.e. market value of operating/invested capital) vs. shareholders' value (i.e. market value of equity)

Let us now illustrate the relationship between the *market value* of operating/invested capital (enterprise value – EV) and equity (price – P), respectively, as defined above and the corresponding *book value* of operating/invested capital (book enterprise value – BEV) and equity (book value of equity – BV), respectively.

Figure 5.2 shows these relationships for the fictitious Chinese company XYZ Group.

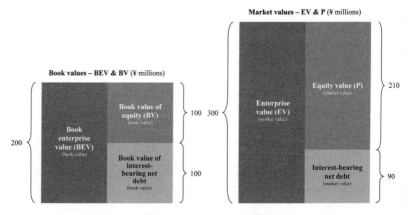

Figure 5.2   XYZ Group – operating/invested capital vs. equity capital, and book value vs. market value, respectively

What is the difference? We will start at square one. Table 5.1 shows the total assets of XYZ Group (specifically, book values).

Table 5.1   XYZ Group – balance sheet as per last fiscal year

XYZ Group Balance sheet (¥ millions)	LFY
Intangible assets	40
Tangible assets	130
Fixed assets	**170**
Inventories	20
Accounts receivable	40
Cash & cash equivalents	20
Current assets	**80**
TOTAL ASSETS	**250**
Equity	**100**
Long-term borrowings	80
Short-term borrowings	40
Interest-bearing debt	**120**
Accounts payable	20
Other current liabilities	10
Current liabilities	**30**
TOTAL EQUITY & LIABILITIES	**250**

In Figure 5.3, we show the exact same figures as per a "cube-shaped" arrangement. That is, we have split the balance sheet from Table 5.1 into an assets side and a liability side.

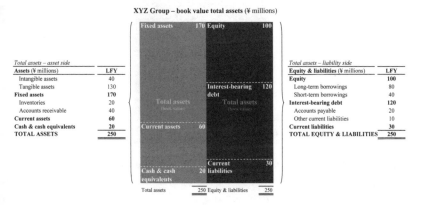

Figure 5.3   XYZ Group – total assets and its funding

In order to illustrate how to get from book value of total assets to book value of operating assets (i.e. book value of operating/invested capital), we rearrange the balance sheet – the line items and numbers remain exactly the same but we have, for pure pedagogical reasons, reshuffled them somewhat. On the asset side we have moved the cash line item to the top, and on the liabilities side we have swapped the location of equity and financial liabilities (see Figure 5.4).

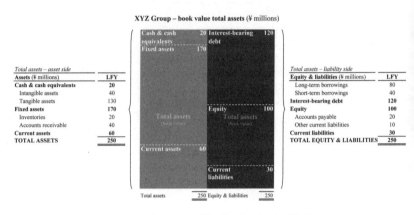

Figure 5.4   XYZ Group – total assets and its funding (reshuffled)

Figure 5.5 demonstrates how we move from total assets as shown in Figure 5.4, first to capital employed and then to operating/invested capital.[2]

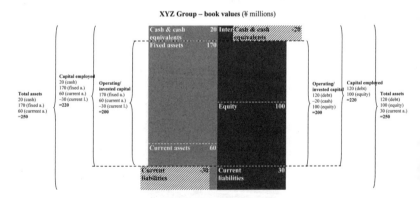

Figure 5.5   XYZ Group – total assets → capital employed → operating/invested capital

---

[2] In the first step, i.e. when identifying the capital employed, we eliminate all debt providers that do not carry claims on the company's operating earnings/cash flows (that is, current liabilities). In the second step, i.e. when identifying the operating/invested capital, we eliminate all cash and cash equivalents not necessary to produce that amount of operating earnings/cash flows.

Consequently, we have defined the book value of operating assets (i.e. the book value of operating/invested capital) in XYZ Group, i.e. the left of the two initially presented "cubes" as shown in Figure 5.6.

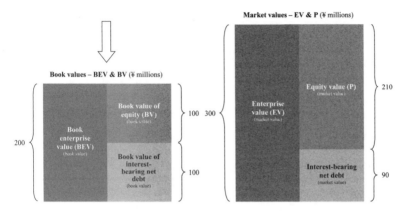

Figure 5.6   XYZ Group – operating/invested capital vs. equity capital, and book value vs. market value, respectively

The book value of operating/invested capital in XYZ Group is therefore calculated at ¥200 million. Given XYZ's ¥100 million book interest-bearing net debt (that is, its ¥120 million in financial liabilities less its ¥20 million in cash and cash equivalents), its book equity value is calculated at ¥100 million.

What about the "cube" on the right-hand side though, i.e. XYZ's *market value* of operating/invested capital and equity capital, respectively? In the first chapter we stated that the market value of a (or any) cash-generating asset, such as a company (or a financial liability for that matter), will equal its projected future returns discounted to a present value by a risk-adjusted rate of return.

Table 5.2 shows the discounted cash flow value of XYZ's operating/invested capital, i.e. its expected free cash flow to operating capital discounted, or present value calculated, by a risk-adjusted required rate of return.[3]

---

[3] A more detailed description of the cash flow valuation concept (with respect to operating/invested capital as well as equity capital), together with relevant definitions, is presented later in the book.

Table 5.2   XYZ Group – discounted cash flow value (i.e. market value) of operating/invested capital (i.e. EV)

XYZ Group	FY+1	FY+2	FY+3	FY+4	FY+5	Terminal year (TY)
Free cash flow to firm – FCFF (¥ millions)	36	38	41	42	43	43
Terminal value = FCFF TY * (1 + g)/(WACC – g) (WACC = 15%, g = 2%)	↓	↓	↓	↓	↓	337 ↓
Free cash flow to firm (FCFF)	36	38	41	42	43	337
Discount factor @ 15% = 1/(1 + WACC)^n	87.0%	75.6%	65.8%	57.2%	49.7%	49.7%
ENTERPRISE VALUE (EV)	**300** = 31 +	29 +	27 +	24 +	21 +	168

The discounted cash flow value of operating/invested capital in XYZ is therefore calculated at ¥300 million. Accordingly, this figure represents the market value of XYZ's operating assets (i.e. its EV) as shown in the figure above (explicitly the "cube" on the right-hand side of Figure 5.6). That the assets in question (i.e. the invested capital) happen to be booked at ¥200 million is, in this respect, more or less irrelevant. As the concerned operating capital, as shown in Table 5.2, is expected to yield a risk-adjusted return of ¥300 million to its owner, the owner of these assets will, if he or she intends to sell them, not accept a price below ¥300 million, i.e. he or she will not accept an offer below the market value.

So what about the market value of *equity* in XYZ? We assume the long-term financial liabilities (a 5-year maturity loan) in XYZ carry a nominal value of ¥80 million and bear a fixed coupon rate (i.e. interest payment) of 5 percent. The annual interest payment in absolute terms is thus calculated at ¥4 million (5% × ¥80 million). We further assume that the market interest rate (i.e. the coupon rate that an investor would receive for an equivalent loan today) has for some reason suddenly risen to 8 percent (and consequently that a lender would now receive ¥6.4 million a year in interest payment, 8% × ¥80 million, if providing an equivalent loan today). Using the same cash flow technique demonstrated above, we can then calculate the new adjusted market value of the XYZ loan. That is, we calculate the present value of the loan at issue using its new adjusted terms (i.e. we discount the fixed ¥4 million coupon rate payment by the currently updated 8 percent market rate instead of the now outdated 5 percent rate) (see Table 5.3).

Table 5.3   XYZ Group – discounted cash flow value (i.e. market value) of long-term debt

XYZ Group

Book value long-term debt (¥ millions)	FY+1	FY+2	FY+3	FY+4	FY+5	FY +5
5% fixed annual coupon rate (payment)	4	4	4	4	4	80
(5% required rate of return)						
Discount factor @ 5% = $1/(1 + 5\%$ required rate of return$)^n$	95.2%	90.7%	86.4%	82.3%	78.4%	78.4%
	↓	↓	↓	↓	↓	↓

VALUE LONG-TERM DEBT   80 = 4 + 4 + 3 + 3 + 3 + 63

- -

XYZ Group

Market value long-term debt (¥ millions)	FY+1	FY+2	FY+3	FY+4	FY+5	FY +5
5% fixed annual coupon rate (payment)	4	4	4	4	4	80
(8% required rate of return)						
Discount factor @ 8% = $1/(1 + 8\%$ required rate of return$)^n$	92.6%	85.7%	79.4%	73.5%	68.1%	68.1%
	↓	↓	↓	↓	↓	↓

VALUE LONG-TERM DEBT   70 = 4 + 3 + 3 + 3 + 3 + 54

Given this – to be honest, quite steep – change in interest rates, the long-term debt decreases in value by ¥10 million (from its recorded ¥80 million book value to the ¥70 million market value above). If at the same time, so as not to complicate the example more than necessary, we assume that the short-term debt carries a variable interest rate (i.e. as the market rate changes, so does the coupon rate accordingly), we can assume its market value to be equivalent to its nominal or book value. From that we can calculate the market value of XYZ's total financial liabilities as ¥110 million (i.e. ¥70 million in long-term debt plus ¥40 million in short-term debt as above).

We can now calculate the equity market value of XYZ Group at ¥210 million, i.e. its calculated ¥300 million EV, in accordance with the previous statement, less its ¥110 million financial debt value as presented above, and, finally, a final ¥20 million addition of cash and cash equivalents (that is, a total interest-bearing net debt position of ¥90 million):

¥ 300 million	Market value of operating/invested capital (i.e. EV)
¥ –70 million	Market value of long-term debt
¥ –40 million	Market value of short-term debt
¥ +20 million	Market value of cash and cash equivalents
¥210 million	**Market value of equity (i.e. P)**[4]

That completes the review.

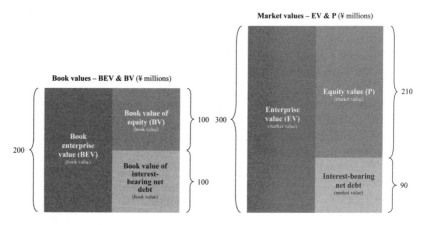

Figure 5.7   XYZ Group – operating/invested capital vs. equity capital, and book value vs. market value, respectively

---

[4] For a listed company, the market value of all outstanding shares, or, alternatively, the market value of equity, is already given. That is, the market value of equity, i.e. "P" (price), for a given listed company, will equal its market capitalization. Following that, the market value of operating/invested capital, i.e. EV (enterprise value), for that company will then be given by its market capitalization (i.e. its P as above) with the addition of, at market value, its interest-bearing net debt. Note, moreover, that the market capitalization of a given listed company, i.e. its market value of equity as set by the stock market, is built on the same basis as that above. That is, the market value of equity (P) for a given listed company represents all its expected cash flows to equity (however, in this case, as anticipated by stock market investors as a collective group rather than by us as in the case presented above) discounted to a present value by the stock market's collective assessment of its relevant required rate of return, i.e. its cost of equity. Notwithstanding this, the absolute level of these two variables, i.e. the stock market's overall assessment of its expected cash flows and discount rate in absolute terms, is not, as in the XYZ Group case, directly observable, but is only implicitly given, or implicitly embedded, in its present market capitalization. Later in this book, we will return to this issue on several occasions and in several forms.

This exercise may possibly appear elementary as well as overly explicit in nature. However, my experience is that the issues above, in reality, and more often than not, are a source of considerable or constant confusion. The presented relationships are very much more obvious and logical when displayed using the images and cubes above, but can be considerably trickier to keep track of in real life, as they normally only occur in terms of myriad different reports and spreadsheets (and, as happens in the real world, are often also of varying structure and quality). Not knowing exactly what you are valuing, i.e. the shares or the business enterprise, and, perhaps, also not knowing exactly what assets are included in or excluded from this business enterprise, and, finally, what values, i.e. book values or market values, we are referring to can give rise to both significant misunderstanding and major miscalculations.

6
The Value Multiples

The value multiples of the comparable companies should be calculated by means of price quotations as per the relevant valuation date. Furthermore, working with the market approach, one may either:

1. derive the market value of the business operations; that is, the market value of operating/invested capital, i.e. the enterprise value (EV) or
2. derive the market value of all outstanding shares, that is, the market value of equity, i.e. the price (P).

These two options also correspond. The value of invested capital, for example, may either be derived by way of a direct approach, that is, by way of value multiples comprising the entire capital structure (i.e. EV multiples), or indirectly, using value multiples comprising solely the equity capital (i.e. P multiples) with the net debt of the subject company added.

Similarly, the equity value may either be derived directly, by value multiples comprising solely the equity capital (i.e. P multiples), or indirectly, by value multiples comprising all invested capital (i.e. EV multiples) and then subtracting the subject company's interest-bearing net debt.

Note, however, that the calculated enterprise value as well as the calculated equity value of any given subject company should be the same, irrespective of the method chosen. That is, the equity value calculated via the indirect approach (i.e. the calculated equity value using EV multiples) should have exactly the same outcome as the equity value calculated via the direct approach (i.e. the calculated equity value using pure P multiples) and vice versa. However, the final statement may be incorrect if the derived P multiples are applied uncritically to the subject company if it has noticeably disparate capital structures to its peers.[1]

In order to avoid erroneous conclusions stemming from capital structure differences between the subject company and that of the peers (and, moreover, to avoid the impact of any extraordinary items further down the income statement), I prefer even to calculate the equity value by way of the first methodology, i.e. to first calculate the value of the business enterprise and then to adjust for (i.e. deduct) interest-bearing net debt.[2]

---

[1] A high level of debt will bring a high level of financial risk (for the equity holders), which, all else being equal, justifies a lower P multiple. Excess cash or non-operating assets may, additionally, result in non-representative P multiples. Differences in leverage between the valuation subject and the peers may also give rise to problems if using market value of equity (i.e. P) in relation to operating base metrics like Sales, EBIT, etc. We will return to all these issues later on.

[2] It must, however, be noted that geared companies may, as a result of interest rates being tax deductible, show higher equity values than equivalent companies with no financial liabilities, all else being equal.

6.1   EV MULTIPLES

EV multiples (enterprise value multiples) state the market value of the business enterprise (i.e. the market value of operating/invested capital) in relation to some appropriate choice of base metric.

Commonly used data from the income and cash flow statements include:

- *Sales:* revenues/turnover
- *EBITDA:* earnings before interest, taxes, depreciation, and amortization
- *EBITA:* earnings before interest, taxes, and amortization
- *EBIT:* earnings before interest and tax
- *FCFF:* free cash flow to firm.

The resultant value multiples are:

- *EV/Sales:* market value of invested capital (EV) in relation to revenues (Sales)
- *EV/EBITDA:* market value of invested capital (EV) in relation to earnings before interest, taxes, depreciation, and amortization (EBITDA)
- *EV/EBITA:* market value of invested capital (EV) in relation to earnings before interest, taxes, and amortization (EBITA)
- *EV/EBIT:* market value of invested capital (EV) in relation to earnings before interest and tax (EBIT)
- *EV/FCFF:* market value of invested capital (EV) in relation to free cash flow to firm (FCFF).

As the numerator (i.e. the EV) represents all investor claims on the business enterprise (i.e. the market value of the capital structure in its entirety – equity capital as well as debt claims), the denominator (i.e. the relevant earnings or cash flow measure) should also represent the return available to all investors (the return available for distribution to shareholders as well as lenders), i.e. not already burdened by interest payments, etc. Consequently, the profit and cash flow measures above (i.e. EBITDA, EBITA, EBIT, and FCFF) are picked at operating level (i.e. before interest payments, etc.) and not at shareholder level (i.e. after interest payments, etc.). It is therefore inappropriate to calculate EV multiples using earnings and cash flow measures of benefit solely to the shareholders (e.g. profit before tax or net income).

Moreover, as the market value of operating/invested capital (EV), as defined before, represents the market value of equity plus the market value of interest-bearing net debt – i.e. via the interest-bearing net debt concept we have deducted cash and cash equivalents from the asset base – the return associated with these cash and cash equivalents (i.e. interest income, etc.) should not be included in the relevant profit or cash flow measure. The numerator and the denominator must go together. From an income statement perspective, this is illustrated in Figure 6.1.

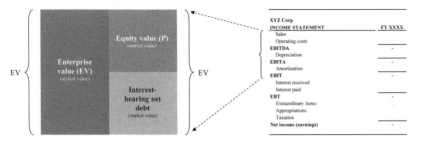

Figure 6.1   Enterprise value (i.e. market value of operating/invested capital) – appropriate base metrics of the income statement

The earnings and cash flow-related variables may be associated with EV for any time period as long as it is with good reason and provided that all companies are handled consistently. Some common examples:

- last fiscal year
- last 12 months
- budget/forecast for next year
- any forecast year following next year.

Value multiples may also be derived from balance sheet data. These multiples are usually obtained by dividing the price quotation as of the valuation date by balance sheet data as of the end of the last fiscal year or as of a date as close to the valuation date as possible. A precondition, however, is that data used for the subject company and the comparables is from the same day. As the comparable companies from which the value multiples are derived are typically listed, and are therefore also bound by strict rules on public disclosure, this will, in practice, imply balance sheet data from the latest published annual or quarterly report.

Commonly used (enterprise value-related) data from the balance sheet statement include:

- *TA:* total assets
- *BEV:* book enterprise value (i.e. book value of operating/invested capital)
- *FA:* fixed assets
- *TFA:* tangible fixed assets.[3]

---

[3] Occasionally, it may be advisable to disconnect intangible assets from tangible assets. Should a company acquire intellectual property rights – for example, a trademark – international

The resultant value multiples are:

- *EV/TA:* market value of invested capital (EV) in relation to total assets (TA)
- *EV/BEV:* market value of invested capital (EV) in relation to book value of invested capital, i.e. book enterprise value (BEV)
- *EV/FA:* market value of invested capital (EV) in relation to (tangible and intangible) fixed assets (FA)
- *EV/TFA:* market value of invested capital (EV) in relation to tangible fixed assets (TFA).

6.2   P MULTIPLES

P multiples (price multiples) state the market value of all outstanding shares (i.e. the market value of equity) in relation to some appropriate choice of base metric.

Commonly used data from the income and cash flow statements include:

- *EBT:* earnings before tax
- *E:* earnings (after tax)
- *FCFE:* free cash flow to equity.

The resultant value multiples are:

- *P/EBT:* market value of equity (P) in relation to earnings before tax (EBT)
- *P/E:* market value of equity (P) in relation to earnings after tax (E)
- *P/FCFE:* market value of equity (P) in relation to free cash flow to equity (FCFE).

The logic is the same as in the case of EV above. As the numerator (i.e. P) represents the market value solely of the equity capital, the denominator (i.e. the earnings or the cash flow measure) should therefore exclude income belonging to other types of investors or financiers, i.e. lenders, etc. The relevant earnings or cash flow measure should thus reflect return solely attributable to the shareholders. Consequently, the profit and cash flow measures above (i.e. EBT, E, and FCFE) are taken at the shareholder level (i.e. after interest payments, etc.) and not at operating level (i.e. before interest payments, etc.). It is therefore inappropriate to calculate P multiples using earnings and cash flow measures

---

accounting standards would typically specify these rights as a recordable asset. If a company were, on the other hand, to invest the same amount of money internally, to build a brand on its own, the accounting standards would typically require these investments to be expensed. As a result, the latter company will, as opposed to the former, report no asset on the balance sheet even though they have invested exactly the same amount of money for exactly the same type of asset.

of benefit to all financiers of the business enterprise.[4] This is illustrated from an income statement perspective in Figure 6.2.

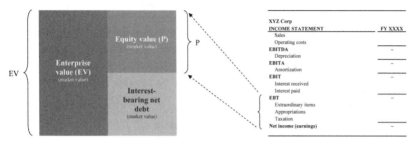

Figure 6.2   Shareholder value (i.e. market value of equity) – appropriate base metrics of the income statement

Commonly used (shareholder value related) data from the balance sheet statement include:

- *BV:* book value (of equity)
- *ABV:* adjusted book value (of equity).

The resultant value multiples are:

- *P/BV:* market value of equity (P) in relation to book value of equity (BV)
- *P/ABV:* market value of equity (P) in relation to adjusted book value of equity (ABV).

In addition, value multiples may also be calculated on more or less industry-specific bases, e.g. number of employees, number of consultants, MWh, number of tons produced, number of subscribers/visitors, etc. These quantities will be of benefit to the entire business entity and are as a consequence not dependent on the financing structure of the company. To put this in other words, they are the result of the business operations in its entirety and not specifically the result of, or distributable to, the company's respective financiers. For example, you can neither divide nor distribute an energy company's production of MWh as one part attributable to the shareholders and the other part attributable to the lenders in the same way you could a profit figure. For that reason, the above-mentioned business-related base metrics should be put into relation with EV

---

[4] To put the subject company and its peers on equal footing, there may also be times when an adjustment for extraordinary income/expenses, appropriations, etc. may be appropriate. If executing such adjustments, one should: (i) make the corresponding adjustments to the peers; and (ii) adjust taxes paid accordingly.

and not P. As a result, should we seek the equity market value (i.e. P) using the above-mentioned base metrics, it is recommended to first calculate the value of the subject company's operations, i.e. its EV, using EV multiples, and then to adjust for (i.e. deduct) the relevant net debt balance.

But what about the frequently used P/Sales ratio (where one does, in fact, mix an equity metric, i.e. P, with an operational metric, i.e. Sales)? Is that wrong? Well, in most cases, yes. The numerator and denominator must cohere, i.e. Sales should be related to EV and not to P. Here is an example to illustrate the problem. First, recall the "cube" discussed earlier (see Figure 6.3).

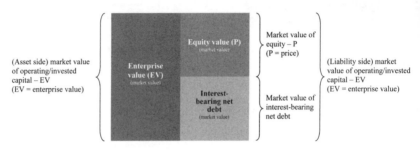

Figure 6.3 Enterprise value (i.e. market value of operating/invested capital) vs. shareholder value (i.e. market value of equity)

Assume that we are asked to calculate the market value of equity in the fictitious privately held German company BQZ GmbH using the market approach. Table 6.1 shows the relevant listed peers of BQZ GmbH.

Table 6.1   Derivation of shareholder value (i.e. market value of equity) in BQZ GmbH – summary of relevant data

Company (€ millions)	Market cap, or price (P)		Interest-bearing net debt		Enterprise value (EV)		Sales	P/ Sales	EV/ Sales
Peer 1	(	100	+	100	=	200	)	240	0.42x	0.83x
Peer 2	(	200	+	200	=	400	)	450	0.44x	0.89x
Peer 3	(	300	+	300	=	600	)	556	0.54x	1.08x
Peer 4	(	300	+	100	=	400	)	535	0.56x	0.75x
Mean									**0.49x**	**0.89x**
Median									**0.49x**	**0.86x**

We note that all comparable companies have a capital structure comprising financial liabilities. For the majority of the listed peers this is a financing mix, at market value, containing approximately 50 percent equity and 50 percent debt (i.e. a capital structure in line with that illustrated in the "cube" above).

Our listed peers are therefore on average (median) valued at 0.49x P/Sales and 0.86x EV/Sales. Turnover (each company's sales figure) is evidently the same, i.e. constant, regardless of whether we calculate the ratio using EV or P. Thus, as EV includes financial liabilities (see the "cube" above), the calculated EV/Sales multiples will be higher than the corresponding P/Sales multiples for leveraged companies, all else being equal. Therefore, as our listed peers have a capital structure comprising approximately 50 percent debt, their EV/Sales multiples will be significantly higher than their corresponding P/Sales multiples.

We now introduce our valuation subject BQZ GmbH into the calculations. BQZ GmbH has €500 million in turnover (Sales) and has chosen to finance its operations solely by equity, i.e. BQZ GmbH is debt-free.

Let us now return to the "cube." BQZ GmbH, which has chosen to finance its operations solely by equity (as is often the case with privately held companies like BQZ GmbH), have a "cube" that looks radically different compared with those of companies which do not. Figure 6.4 shows the "cube" for a company with a capital structure of 50 percent debt, and the corresponding "cube" for the all-equity financed BQZ GmbH.

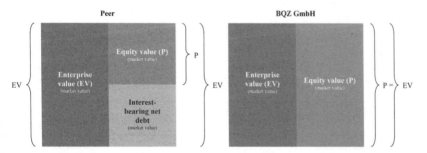

Figure 6.4   Enterprise value (i.e. market value of operating/invested capital) vs. shareholder value (i.e. market value of equity) – illustration of different capital structures for the same type of business

Consequently, should the company in question not be funded by any financial liabilities, its enterprise value will then equal its shareholder value.[5]

---

[5] Should the company in question have no financial liabilities and also hold liquid assets and/or other financial assets, then the equity value will naturally be greater than the invested capital value.

So, how will this affect the appropriate equity value of BQZ GmbH? As discussed at the beginning of this chapter, there are two market approach alternatives for deriving the equity value of a company. Either:

1. we derive the equity value directly using P multiples or
2. we derive the value of the shares indirectly using EV multiples (i.e. first deriving the enterprise value, and then adjusting for (i.e. subtracting) the interest-bearing net debt).

We have the following data on BQZ GmbH and its peers:

- From the table above, the derived median peer group P/Sales multiple is 0.49x.
- From the table above, the derived median peer group EV/Sales multiple is 0.86x.
- BQZ GmbH's sales are €500 million.
- BQZ GmbH's interest-bearing net debt is €0 million.

Consequently, we note that the equity value of BQZ GmbH is calculated at €246 million using the direct approach (i.e. by way of the P/Sales multiple). On the other hand, if we calculate the equity value of BQZ GmbH using the EV/Sales multiple and then adjust for its current net debt position, the corresponding result is €431 million (see Table 6.2). Had we not used the EV multiple, we would have underestimated the equity value of BQZ GmbH by €185 million.

Table 6.2   Derived shareholder value (i.e. market value of equity) in BQZ GmbH – value effects as a result of differing capital structure between the valuation subject and its peers

BQZ GmbH (€ millions)	P/ Sales	EV/ Sales
Derived value multiple	0.49x	0.86x
Sales of BQZ GmbH	500	500
Enterprise value (market value of invested capital)	n.a.	431
Interest-bearing net debt	n.a.	0
Price (market value of equity)	**246**	**431**

The reason for this phenomenon is that the price component (P) represents only the shareholder's claims on the company, and so interest payments, etc., have been deducted from the expected cash flows (therefore the higher the leverage, i.e. the higher the interest payments, the lower the shareholder's residual, i.e. the lower the price, all else being equal). As the peers presented above are geared, their P will have been charged with interest payments, etc., compared with an ungeared peer (for example, BQZ GmbH). Hence, if the subject company has no debt, i.e. no interest payments, then its proper value multiple should match that of an equivalent ungeared peer, i.e. it should be valued on a debt-free basis (or to put it another way, an EV multiple is appropriate).

As a result, the problem above is not isolated to the P/Sales multiple. Given that the valuation subject and its peers do not have identical capital structures, all multiples that mix a metric specifically of benefit to the shareholders (i.e. P) with a metric of benefit to all providers of capital (e.g. sales, number of employees, MWh, subscribers, EBITDA, EBIT, etc.) will suffer from this problem. The only time that these effects do not occur is when the valuation subject and its peers all have exactly the same capital structure, all else being equal. However, as this is *far* from always the case (especially when working with unlisted companies), it may be advisable, when making use of an operational base metric as mentioned above for valuation purposes, to use the EV even though in reality we are targeting the equity value.

6.3   OTHER DETAILS TO CONSIDER

Multiples and values (EV as well as P) are generally calculated on an operating basis – i.e. typically non-operating items, such as pleasure boats, private jets, non-operating real estate, etc. (i.e. assets with no clear or obvious link to the core business of the company), are normally dealt with separately.

Moreover, when dealing with assets on an individual basis, the numerator and the denominator must (in order to not engage in double counting) go hand-in-hand. Suppose that the company in question owns a property which it makes use of in its everyday business. If one chooses to value this property separately (i.e. to apply a "sum-of-the-parts valuation"), one cannot, when valuing the remaining business operations, have a "rent-free" line item in the profit/cash flow statement. In other words, one cannot have a higher level of profit/cash flow than would have otherwise been the case just as a result of the owned or "rent-free" property. Either:

1. you let the cost reduction, due to the owned property, remain in the profit or cash flow statement (i.e. you let the profit/cash flow base metric reflect the fact that the company does not have to pay rent to itself), which, accordingly, would suggest that it cannot be credited any "extra" value of the property itself, or, alternatively

2. you do the opposite, i.e. you increase the operating cost base by a notional market rent of the property at issue and recalculate a new business value

(which will then, of course, be lower than in the case above as we have increased the operating costs by the market rent of the concerned property), and then add that amount to the estimated market value of the concerned property.

Whichever of these two options you choose, the overall result (i.e. the total value of the business including the property at issue) has to be exactly the same. You cannot "rent" for free from yourself and simultaneously be credited with the market value of the property concerned. The market value of the property is built upon the premise that it can generate external rental income, which is not possible if the property owner already rents to himself for "free" (i.e. one cannot have one's cake and eat it).

As a final note to this chapter, it is also important to stress that income data on the valuation subject as well as on the peers can refer to different time periods than the standard 12 months (January 1 to December 31). Companies may, for various reasons (being newly set up, switching from split financial year to calendar year, etc.), occasionally present a different stretch of time period in relation to each other.

7

The Value Drivers

All value multiples are influenced by one or more primary value drivers (in addition to risk, which we will return to in a later chapter). Moreover, the value drivers of the respective multiples are unique or individual, i.e. they have a direct link to the specific variables building the concerned multiple. Typically, the simple rule of "the higher the level of value driver, the higher the level of value multiple" applies. Listed below are the most important (i.e. the primary) value drivers of the previously presented value multiples.

7.1 PRIMARY VALUE DRIVERS OF THE EV MULTIPLES

- *EV/Sales:* expected operating margin (e.g. EBITDA%, EBITA%, EBIT%) and revenue growth, respectively
- *EV/EBITDA:* expected growth in earnings before interest, taxes, depreciation, and amortization
- *EV/EBITA:* expected growth in earnings before interest, taxes and amortization
- *EV/EBIT:* expected growth in earnings before interest and tax
- *EV/FCFF:* expected growth in free cash flow to firm
- *EV/TA:* expected return on total assets[1]
- *EV/BEV:* expected return on book operating/invested capital (i.e. expected return on book enterprise value)[2]
- *EV/FA:* expected return on fixed assets[3]
- *EV/TFA:* expected return on tangible fixed assets.[4]

---

[1] Earnings before interest and tax plus financial income (as the capital base, hence total assets, includes cash and financial assets, the corresponding income measure should do the same, i.e. comprise the expected return of these cash and financial assets) in relation to average assets over the fiscal year (the ratio may, moreover, be calculated before as well as after taxes).

[2] Earnings before interest and tax (as the capital base, hence operating/invested capital, does not include cash and financial assets [and so we have in and with the application of the interest-bearing net debt concept deducted cash and financial assets from the total amount of financial debt], so the corresponding income measure should not do so either, i.e. comprise the expected return of these excluded cash and financial assets) in relation to average operating/invested capital over the fiscal year (the ratio may, moreover, be calculated before as well as after taxes).

[3] Earnings before interest and tax in relation to average tangible and intangible assets over the fiscal year (the ratio may, moreover, be calculated before as well as after taxes).

[4] Earnings before interest and tax (possibly adjusted for items relating to the intangible assets, excluded in the asset base) in relation to average tangible assets over the fiscal year (the ratio may, moreover, be calculated before as well as after taxes).

7.2   PRIMARY VALUE DRIVERS OF THE P MULTIPLES

- *P/EBT:* expected growth in earnings before tax
- *P/E:* expected growth in earnings (after tax)
- *P/FCFE:* expected growth in free cash flow to equity
- *P/BV:* expected return on book value (of equity)[5]
- *P/ABV:* expected return on adjusted book value (of equity).[6]

7.3   ASSUMPTIONS REGARDING VALUE DRIVERS

Any conclusions in terms of expected growth, margins, etc., may be drawn on historical as well as on forward-looking data. What matters is not what data is used, but that the result is representative of the most likely future scenario. The value of any company, as stated at the very beginning of this book, will always (that is, under a going concern assumption) equal its expected *future* returns discounted to a present value by way of a risk-adjusted rate of return.

Should you have access to forward-looking data (e.g. company business plans, market forecasts by industry associations, reports by equity analysts, etc.), this would be a good starting point. Any figures should, however, be subject to a thorough reasonability assessment before they are applied.

If such information is not available, historical data may be used if it can be deemed representative of the concerned company's or companies' future growth and earnings potential (i.e. by that, we implicitly assume the future to be in line with the history).[7]

Should there be a great difference between the actual historical performance and the expected future development of the concerned company or companies, the divergence must be investigated. The history/future bridge therefore needs to be transparent as well as explained.

Moreover, should the valuation subject in question consist of several divisible companies (such as a group) or units, in which business models as well as value driver levels differ significantly, it may be advisable to break the valuation up into the respective companies or business units. Rather than valuing the entire group as a single unit (using one homogeneous peer group and, consequently, only one absolute level of value driver(s)), one is given the option of deriving the corresponding group value via a peer group tailored by group company or business unit. Such a "sum-of-the-parts valuation" may help to highlight companies and business areas as part of a larger group structure, where their unique level of value driver(s) may justify a higher or

---

[5] Earnings after tax in relation to average book equity over the fiscal year.

[6] Earnings after tax in relation to average adjusted book equity over the fiscal year.

[7] Should this not be the case, however, the historical figures are not relevant and it would clearly be wrong to use them.

lower valuation than that given by the corresponding figures of the group. The resultant Group value (i.e. the total value of the company) should, however, be the same, irrespective of the applied methodology; otherwise one has made a mistake somewhere.

8

Applying the Market Approach in Practice

To make the market approach valuation process easier to comprehend, let us take a fictitious case study to illustrate the proper way to go about it.

8.1   THE CASE STUDY

The valuation subject in question is a privately held U.S.-based engineering company, Engineering Corp (see Table 8.1). Now suppose that you, as the sole owner of all outstanding shares, want to know what your business is really worth. How then do you go about this?

Table 8.1   Engineering Corp – historical data and forecasts

Engineering Corp INCOME STATEMENT ($ millions)	FY–2	FY–1	LFY
Sales	1,144	1,244	1,500
Operating costs	–952	–1,019	–1,193
Earnings before interest, taxes, depreciation, and amortization (EBITDA)	**192**	**225**	**307**
Depreciation	–41	–43	–53
Earnings before interest, taxes, and amortization (EBITA)	**151**	**182**	**255**
Amortization	0	0	0
Earnings before interest and tax (EBIT)	**151**	**182**	**255**
Results of non-consolidated participating interests	0	0	0
Interest received	1	1	0
Interest paid	–22	–22	–17
Earnings before tax (EBT)	**130**	**161**	**238**
Extraordinary income	8	0	0
Appropriations	0	0	0
Taxation	–53	–64	–92
Minority interest	0	0	0
Net income (earnings)	**84**	**97**	**146**

(Continued)

Table 8.1   (*Continued*)

Engineering Corp

BALANCE SHEET ($ millions)	FY–2	FY–1	LFY
Goodwill	0	0	0
Intangible and tangible assets	610	610	611
Financial fixed assets	0	0	0
Fixed assets	**610**	**610**	**611**
Inventories	216	235	283
Accounts receivable	313	340	410
Other current assets	128	139	168
Cash & cash equivalents	78	44	41
Current assets	**734**	**758**	**902**
TOTAL ASSETS	**1,344**	**1,367**	**1,513**
Equity	**510**	**486**	**510**
Minority interest	**0**	**0**	**0**
Provisions	**0**	**0**	**0**
Short- and long-term interest-bearing debt	**292**	**291**	**292**
Other current liabilities	430	468	564
Accounts payable	112	122	147
Current liabilities	**542**	**590**	**711**
TOTAL EQUITY AND LIABILITIES	**1,344**	**1,367**	**1,513**

FORECAST ($ millions)	FY+1	FY+2	FY+3
Sales	1,748	1,957	2,081
Revenue growth (compounded annual growth rate, LFY starting point)	16.5%	14.2%	11.5%
EBITDA	395	472	527
EBITDA growth (compounded annual growth rate, LFY starting point)	28.5%	23.9%	19.7%
EBITDA margin	22.6%	24.1%	25.3%
EBIT	334	403	454
EBIT growth (compounded annual growth rate, LFY starting point)	31.0%	25.7%	21.2%
EBIT margin	19.1%	20.6%	21.8%
Net income (earnings)	189	231	272
Net income growth (compounded annual growth rate, LFY starting point)	30.2%	25.8%	23.1%
Net margin	10.8%	11.8%	13.1%

We are instructed to use value multiples derived from comparable listed companies to calculate the market value (the fair market value) of 100 percent of the shares (i.e. a non-marketable majority interest) in Engineering Corp as of the first day of fiscal year +1 (i.e. January 1, FY+1).[1]

---

[1] Should we have another valuation date, such as 3 months into FY+1, the share price of the peer(s) as of this date should be applied (i.e. the share price(s) as of April 1, FY+1), rather than the first day of FY+1 (i.e. the share price(s) as of January 1, FY+1) as in this case.

For the assignment we have put together a peer group of publicly listed U.S. engineering companies. In line with previous reasoning, historical data as well as forecasts should be reviewed and, if warranted, these should be adjusted in an appropriate manner before application. To simplify matters, we assume that all data in Tables 8.2 and 8.3 has been subject to such a reasonability assessment.

Table 8.2   Selected value multiples – EV and P

Company	Enterprise value (EV) ($ millions)	Market cap (P) ($ millions)	EV/ Sales	EV/ EBIT	EV/ BEV	P/E	P/BV
	Valuation date	Valuation date	LFY	LFY	LFY	LFY	LFY
Peer 1	46,152	44,301	2.30x	18.1x	5.3x	32.5x	6.5x
Peer 2	133,930	149,849	2.65x	18.9x	11.4x	32.5x	5.4x
Peer 3	5,201	3,787	0.40x	8.1x	1.2x	12.6x	1.2x
Peer 4	177,892	169,639	2.46x	15.2x	5.2x	26.9x	6.5x
Peer 5	14,738	14,631	2.70x	11.6x	6.3x	20.5x	6.6x
Peer 6	69,004	69,538	1.30x	11.6x	3.7x	20.4x	3.7x
Peer 7	25,093	15,518	0.93x	15.3x	1.3x	27.1x	1.6x
Peer 8	18,333	16,383	0.97x	13.9x	2.1x	24.4x	2.5x
Peer 9	2,046	2,014	1.35x	14.6x	4.8x	24.1x	5.1x
Peer 10	1,070	840	0.51x	6.8x	1.0x	10.0x	1.0x
Mean	49,346	48,650	1.56x	13.4x	4.2x	23.1x	4.0x
Median	21,713	15,950	1.33x	14.2x	4.3x	24.2x	4.4x
Engineering Corp	n.a.	n.a.	n.a.	n.a.	n.a.	n.a.	n.a.

Table 8.3   Selected key ratios – value drivers

Company	Expected EBIT margin	Expected revenue growth	Expected EBIT growth	Expected EBIT growth	Expected ROOC/ ROIC	Expected earnings growth	Expected ROE
	FY+1 to FY+3	LFY to FY+3	LFY to FY+3	FY+3	FY+1 to FY+3	LFY to FY+3	FY+1 to FY+3
Peer 1	14.9%	16.5%	23.0%	15.1%	24.0%	26.7%	39.7%
Peer 2	18.6%	10.2%	21.9%	19.1%	51.0%	22.0%	31.0%
Peer 3	6.7%	4.1%	13.4%	5.0%	17.1%	15.0%	19.0%
Peer 4	20.8%	6.6%	16.5%	6.6%	27.8%	19.7%	34.0%
Peer 5	26.6%	7.9%	13.6%	7.7%	37.8%	15.9%	42.0%
Peer 6	14.0%	3.3%	11.8%	2.6%	22.6%	14.1%	19.9%
Peer 7	8.7%	2.8%	21.7%	13.0%	7.0%	25.6%	12.7%
Peer 8	8.8%	6.4%	19.0%	11.0%	12.6%	23.2%	20.4%
Peer 9	10.0%	16.7%	22.7%	18.7%	33.0%	25.1%	38.0%
Peer 10	10.5%	4.4%	13.2%	3.0%	18.4%	14.8%	21.0%
Mean	14.0%	7.9%	17.7%	10.2%	25.1%	20.2%	27.8%
Median	12.3%	6.5%	17.7%	9.4%	23.3%	20.8%	26.0%
Engineering Corp	20.5%	11.5%	21.2%	12.7%	29.7%	23.1%	43.0%

8.1.1   EV/Sales

$$EV/Sales = \frac{\text{Enterprise value (market value of operating/invested capital)}}{\text{Sales (revenues)}}$$

From the table above we collect the EV/Sales multiples (EV/Sales based on sales last fiscal year) for the peers (Table 8.4).

Table 8.4   EV/Sales

Company	EV/Sales
	LFY
Peer 1	2.30x
Peer 2	2.65x
Peer 3	0.40x
Peer 4	2.46x
Peer 5	2.70x
Peer 6	1.30x
Peer 7	0.93x
Peer 8	0.97x
Peer 9	1.35x
Peer 10	0.51x
Mean	1.56x
Median	1.33x
Engineering Corp	n.a.

The peers are valued at EV/Sales multiples in the range of 0.40x to 2.70x, with mean and median values of 1.56x and 1.33x, respectively. This means that the comparable companies' invested capital on average and in median is market valued at 1.56x and 1.33x revenues, respectively. Hence:

The median EV/Sales multiple of the peer group: **1.33x**
Engineering Corp's turnover – Sales ($ millions): **1,500**

Consequently, applying the median EV/Sales multiple of the peer group to our valuation subject, Engineering Corp, we arrive at the following estimated value:

$$1.33 \times \$1,500 \text{ million} = \$1,995 \text{ million}$$

The calculated $1,995 million value refers to the market value of Engineering Corp's invested capital. If we wish to estimate the market value of

Engineering Corp's equity capital, we need to adjust for its interest-bearing net debt (Figure 8.1).

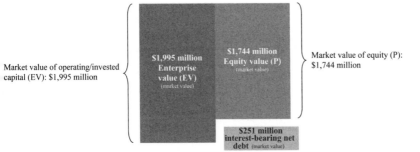

Figure 8.1   Enterprise value (i.e. market value of operating/invested capital) vs. shareholder value (i.e. market value of equity) – the shareholder value of Engineering Corp

The market value of Engineering Corp's equity capital (market value of all outstanding shares) is thus calculated at $1,744 million:

$1,995 million	Market value of operating/invested capital (EV)
$ –251 million	Market value of interest-bearing net debt
$1,744 million	**Market value of equity (P)**

However, as seen in Table 8.4, the distribution of the peers in terms of EV/Sales is quite large (in the range of 0.40x to 2.70x, with mean and median values of 1.56x and 1.33x respectively). It is, of course, no coincidence that Peer 5 is valued at 2.70x Sales whereas Peer 3 is valued at just 0.40x Sales. The divergence is due to the level of value driver(s). As regards the size of the EV/Sales multiple, the most important value drivers (in addition to risk) are expected operating margin and revenue growth. Consequently, we need to take the analysis farther. We start with operating margin.

(a) Operating margin (EBIT%) as key value driver

We have noted that the peer group shows a wide distribution in terms of EV/Sales multiple. What, then, about the operating margin? In Table 8.5 we have supplemented the EV/Sales multiples with the respective companies' expected average operating margin (EBIT margin) for the coming three years (fiscal years +1 to +3).

Table 8.5   EV/Sales – value multiple and
expected operating margin (EBIT%)

Company	EV/Sales	Expected EBIT margin
	LFY	FY+1 to FY+3
Peer 1	2.30x	14.9%
Peer 2	2.65x	18.6%
Peer 3	0.40x	6.7%
Peer 4	2.46x	20.8%
Peer 5	2.70x	26.6%
Peer 6	1.30x	14.0%
Peer 7	0.93x	8.7%
Peer 8	0.97x	8.8%
Peer 9	1.35x	10.0%
Peer 10	0.51x	10.5%
Mean	1.56x	14.0%
Median	1.33x	12.3%
Engineering Corp	n.a.	20.5%

Looking at Table 8.5, we note that the peers are widely distributed in terms of expected operating margin as well. Expected operating margins are in the range of 6.7 percent to 26.6 percent, with an estimated average and median of 14.0 percent and 12.3 percent, respectively. So what does this suggest?

Figure 8.2 shows the EV/Sales multiples of the peers plotted against the expected operating margin presented in Table 8.5. It is up to the analyst concerned, depending on the specific conditions of the subject company and its industry, to decide whether the margin should be before or after depreciations and amortizations. However, it should nonetheless be a performance measure before financial items (interest, etc.) as it is the business enterprise, not the equity capital, that is being valued. In accordance with discussions in Chapter 6, enterprise value multiples represent the business entity in its entirety (in the form of fixed assets and net working capital on the asset side, and its corresponding funding, i.e. equity and net financial liabilities, on the liabilities side). The financial metric (i.e. the measure of performance) chosen should accordingly be a performance measure of benefit to all financiers of the business enterprise in question, i.e. shareholders as well as lenders, and hence a performance measure not already burdened by interest expenses, etc.

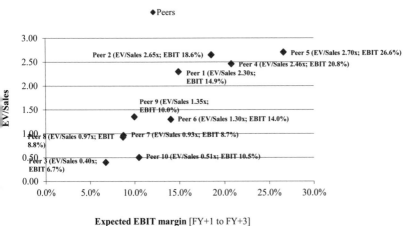

Figure 8.2   EV/Sales – EV/Sales vs. operating margin (EBIT%)

As can be seen in Figure 8.2, the relationship is quite clear: the higher the operating margin, the higher the EV/Sales multiple. The link is logical as investors are likely to be willing to pay more per dollar of sales, the higher the expected return of that dollar of sales. Consequently, Peer 5, valued at 2.70x Sales, is expected to show a 26.6 percent operating margin, whereas Peer 3, valued at only 0.40x Sales, is expected to show a mere 6.7 percent operating margin. Put another way, Peer 5 is expected to "earn" 26.6 cents of operating profit per dollar of sales, whereas Peer 3 is expected to "earn" only 6.7 cents of operating profit per dollar of sales.

What impact will this relationship have on our conclusions with regards to the applicable EV/Sales multiple for Engineering Corp?

In the scatter chart we insert a trend line (i.e. a regression line). As shown in Figure 8.3, Engineering Corp is expected, over the next three years, to show an average operating margin of 20.5 percent. We therefore follow the x-axis of the graph until we reach an operating margin of 20.5 percent. We then move upwards until we reach the regression line. From this point we move to the y-axis to read the given level of EV/Sales multiple.

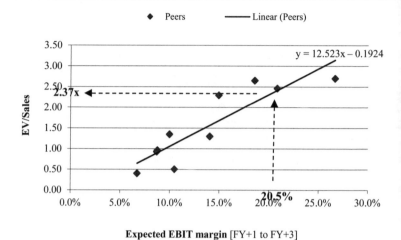

Figure 8.3   EV/Sales – derivation of appropriate value multiple using expected operating margin

Explicitly (as noted in the upper right-hand side of Figure 8.3), the regression is set at y = 12.523x – 0.1924, where y equals EV/Sales and x equals operating margin. The 12.523 figure denotes the slope of the regression line. Thus each percentage point (0.01) increase or decrease in operating margin will justify a 0.12523x EV/Sales increase or decrease. The –0.1924 figure denotes the intercept – the point at which the regression line crosses the y-axis, or put another way, the level of y (EV/Sales) when x (the operating margin) equals zero. As noted, the intercept of this regression is negative (–0.1924). A company with an expected operating margin over the coming three years at 0.0 percent would then, according to the regression above, be justified as valued at –0.1924x EV/Sales, i.e. that company's value is calculated as negative. A company not expected to show future profits will, of course, have no value. However, companies may, over some periods, report no profit or even report great losses without seeing their value turn to zero.[2]

---

[2] Here is an implied assumption that the concerned company can be expected, at some future date (i.e. outside of our forecast period), to reach (or at least have the possibility to reach) future positive cash flows. This effect can be captured by an extended forecast period. However, the risks associated with, or the required rate of return for, a "turnaround" candidate is high, and so its resultant value (i.e. its value multiple) is justified at a low, all else being equal. Alternatively, if one prefers a stock option point of view – as the equity value can, as a result of shareholders limited liability, never be less than zero – there will always (or until the company in question physically goes bankrupt), regardless of how poorly the company performs, be a possibility (i.e. an option) for future positive cash flows. The value of this option will at all times be positive (however, it will most likely also be very low). Consequently, the regression line is, in reality, not straight but curved, i.e. it will level off as we approach zero on the x-axis.

The regression is derived on the basis of the comparable companies' expected level of performance. Deriving appropriate value multiples by way of regression analysis is therefore best suited to a subject company that does not show too different expectations as regards the future level of value driver(s) in relation to its peers. Valuing a company with an expected operating margin of 1.0 percent over the next three years using the regression above may thus very well be inappropriate. Anyway, let us apply the data for our subject company Engineering Corp to the equation and achieve y (i.e. the justified EV/Sales multiple for valuing Engineering Corp).

The regression:

y   = the dependent variable (in this equation, the EV/Sales multiple)
12.523 = the slope of the regression line
x   = the independent variable (in this equation, the expected operating margin)
−0.1924 = the intercept (i.e. the level of y when x equals zero)

The result:

x = 0.205 (the 20.5 percent expected average operating margin of Engineering Corp FY+1 to FY+3)
y = 12.523x − 0.1924
y = 12.523 × 0.205 − 0.1924
y = 2.37

Engineering Corp, with a 20.5 percent expected average operating margin for the coming three years, is thus, all else being equal, warranted a valuation at about 2.37 times its last reported sales.

This provides us with the following revised data (the initial unrevised valuation is shown in brackets):

Derived EV/Sales multiple (at given operating margin): **2.37x** (1.33x)
Engineering Corp's turnover – Sales ($ millions):   **1,500** (1,500)

Applying this "operating margin adjusted" EV/Sales multiple to our valuation subject, Engineering Corp, we arrive at the following adjusted value (market value of operating/invested capital):

2.37 × $1,500 million = $3,555 million
(1.33 × $1,500 million = $1,995 million)

The calculated value of Engineering Corp's invested capital thus increases by $1,560 million ($3,555 million – $1,995 million). Had we valued the company using the initial unrevised 1.33x multiple (i.e. the median peer group multiple), without regard for, among other things, the expected operating margin value driver, all else being equal (which in this case also means ignoring value driver no. 2, expected revenue growth), we would have underestimated the value of Engineering Corp's invested capital by $1,560 million.

(b) Revenue growth as key value driver

We now conduct a similar analysis as above, except that we replace the operating margin value driver with the revenue growth value driver – the higher the expected growth per dollar of sales, the higher the price per dollar of sales, all else being equal. We illustrate this with a very simple example: suppose we have two otherwise similar companies but with significantly different growth expectations. Company A is, over the coming year, expected to grow in terms of sales by 0 percent, whereas the corresponding growth expectation for Company B is 100 percent. Suppose further that both companies are expected to show stable operating margins. Company B is therefore, over the coming year, as an effect of a 100 percent expected revenue growth at a constant margin, expected to double its operating profit, whereas Company A, as an effect of 0 percent expected revenue growth at a likewise constant margin, is expected to report zero earnings growth. The outcome equals that of the operating margin case above, i.e. all else being equal, a high expected return will bring about a high valuation.[3] In other words, just as with the operating margin value driver, investors are likely willing to pay more, all else being equal, for a high-yielding asset compared with a low-yielding one.

In Table 8.6 we have supplemented the EV/Sales multiples from before with each company's compounded annual growth rate (CAGR) in revenues for the last fiscal year to fiscal year +3. It should be (as with the operating margin value driver previously) *expected* growth (note: if no forecasts are available, you may accept historical figures, but only after extensive consideration whether they are considered a good proxy for future growth).

---

[3] The example above includes, among other things, an assumption of a constant capital base. In isolation, this is, of course, an unreasonable assumption. To double the turnover without a corresponding investment in operating assets is not the easiest of tasks. However, even under normal conditions, i.e. when an expected revenue growth is accompanied by a corresponding growth in assets, sales growth is value driving, i.e. value multiple driving, if that growth is value-creating (that is, if the investments in question are expected to generate a return greater than the corresponding cost of capital, more on cost of capital later).

Table 8.6 EV/Sales – value multiple and expected revenue growth

Company	EV/Sales LFY	Expected revenue growth LFY to FY+3
Peer 1	2.30x	16.5%
Peer 2	2.65x	10.2%
Peer 3	0.40x	4.1%
Peer 4	2.46x	6.6%
Peer 5	2.70x	7.9%
Peer 6	1.30x	3.3%
Peer 7	0.93x	2.8%
Peer 8	0.97x	6.4%
Peer 9	1.35x	16.7%
Peer 10	0.51x	4.4%
Mean	1.56x	7.9%
Median	1.33x	6.5%
Engineering Corp	n.a.	11.5%

A regression analysis does show a relationship between EV/Sales and expected revenue growth, but the link is not as clear-cut as in the case of operating margin previously. Nevertheless, the higher the expected revenue growth, the higher the EV/Sales multiple (Figure 8.4).

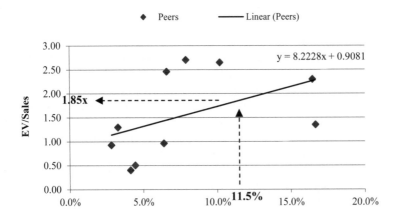

Figure 8.4 EV/Sales – derivation of applicable value multiple using expected revenue growth

Engineering Corp has an expected average annual growth rate in Sales over the next three years of about 11.5 percent. Using this, we can perform the same kind of value derivation as we did for EV/Sales vs. operating margin. We follow the x-axis of the graph until we reach the 11.5 percent figure. We then move up the graph until we reach the regression line. From this point we move to the y-axis to read the given level of the EV/Sales multiple. Engineering Corp, with an 11.5 percent expected average annual growth rate in Sales for the coming three years is, all else being equal, warranted a valuation of about 1.85 times its last reported sales.

This provides us with the following revised data (the initial unrevised valuation is shown in brackets):

Derived EV/Sales multiple (at given revenue growth): **1.85x** (1.33x)
Engineering Corp's turnover – Sales ($ millions): **1,500** (1,500)

Consequently, applying this "revenue growth adjusted" EV/Sales multiple to our valuation subject, Engineering Corp, we arrive at the following adjusted value (market value of operating/invested capital):

1.85 × $1,500 million = $2,775 million
(1.33 × $1,500 million = $1,995 million)

The calculated value of Engineering Corp's invested capital therefore increases by $780 million ($2,775 million less $1,995 million). Had we valued the company using the initial unrevised 1.33x multiple (i.e. the median peer group multiple), that is, without regard for the expected revenue growth value driver, all else being equal (which in this case also means ignoring value driver no. 1, expected operating margin), we would have underestimated the value of Engineering Corp's invested capital by $780 million.

The EV/Sales multiple thus has two primary value drivers: operating margin and revenue growth. However, as seen in the calculations and graphs above, the spread of the EV/Sales multiple above and below the regression line as well as the derived value, in terms of value driver no. 1 (operating margin) and value driver no. 2 (revenue growth), differs significantly (the regression EV/Sales vs. operating margin thus indicated an "extra" $1,560 million in value compared with that given solely by the pure peer group median, whereas the regression EV/Sales vs. expected revenue growth only indicated an equivalent $780 million in "extra" value). Why is that? We need to return to the first graph, EV/Sales vs. operating margin (Figure 8.5).

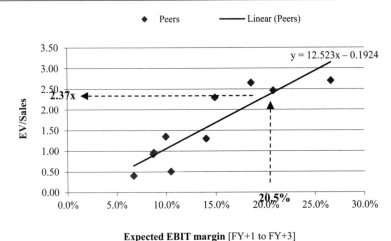

Figure 8.5 EV/Sales – derivation of applicable value multiple using expected operating margin

As noted, the EV/Sales vs. operating margin regression is set at y = 12.523x – 0.1924.

The regression:

y   = the dependent variable (in this equation, the EV/Sales multiple)
12.523 = the slope of the regression line
x   = the independent variable (in this equation, the expected operating margin)
–0.1924 = the intercept (i.e. the level of y when x equals zero)

The result:

x = 0.205 (the 20.5 percent expected average operating margin of Engineer-ing Corp FY+1 to FY+3)
y = 12.523x – 0.1924
y = 12.523 × 0.205 – 0.1924
y = 2.37

At an expected operating margin of 20.5 percent, the justified EV/Sales multi-ple of Engineering Corp is thus calculated at 2.37x (12.523 × 0.205 – 0.1924). In the equation above we substituted the term x with Engineering Corp's 20.5 percent expected operating margin. Therefore y (the EV/Sales multiple in this regression) is at any given level of x (the operating margin in this regression) driven by the slope of the regression line. Consequently, the greater the slope of the regression line, the greater the effect on y from changes in x. Let us now turn to the corresponding findings of the EV/Sales vs. expected revenue growth regression (Figure 8.6).

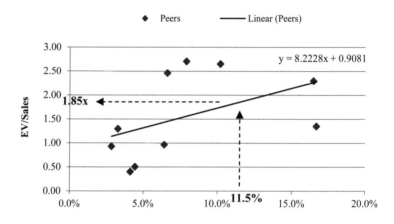

Figure 8.6   EV/Sales – derivation of applicable value multiple using expected revenue growth

As noted, the EV/Sales vs. expected revenue growth regression is set at y = 8.2228x + 0.9081.
The regression:

y   = the dependent variable (in this equation, the EV/Sales multiple)
8.2228 = the slope of the regression line
x   = the independent variable (in this equation, the expected *revenue growth*)
0.9081 = the intercept (i.e. the level of y when x equals zero)

The result:

x = 0.115 (the 11.5 percent expected annual revenue growth rate of Engineering Corp LFY to FY+3)
y = 8.2228x + 0.9081
y = 8.2228 × 0.115 + 0.9081
y = 1.85

Hence, at an 11.5 percent expected revenue growth, the applicable EV/Sales multiple of Engineering Corp is calculated at 1.85x (8.2228 × 0.115 + 0.9081). In the equation above, we substituted the term x with Engineering Corp's 11.5 percent expected revenue growth. We could then see that this equation has a lower slope of regression line as well as a higher intercept than the previous one. This means that the leverage (i.e. the significance) of a higher level of x is less, in terms of outcome on y, when looking at EV/Sales vs. revenue growth than when looking at EV/Sales vs. operating margin.

Or in plain English, it is not the sales in itself that justify the value, but instead the result, or the cash flow, of that sales, hence the importance of the operating margin value driver on the EV/Sales multiple. Therefore we first have to turn the sales figure into a profit figure (that is consequently what we do when we apply the operating margin value driver), then, as step two, the revenue growth value driver will reflect the value of expected growth in that profit figure.

In addition, Engineering Corp happens to have a significantly higher level of x in terms of expected operating margin in relation to its corresponding average peer, than the corresponding level of x in terms of expected revenue growth. In other words, Engineering Corp has, in relation to its comparables, a very high expected operating margin but only a high expected level of revenue growth. A significant slope of regression line in combination with a high level of x therefore has a powerful impact on y.

This is why the two regressions, when compared with the initial median-based, unrevised 1.33x EV/Sales multiple, resulted in significantly different upward value adjustments (that is, the EV/Sales vs. operating margin regression, in isolation, gave rise to a $1,560 million value contribution, whereas the EV/Sales vs. revenue growth regression, in isolation, only gave rise to a corresponding $780 million value contribution).

Hence the regressions presented above can only capture one variable, i.e. one value driver, at a time (either operating margin or sales growth). In consequence, the EV/Sales vs. operating margin regression failed to capture the value increase due to greater expected sales growth versus the average peer, in the same way that the EV/Sales vs. revenue growth regression failed to capture the value increase due to greater expected operating margin versus the average peer. As the slope of the regression line as well as the absolute level of the value driver for our valuation subject, Engineering Corp, was greater in the EV/Sales vs. operating margin regression when compared with the corresponding slope of regression line and value driver for the EV/Sales vs. revenue growth regression, the resulting value effect of not capturing operating margin as a value driver was greater than that of not capturing expected revenue growth as a value driver.

This may also be seen clearly by the comparable companies' spread above or below the regression line as shown in the respective graphs. The EV/Sales vs. operating margin regression, for example, presupposes revenue growth exactly in line with that of the average peer. Thus for each value point (i.e. EV/Sales multiple) that by means of the regression line can be derived from each level of value driver (i.e. operating margin), revenue growth perfectly in line with that of the average peer is assumed. Consequently, the same relationship but reversed applies to the EV/Sales vs. revenue growth regression. In other words, for each value point (i.e. EV/Sales multiple) that by means of the regression line can be derived from each level of value driver (in this case *expected revenue growth*), an *operating margin* perfectly in line with that of the average peer is assumed.

We find the average LFY to FY+3 expected revenue growth of our peers to be 7.9 percent. Companies with an expected revenue growth rate in line with that exact average (i.e. those with an expected revenue growth rate LFY to FY+3 at about 7.9 percent) will therefore be placed in the EV/Sales vs. operating margin graph if not directly on, then at least very close to, the regression line. Companies with an expected revenue growth rate above or below that 7.9 percent will accordingly be placed above or below that same regression line, all else being equal (in principle disregarding the potential differences in risk profile, which we will return to later).

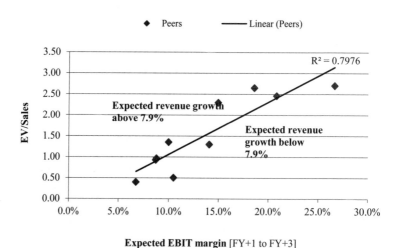

Figure 8.7   EV/Sales vs. operating margin – disparities between the peer concerned and the average peer, in terms of expected revenue growth, will drive the resulting justified multiple above or below that provided by the pure regression line (i.e. by that provided by expected operating margin)

The distribution above or below the regression line, owing to different growth expectations, as noted in Figure 8.7 (the EV/Sales vs. operating margin regression) is the reverse of what is seen in regression 2 (the EV/Sales vs. revenue growth regression, see Figure 8.8). In other words, just as companies with different growth expectations (relative to the comparable companies' corresponding average) in regression 1 above are placed above or below the regression line, companies with different margin expectations (relative to the comparable companies' corresponding average) in regression 2 are placed above or below that regression line, all else being equal (in principle disregarding potential risk differences, which we will return to later).

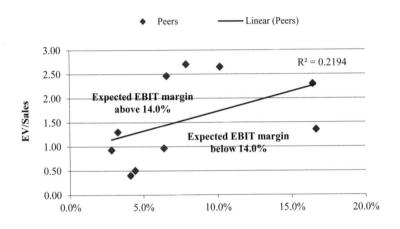

Figure 8.8 EV/Sales vs. revenue growth – disparities between the peer concerned and the average peer, in terms of expected operating margin, will drive the resulting justified multiple above or below that provided by the pure regression line (i.e. by that provided by expected revenue growth)

As noted above, the observations (i.e. the comparables) are more centered on the regression line in terms of the operating margin value driver than in terms of the revenue growth value driver. Specifically, the so-called coefficient of determination (R^2) is higher for the operating margin value driver than for the revenue growth value driver (R^2 of 0.7976 vs. 0.2194). R^2 refers to that part of the dependent variable's variance (in this case the EV/Sales multiple's variance) explained by the independent variable (in this case, operating margin and revenue growth). The value may vary between 0.00 (no correlation at all) and 1.00 (100 percent correlation). Therefore, if R^2 is calculated at 1.00, all changes in the dependent variable are explained by changes in the independent variable. A high R^2 is essential for the regressions to be reliable on their own.[4]

Our EV/Sales vs. operating margin and EV/Sales vs. revenue growth regressions showed R^2s of 0.7976 and 0.2194, respectively, suggesting that changes in the EV/Sales multiple are 79.76 percent explained by changes in the operating margin, and 21.94 percent by changes in revenue growth, when dealt with in isolation.[5] In conclusion, the coefficient of determination is thus significantly higher for EV/Sales vs. operating margin than for EV/Sales vs. revenue growth.

The importance of a high R^2 may also be understood by just physically looking at the two graphs above. If we were to introduce one or maybe two "outliers" (i.e. comparable companies whose multiple cannot be explained by the relevant operating margin and sales growth value drivers) in each regression, where its location would imply a position far down in the right-hand corner of the respective graphs, the EV/Sales vs. operating margin regression would most likely remain relatively unchanged, whereas the EV/Sales vs. revenue growth regression would possibly "tip over" (i.e. turn horizontal or become even negative). The EV/Sales vs. revenue growth regression is therefore significantly more sensitive than the EV/Sales vs. operating margin regression to unexplainable outliers or disorders of capacity/potential to unjustifiably drive the slope of the regression line up or down.

If we now wish to derive an applicable EV/Sales multiple for Engineering Corp, reflecting both the operating margin and revenue growth value drivers, we will therefore be forced to adjust the hitherto one-dimensional graphs. We can then either modify regression 1 (EV/Sales vs. operating margin) for differences in expected revenue growth or we can modify regression 2 (EV/Sales vs. revenue growth) for differences in expected operating margin.

Hence, in theory, it makes no difference if, when deriving the value of a given company, we opt to use the EV/Sales vs. operating margin regression and adjust for divergent revenue growth expectations in relation to the average peer, or if we alternatively apply the EV/Sales vs. revenue growth regression and adjust for divergent operating margin expectations, in relation to the average peer. However, as both the slope of the regression line and the coefficient of determination for Engineering Corp are significantly higher for operating

---

[4] It is important to note that a high coefficient of determination does not necessarily equal a high slope of the regression line. The coefficient of determination only describes the centering of the observations (around the regression line), not the actual slope of the line. Hence, it is possible to show a sharp slope of the regression line and at the same time have a low coefficient of determination, or vice versa. However, if the former applies, the equation (and therefore also the derived value multiple) is probably not reliable and should not be utilized.

[5] There is a possibility of capturing through multiple linear regression analysis more than one explanatory variable in the same regression. However, this methodology is mathematically somewhat more complex and, moreover, may in the end not even solve the problem – more on this later.

margin as a value driver than for revenue growth as a value driver, it may consequently be better to use the former as a starting point for adjustment.

It may additionally be stated that the operating margin value driver in real life, just as in the Engineering Corp case above, tends to provide very good correlation, whereas the revenue growth value driver tends to give a less clear relationship. Thus, as indicated previously, the EV/Sales multiple is first and foremost generally driven by operating margin, and secondly by sales growth. Consequently, it is usually more advantageous to use the EV/Sales vs. operating margin regression and adjust for any growth abnormalities versus the average peer than to use the EV/Sales vs. revenue growth regression and adjust for any operating margin discrepancies versus the average peer. Then again, no matter what approach is taken, the outcome (that is, the resulting value) has to be exactly the same; otherwise we have made a mistake somewhere.

This implies that for Engineering Corp we need to supplement the previously performed value calculation based on EV/Sales vs. operating margin with an analysis of expected revenue growth. If the expected revenue growth of Engineering Corp should prove noticeably different to that indicated by its average peer, we would run the risk of over- or undervaluing the company if we did not consider these differences. Based on the results of this analysis, we may be forced to revise the 2.37x EV/Sales multiple that we previously derived from the expected operating margin value driver.

From Table 8.6 we learn that the expected average annual sales growth of the peers over the coming three years is 7.9 percent, whereas the corresponding revenue growth of Engineering Corp is 11.5 percent. The condition "all else being equal," under which we previously derived Engineering Corp's applicable EV/Sales multiple using expected operating margin, therefore no longer applies. Engineering Corp's higher expected revenue growth compared with the average peer's thus causes the appropriate EV/Sales vs. operating margin regression for the valuation of Engineering Corp to "shift" upwards.

How much then should the regression line shift due to Engineering Corp's higher expected revenue growth versus the average peer (which thus forms the basis of the initial unrevised regression)? If we can identify similar companies (i.e. reasonably similar operations, not overly divergent margins, etc.) that have significantly different growth expectations, we may, on the basis of their relative positions in terms of the EV/Sales multiple, get an indication of the importance of growth.

In Table 8.6, and as illustrated in Figure 8.9, we note that Peers 1, 2 and 9 have an expected revenue growth significantly above that of the corresponding average peer and that these companies, as a result, also rank above the regression line. Peers 3, 6 and 10, on the other hand, have an expected revenue growth considerably below that of the same average peer, meaning they rank below the regression line.

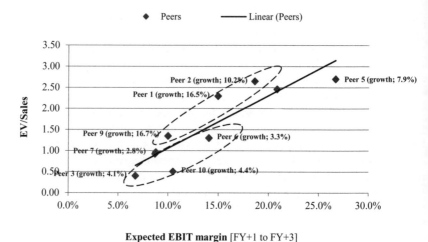

Figure 8.9   EV/Sales vs. operating margin – an expected revenue growth above or below that provided by the average peer will justify a valuation (i.e. a value multiple) above or below that provided by the (thus one-dimensional) EV/Sales vs. operating margin regression line

We may also note that in Peers 5 and 7 we have two so-called "outliers." These companies therefore have an expected revenue growth in line with and substantially below that of the corresponding peer group average but are nonetheless located below and directly on the regression line. For these particular companies in this particular regression there are therefore some unidentified factor(s) driving the resulting EV/Sales multiples below and above that justified solely by expected operating margin and revenue growth. The EV/Sales multiple is, alongside risk, primarily driven by operating margin and revenue growth and secondarily affected by other factors.[6]

In addition, permanent and/or temporarily (if that should be the case) discrepancies between the valuation subject and its peers in terms of fixed assets, working capital requirements, taxes, etc., may also justify a value deviation in relation to that given purely by prime value drivers. These factors will, however, affect all multiples, or the overall appraised value, in unison. In other words, the estimated value of these deviations, whether in absolute dollars or in percentage terms, will affect all multiples or all calculated values

---

[6] For a description of the variables and relationships that drive the EV/Sales multiple, see the Appendix.

alike.[7] Moreover, the individual values of the respective peers may also have been influenced by more or less "soft" factors, such as takeover speculation, value-destroying conflicts of management and board, etc. When dealing with such a complicated issue as a company's value, such "noise" might always be present. Thus minor discrepancies, in accordance with above, can never be completely ruled out.

Our valuation subject, Engineering Corp, has an 11.5 percent expected annual revenue growth for the coming three-year period, i.e. in line with Peers 1, 2 and 9. This indicates a regression line shift at a level somewhere in line with that of these three peers. That is, based on the analysis above, we manually shift the regression line by making a subjective assessment of a relevant regression line shift to a level in line with these three peers that we consider most comparable to Engineering Corp in terms of expected revenue growth (Figure 8.10).

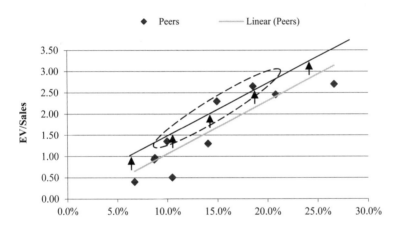

Figure 8.10   EV/Sales vs. operating margin – shifting the regression line, by hand, in order to reflect the unique conditions of the valuation subject in terms of expected revenue growth in relation to the corresponding average peer

---

[7] Let us take working capital as a concrete example. Should the valuation subject in question have, for example, a $10 million working capital deficit compared with its peers, then the resulting value, as calculated using the multiples presented above, should be adjusted downward accordingly, i.e. by $10 million. Similarly, the value of, for example, disparate tax rates (should the peer group consist of companies of varying nationalities and tax rates) may be derived in either absolute or percentage terms (preferably using a discounted cash flow approach, more on which can be found later on in this book).

Thus for each given level of operating margin, and an 11.5 percent average annual expected revenue growth rate for the coming three years, a new equilibrium is set. The regression line now takes into account both the operating margin (at any given level within the specified range) and revenue growth (but still at an 11.5 percent fixed level) value drivers, all else being equal. By hand we have therefore shifted the regression line from its unrevised form (reflecting a 7.9 percent expected revenue growth as given by the average peer) to instead reflect the 11.5 percent expected revenue growth of our valuation subject, Engineering Corp.

We may now use this "growth-adjusted" regression line to execute a "new" derivation of an applicable EV/Sales multiple for Engineering Corp by means of expected operating margin (though now also taking into account the EV/Sales multiple's supplementary prime value driver, expected revenue growth).

As previously recognized, Engineering Corp is expected over the coming three years to have a 20.5 percent operating margin. If we perform the same type of value derivation as above and use this new "growth-adjusted" regression line, we thus find the resulting applicable EV/Sales multiple to be about 2.75x (Figure 8.11).

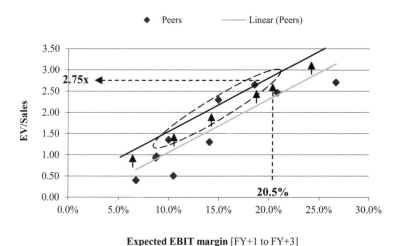

Figure 8.11   EV/Sales vs. operating margin – deriving the appropriate value multiple using a "growth-adjusted" EV/Sales vs. operating margin regression

We can then conclude that Engineering Corp, at an expected operating margin and revenue growth of 20.5 percent and 11.5 percent, respectively, can be justified, all else being equal, at a valuation of about 2.75 times its last reported sales. Then we will have the following revised data (our previous value calculation, which took into account the expected operating margin value driver but not the expected revenue growth value driver, is shown in brackets):

Derived EV/Sales multiple (at given operating margin and
revenue growth):   **2.75x** (2.37x)
Engineering Corp's turnover – Sales ($ millions):   **1,500** (1,500)

Consequently, applying this "operating margin and revenue growth-adjusted" EV/Sales multiple to Engineering Corp, we arrive at the following adjusted value (market value of operating/invested capital):

$$\textbf{2.75} \times \textbf{\$1,500 million} = \textbf{\$4,125 million}$$
$$(2.37 \times \$1,500 \text{ million} = \$3,555 \text{ million})$$

The calculated value of Engineering Corp's invested capital thus increases by a further $570 million (i.e. $4,125 million less $3,555 million). Had we valued the company using the expected operating margin value driver but not the expected revenue growth value driver, we would, all else being equal, have underestimated the value of Engineering Corp's invested capital by $570 million or, alternatively, approximately 15 percent.

It is also important to note that, in a broad perspective, only organic (i.e. internally generated) growth drives value. Growth by acquisitions may in general be considered as realized (unless it can be justified otherwise) on the basis of market value. This relationship will, for that matter, apply to all value multiples driven by growth. For example, the EV/EBIT multiple is primarily driven by expected growth in EBIT. Should that growth be entirely the result of expected acquisitions (i.e. without organic growth, supplementary bonus synergies or streamlining benefits), its contributory value will be zero. That is, the net present value of the cash flows that the acquisition subject is expected to provide to the transferee, i.e. the surplus value of the growth, will therefore be equivalent to the purchase price paid (i.e. the market price) for the subject company in question. The only value-creating element of an acquisition (unless you have, for some reason, been lucky enough to buy at a bargain price) is consequently identified as supplementary synergies or streamlining benefits (i.e. the value of expected synergies and streamlining that you as an acquirer did not have to give away to the concerned seller when negotiating the final purchase price of the acquisition at issue). This may be in the form of either a reduced risk exposure (i.e. a lower cost of capital) or increased expected cash flows. Consequently, if there are no supplementary synergies or streamlining benefits (i.e. greater expected cash flows or a reduced risk exposure) to be gained from the prospective acquisition, then the growth is, in conjunction with its accompanying purchase price, a "zero sum game."

The relationships presented above are correct in theory. In reality, as is evident from the analysis above, it can be quite challenging to estimate, with mathematical exactness (on the basis solely of the comparable companies' prevailing price quotations), how much up or down the EV/Sales vs. operating margin regression line should shift.[8] The theoretically correct solution of the problem above would, of course, be a multiple linear regression analysis (whereby all relevant, i.e. all selected, variables would be captured at the same time, i.e. in the same regression). However, the methodology is mathematically somewhat more complex.

In addition, as is also the overall theme of this entire book, the calculated value of the same valuation subject, as derived by the same analyst under the same valuation purpose, must be the same, irrespective of applied methodology or multiple, otherwise you have made a mistake somewhere. Consequently, if the values given by the respective multiple linear regressions do not correspond – that is, if the valuation of the subject in question, despite the use of multiple linear regression, results in different values depending on what multiple is applied (which, by the way, with close to 100 percent certainty will also be the case) – we are back to square one. We will then be forced to individually analyze and adjust the respective multiples by hand until the resulting company value (i.e. the calculated value of the subject company) proves the same, regardless of the applied multiple (or methodology, for that matter). We will return to this matter again and again in this book.

Thus, however pleasing the idea might be, there will never be a single generic formula or model that can, in one stroke, eliminate or solve all of the tough decisions and judgments of a complex valuation. Numerous people have attempted to automate the valuation process by way of pure mathematics, but purely and mechanically inserting numbers into a model (however complex and fancy that model may be) is not and will never be a valuation. – Or put another way, if the result is wrong, it does not matter that the mathematics are correct.

In order to verify the accuracy of the analysis above, we execute a corresponding adjustment of the EV/Sales vs. revenue growth regression in accordance with the technique above, due to differing levels of expected operating margin relative to the average peer. Therefore, if everything works out in accordance with reasoning above, the 2.75x EV/Sales multiple above that has been derived from the EV/Sales vs. operating margin regression (adjusted for differing growth expectations versus the corresponding average peer) will be more or less exactly the same as that derived from the EV/Sales vs. revenue growth regression (instead adjusted for a differing expected operating margin versus the corresponding average peer).

In Table 8.5, and as illustrated in the EV/Sales vs. revenue growth regression in Figure 8.12, we note that Peers 2, 4 and 5 have an expected operating

---

[8] The mathematically exact regression line shift for the valuation subject in question may, however, be derived by means of a discounted cash flow analysis (DCF approach). We will return to this technique later.

margin substantially above that of the corresponding 14.0 percent peer group average. We also note that this group of companies is indeed to be found high above the regression line. Peers 3, 7, 8, 9 and 10 have, on the other hand, an expected operating margin significantly below that of the average peer and are thus located far below the same regression line. The remaining two peers (Peers 6 and 1) have an expected operating margin in line with that of the 14.0 percent peer group average (at 14.0 percent and 14.9 percent, respectively) and are, accordingly, located more or less right on the regression line. Our valuation subject, Engineering Corp, has a corresponding expected operating margin of 20.5 percent, i.e. in line with that of Peers 2, 4 and 5.

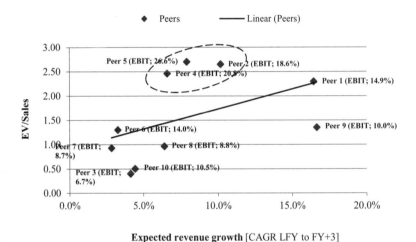

Figure 8.12   EV/Sales vs. revenue growth – an expected operating margin above or below that provided by the average peer will justify a valuation (i.e. a value multiple) above or below that provided by the (one-dimensional) EV/Sales vs. revenue growth regression line

This indicates a regression line shift somewhere in line with these three peers. For each given level of expected revenue growth and a 20.5 percent average expected operating margin for the coming three years, a new equilibrium is set. In other words, the regression line now takes into account both the revenue growth value driver (at any given level within the specified range) and the operating margin value driver (but still at a 20.5 percent fixed level), all else being equal. We therefore shift the regression line by hand from what it reflects in its unrevised form (the 14.0 percent expected operating margin of the average peer) to instead reflect the 20.5 percent expected operating margin of our valuation subject, Engineering Corp (Figure 8.13).

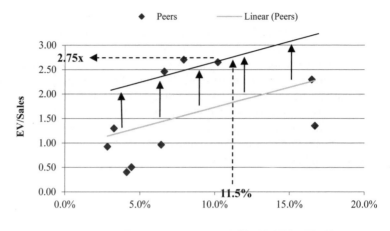

Figure 8.13   EV/Sales vs. revenue growth – deriving the appropriate value multiple using an "operating margin adjusted" EV/Sales vs. revenue growth regression

The "operating margin adjusted" EV/Sales vs. revenue growth regression above thus indicates that Engineering Corp, at expected revenue growth and operating margin of 11.5 percent and 20.5 percent, respectively, is justified at a valuation about 2.75 times its last reported sales, all else being equal. This is in line with the 2.75x EV/Sales multiple that we just derived using the parallel "revenue growth adjusted" EV/Sales vs. operating margin regression.

We can therefore conclude that it makes no difference when deriving an appropriate EV/Sales multiple for our valuation subject whether we apply the EV/Sales vs. operating margin regression and adjust this for differing revenue growth expectations, or whether we apply the analogous (i.e. mirrored) EV/Sales vs. revenue growth regression and adjust this for differing operating margin expectations. However, as both the slope of the regression line and the coefficient of determination of our publicly traded engineering companies are, as discussed previously, significantly higher in terms of the operating margin value driver than the revenue growth value driver, it is more appropriate to use the former as a starting point for adjustment.

Both assessments will nonetheless result in the exact same 2.75x EV/Sales multiple; they have to, otherwise we have made a mistake somewhere. In other words, we would have (indirectly, i.e. by just moving from one regression to another) changed our view of the company's expected development, which consequently would not be a correct cause of action if no such changes have occurred. And, to avoid all doubt, should such changes *have* occurred, we would be obliged to implement exactly the same changes to both regressions and their resulting values would still prove exactly the same, but, of course, different to that before the alleged changes. Again, bear in mind that the two regressions above are a mirror image of each other, and so, all else being equal, they should result in exactly the same value.

To conclude this section, the only time it would have been acceptable to derive the value of Engineering Corp directly, i.e. using the unadjusted 1.33x EV/Sales peer group median multiple, would be if our subject company were to have the exact same expectations for operating margin and revenue growth, all else being equal (i.e. in essence disregarding risk, to which we will return later), as the average peer (because it is from the average peer that the 1.33x value multiple has been derived). At the point that any value driver(s) of the subject company start to depart from the average peer, we run the risk of over- or undervaluing the company if deriving its value using an unadjusted average or median peer group multiple.[9]

8.1.2   EV/EBIT

$$EV/EBIT = \frac{\text{Enterprise value (market value of operating/invested capital)}}{\text{EBIT (earnings before interest and tax)}}$$

If an income measure before depreciation, and amortization – i.e. EBITDA (earnings before interest, taxes, depreciation, and amortization) – or an income measure before just amortization – i.e. EBITA (earnings before interest, taxes and amortization)[10] – is deemed more proper, it can then equally well be used.

If the subject company and its peers show different levels of depreciation as a result of different accounting principles or the current level of depreciation is not representative in a forward-looking perspective, EBITDA may be

---

[9] On the same subject, one can mention the advocacy of Sales multiples for loss-making companies. Some argue that the Sales multiple is a good option should the company demonstrate losses, i.e. should the company show negative (unusable) earnings multiples. The problem, however, with such reasoning is that the Sales multiple of a profitable company is not immediately comparable with that of a corresponding loss-making company. In order to properly value a loss-making company using a Sales multiple, a peer group of similar characteristics is required (that is, the peers also need to be loss-making, all else being equal), otherwise we run the risk of overvaluation.

[10] In accordance with international accounting standards, acquisition goodwill is not amortized on a regular basis. Instead, the earnings capacity that the goodwill represents should be tested for impairment at least once a year. Should the asset in question be deemed impaired, i.e. its earnings capacity has deteriorated to such an extent that its book value is estimated to exceed its economic value, then a write-down is warranted. Should the asset, on the other hand, be deemed unimpaired, no write-down or amortization is required. Should the latter be the case, then that company's EBIT and EBITA will be on a par with one another. Consequently, should any of the comparable companies (which could very well be the case if using multiples derived from transactions involving privately held companies), or the valuation subject, comply with an accounting standard that dictates regular goodwill amortization, it may be advisable to use EBITA rather than EBIT.

preferable.[11] However, as depreciation, in general, indicates the required level of capital requirement – that is, the required level of production resources (as depreciations are a mirror image, i.e. a direct derivative, of capital expenditure) – EBIT is normally the preferred choice. Companies with a low level of depreciation (that is, low capital requirements) will thus more or less show EBITDA and EBIT multiples at the same level, whereas more or less exactly the same companies but with a high level of depreciation (i.e. high capital expenditure) will show EBITDA and EBIT multiples at substantially different levels. An EBITDA multiple derived from a peer of low capital requirements is therefore not directly applicable to a company with a high capital requirement that is similar in other respects, and vice versa.

In addition, otherwise comparable companies may also produce widely different value multiples simply as a result of the choice of production strategy. Should a company opt to purchase its production facilities (i.e. its factories, machinery, and equipment, etc.), the "cost" of these resources will, in essence, be reflected in its resulting depreciations. Consequently, that company's EBIT will be significantly lower than its corresponding EBITDA. If another company, all else being equal, instead opts to lease or outsource its production facilities, the "cost" of these resources will, in contrast, be reflected in increased operating expenses. As a result, that company's EBIT and EBITDA will, in essence, be exactly the same as one another. That is, the line item separating EBIT from EBITDA (disregarding potential amortization), i.e. depreciations, is moved up to the operating expenses line. As a result, these two otherwise identical companies will produce significantly divergent EBITDA multiples. However, their EBIT multiples will (disregarding the financing costs implicitly embedded in the lease fee but not in the corresponding depreciations) be basically the same.

The EV/EBIT multiple, and its accompanying premier value driver expected growth in EBIT, of Engineering Corp's peers are presented in Table 8.7 (specifically, as given by our analysis of Engineering Corp and its comparable companies, compounded annual growth rate, CAGR, LFY to FY+3).

---

[11] Note that any differences in depreciation policy applied need not, in a long-term perspective, necessarily be a problem. If two companies, with the application of fundamentally different depreciation policies, invest on a regular basis, and to the same amounts, in accordance with given policy, these companies will, over time, all else being equal, report annual depreciations on the same absolute level.

Table 8.7 EV/EBIT – value multiple and expected EBIT growth

Company	EV/EBIT LFY	Expected EBIT growth LFY to FY+3
Peer 1	18.1x	23.0%
Peer 2	18.9x	21.9%
Peer 3	8.1x	13.4%
Peer 4	15.2x	16.5%
Peer 5	11.6x	13.6%
Peer 6	11.6x	11.8%
Peer 7	15.3x	21.7%
Peer 8	13.9x	19.0%
Peer 9	14.6x	22.7%
Peer 10	6.8x	13.2%
Mean	13.4x	17.7%
Median	14.2x	17.7%
Engineering Corp	n.a.	21.2%

The peers are thus valued at EV/EBIT multiples in the range of 6.8x to 18.9x, with a mean and median value at 13.4x and 14.2x, respectively. Therefore the comparable companies' invested capital on average and in median is market valued at 13.4 and 14.2 times its last reported operating profit (i.e. its EBIT), respectively. Figure 8.14 shows the EV/EBIT multiples of the peers plotted against expected growth in EBIT as presented in Table 8.7.

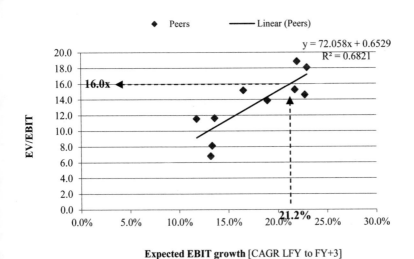

Expected EBIT growth [CAGR LFY to FY+3]

Figure 8.14 EV/EBIT – derivation of applicable value multiple using expected EBIT growth

Engineering Corp has an expected average annual growth rate in EBIT for the coming three years at about 21.2 percent. Using that we can perform the same type of value derivation as we did with EV/Sales vs. operating margin and EV/Sales vs. expected revenue growth earlier. We follow the x-axis of the graph until we reach the 21.2 percent figure and then move up the graph until we reach the regression line. From this point we move to the y-axis to read the given level of EV/EBIT multiple. Engineering Corp, with a 21.2 percent expected average annual growth rate in EBIT for the coming three years, is, all else being equal (which, again, primarily concerns potential risk differences, which we will return to later), justified a valuation at about 16.0 times its last reported EBIT.

This provides us with the following data:

Derived EV/EBIT multiple (at given EBIT growth):   **16.0x**
Engineering Corp's operating profit – EBIT ($ millions): **255**

Consequently, applying this "EBIT growth-adjusted" EV/EBIT multiple to our valuation subject, Engineering Corp, we arrive at the following value (market value of operating/invested capital):

$$16.0 \times \$255 \text{ million} = \$4,080 \text{ million}$$

The enterprise value of Engineering Corp (i.e. the market value of its operating/invested capital) is calculated at $4,080 million, using an "EBIT growth-adjusted" EV/EBIT multiple.

Had we valued the company using the initial unrevised 14.2x multiple (i.e. the median peer group multiple), without regard for the expected growth in EBIT value driver, all else being equal, we would therefore have underestimated the value of Engineering Corp's invested capital by $459 million (i.e. $4,080 million less $3,621 million).

The chief value driver of the EV/EBIT multiple is thus growth in operating profit (i.e. EBIT growth), again disregarding risk (which we will return to later). Accordingly, a high level of EBIT growth will justify a high EV/EBIT multiple. Growth in EBIT may be created, on existing revenues and assets respectively, either by an improved margin (that is, higher earnings on the basis of existing revenues/sales) or an improved capital turnover (that is, higher turnover, i.e. revenues/sales, on the basis of existing assets) or, alternatively, by expected return on future investments.[12] The EV/EBIT multiple, and its ac-

---

[12] In this context it is important to note that the multiple is only driven by value-creating growth (that is, value-creating investments). In other words, if a company brings growth in EBIT by investments in poorly performing assets, this growth will not be value-driving (nor value multiple-driving). If the company in question were to sink funds into unprofitable investments (meaning investments that do not produce income enough to meet the corresponding cost of capital, more on which later), the resulting growth will not drive the multiple. However, in absolute dollars,

companying expected growth in EBIT value driver, is thus capable of seizing, or gathering together, all these factors into one single regression (unlike the EV/Sales multiple, which also had multiple underlying prime value drivers, i.e. operating margin and sales growth).

That the coefficient of determination (R^2) is "only" 0.6821 (though, in reality, this is quite a high R^2), i.e. that "only" 68.21 percent of the variations in EV/EBIT is explained by variations in expected EBIT growth, can be explained by the growth seen in the graph above (i.e. the growth that the respective multiples is plotted against) is given. The above regression is thus based on the assumption that the benchmark companies, for the given/fixed growth in the graph, reinvest (in net fixed assets and working capital) about the exact same proportion of their operating profit after tax. Let us delve deeper into this. Growth in EBIT is stated mathematically with the following relationship:[13]

$$g = NIR \times ROIC$$

where:

g   = growth in EBIT

NIR = net investment ratio (i.e. gross investments in fixed assets, less depreciation, and net working capital in relation to EBIT after tax)

ROIC = return on invested capital (in this case, return on reinvested capital, i.e. reinvested EBIT after tax as per above)

Based on the relationship above, a company may, as a result of a higher expected return on invested capital, ROIC (or to be exact, ROIC on reinvested earnings/capital; that is, ROIC on future net investments), for the exact same amount of money (i.e. at the exact same reinvestment ratio) generate a higher expected growth than a company equivalent in all other respects but with a lower expected ROIC: suppose we have two identical companies, the only difference being that company 1 ("Alpha") has an expected ROIC of 10 percent for future investments, whereas company 2 ("Beta") has a corresponding expected ROIC of 20 percent. Moreover, both companies are expected to show a $100 million operating profit after tax (i.e. EBIT after tax). If both now opt to

---

the company will nonetheless show a growing operating income (that is, the "unprofitable" investments will, of course, in absolute terms, give rise to a higher future EBIT), but that will not be sufficient enough to cover the accompanying cost of capital (i.e. its required rate of return). Consequently, this growth will not be value-creating (it will actually be value-destroying), and so it will not be value multiple driving either.

[13] Assuming the company in question cannot create growth through increased return on existing revenues and assets. A company may, beyond new investments, also generate earnings growth through a greater return on existing assets and turnover (thus a higher capital turnover or a higher margin on existing assets and revenues, respectively), i.e. by way of a greater return on current invested capital – ROIC (at least in the short term; long-term earnings growth cannot, however, be generated by anything other than new net investments).

reinvest 50 percent of their $100 million EBIT after tax, they will, in absolute terms, net invest $50 million. The remaining $50 million may accordingly be "distributed" as free cash flow to firm (FCFF). They will thus recognize exactly the same FCFF, i.e. $50 million, but with a significantly different expected growth rate in EBIT as per the formula above:

(a) Alpha

$$g = \text{NIR} \times \text{ROIC}$$

$$g = 50\% \times 10\%$$

$$g = 5\%$$

(b) Beta

$$g = \text{NIR} \times \text{ROIC}$$

$$g = 50\% \times 20\%$$

$$g = 10\%$$

Both Alpha and Beta are thus expected to generate exactly the same free cash flow for their owners (i.e. $50 million in FCFF). Despite the same $50 million reinvestment, however, Beta is expected, owing to its higher expected ROIC, to increase its earnings by $10 million (i.e. Beta's $100 million in EBIT after tax times its 10 percent expected growth rate as per above), whereas Alpha is only expected to increase its earnings by $5 million (i.e. Alpha's $100 million in EBIT after tax times its 5 percent expected growth rate). As a consequence, Beta will create more value for its owners than Alpha.

Now we come to the actual point. If we turn the reasoning above around, the comparable companies' spread above and below the regression line, i.e. the subject of the somewhat low coefficient of determination of the EV/EBIT vs. expected growth in EBIT regression, may then be explained as follows: if growth is given (i.e. fixed) and other assumptions are unchanged, the regulator then becomes the reinvestment ratio. In other words, if Alpha and Beta are expected to show exactly the same growth rate, they will then demonstrate a divergent reinvestment ratio, rather than a differing growth rate as in the opening case. Accordingly, using the equation above we solve the reinvestment ratio, i.e. NIR, by dividing both sides by ROIC:

$$g = \text{NIR} \times \text{ROIC}$$

$$NIR = \frac{g}{ROIC}$$

To illustrate, let us assume that Alpha and Beta are expected to show a 5 percent growth rate, i.e. we assume that both are expected to reinvest as much EBIT after tax as necessary to reach a 5 percent growth rate. Based on this and otherwise unchanged assumptions as per above, Alpha and Beta's resulting "new" (i.e. required) reinvestment ratio is calculated as follows:

(c) Alpha

$$NIR = \frac{g}{ROIC}$$

$$NIR = \frac{5\%}{10\%}$$

$$NIR = 50\%$$

(d) Beta

$$NIR = \frac{g}{ROIC}$$

$$NIR = \frac{5\%}{20\%}$$

$$NIR = 25\%$$

Beta may, as a result of its higher expected profitability on future investments (i.e. thanks to its higher expected ROIC on new investments), achieve exactly the same expected growth (i.e. a 5 percent growth rate) as Alpha, but using half the amount of money (i.e. at $25 million in reinvestments vs. Alpha's corresponding $50 million). The amount (i.e. the net $25 million as per above) that Beta therefore "saves" is added to its "distributable" free cash flow (that is, its FCFF), meaning that Beta's FCFF will total $75 million compared with $50 million for Alpha. As Beta has exactly the same expected growth rate (i.e. the 5 percent as per above) as Alpha, but a higher expected free cash flow (i.e. $75 million vs. $50 million), Beta is justified at a premium valuation relative to its expected operating profit (i.e. relative to its EBIT). If a greater proportion of the concerned company's EBIT, at a given expected growth, may be "distributed" as FCFF, its EBIT is accordingly justified at a premium valuation.[14]

To conclude, if we now apply this reasoning to our EV/EBIT vs. expected growth in EBIT regression graph, we can note that the growth rate of each comparable company is given (i.e. set). If we were to include Alpha and Beta in this regression graph and both opted to grow by 5 percent (i.e. both "chose" to reinvest enough EBIT after tax to reach a 5 percent growth rate), their level of prime value driver (i.e. their level of "g") in the concerned regression would thus be exactly the same (that is, both Alpha and Beta would show 5 percent expected growth in EBIT as per above). Beta would, however, in accordance with the reasoning above, have a $25 million higher expected free cash flow than Alpha (i.e. $75 million vs. $50 million for Alpha) but both would have exactly the same expected $100 million EBIT after tax. Beta would also be justified at a valuation premium (in relation to its EBIT); that is, it would be justified with a higher EV/EBIT multiple than Alpha. This would consequently warrant a position high above Alpha in the graph above owing to Beta's higher level of "distributable" free cash flow for the given 5 percent growth rate. If for the sake of the argument we also assume that all peers have, on average, (net investment ratio) conditions in line with Alpha, Beta would also be located high above the regression line although its prime value driver, i.e. its expected growth in EBIT, again, would indicate a valuation in line with that given solely by its expected growth, i.e. a valuation in line with Alpha and the regression line.

The relationship above (the derivation of an appropriate EV/EBIT multiple for the company in question using expected growth in EBIT) is thus based on the assumption that the valuation subject in question, for the expected growth given in the scatter chart, reinvests (or if one wants to reverse the reasoning, is able to "distribute," to its owners, by way of free cash flow) about the same proportionate share of its EBIT as the average peer.

In this context it is also important to reiterate that, as with the EV/Sales multiple earlier, chief value driver is not exactly the same as sole value driver.

---

[14] Alternatively, Beta may equally well opt to keep its 50 percent investment ratio, as in the opening example, and will thus experience a higher expected growth rate than Alpha. Beta may therefore choose to (in theory at least; in reality there may not be two such clear-cut alternatives) either boost its free cash flow in relation to Alpha (i.e. its FCFF) or boost its EBIT growth (i.e. its "g"). Notwithstanding that, should Beta have the opportunity to invest more funds into high-yielding projects such as this (i.e. should Beta be faced with a great number of attractive projects as that above), it would be rational for the company to choose a higher growth rate (g) instead of a higher free cash flow to firm (FCFF). If the expected return on reinvested capital (ROIC) is calculated to exceed its corresponding cost of capital (WACC), this option will increase the shareholders' wealth (we will return to the concept of required rate of return, or cost of capital, later).

Therefore, in addition to those presented above, there may be additional causes in relation to that given by the pure regression line for possible deviations.[15]

8.1.3 EV/BEV

$$EV/BEV = \frac{\text{Enterprise value (market value of operating/invested capital)}}{\text{Book enterprise value (book value of operating/invested capital)}}$$

Should the concerned company's book assets be central to its activities, focus may be put on key ratios of balance sheet data.

Knowledge-based companies, i.e. by and large personnel-intensive companies, should not first and foremost be valued using multiples and key ratios of book values. The key assets of these companies are staff and non-book intangible assets (such as established structure capital, trademarks, customer relations, etc.) and these assets are, as we know, not normally accounted for in the balance sheet.[16] This is, however, just a methodology problem, i.e. the risk of making mistakes may increase. The resulting value should, however, not be affected. That is, the calculated value of a given knowledge-based company, as calculated by the same analyst under the same valuation purpose, should, again, be exactly the same whether derived by multiples based on book assets or multiples based on earnings (or any other base metric, for that matter); otherwise we have made a mistake somewhere. Hence, the value of a given company, under a set valuation purpose and an accompanying given expected development, is what it is. That value will only change if the underlying value drivers (i.e. expected growth, profitability, risk exposure, etc.) of the concerned company were to change. In conclusion, the level or the development of the subject company's value driver(s) can never be dependent upon (i.e. can never be driven by) the analyst's choice of valuation multiple (or choice of valuation methodology, for that matter), or, put in other words: *the value multiple is just an instrument to identify that value, not a value driver in itself.*

The EV/BEV multiple, and its accompanying premier value driver expected return on operating/invested capital (i.e. ROOC or, alternatively, ROIC), of Engineering Corp's peers is presented in Table 8.8 (specifically, as given by our analysis of Engineering Corp and its comparable companies, average annual ROIC FY+1 to FY+3).

---

[15] For a description of the variables and relationships that drive the EV/EBIT multiple, see Appendix.

[16] Acquired intangible assets of this type may, however, be recorded on the balance sheet. Notwithstanding that, these rarely have the same significance as those incurred internally.

Table 8.8   EV/BEV – value multiple and expected return on operating/invested capital (i.e. ROOC or, alternatively, ROIC)

Company	EV/BEV LFY	Expected ROOC/ ROIC FY+1 to FY+3
Peer 1	5.3x	24.0%
Peer 2	11.4x	51.0%
Peer 3	1.2x	17.1%
Peer 4	5.2x	27.8%
Peer 5	6.3x	37.8%
Peer 6	3.7x	22.6%
Peer 7	1.3x	7.0%
Peer 8	2.1x	12.6%
Peer 9	4.8x	33.0%
Peer 10	1.0x	18.4%
Mean	4.2x	25.1%
Median	4.3x	23.3%
Engineering Corp	n.a.	29.7%

The peers are thus valued at EV/BEV multiples in the range of 1.0x to 11.4x, with a mean and median value at 4.2x and 4.3x, respectively. This means that the comparable companies' operating/invested capital on average and in median is market valued at 4.2 and 4.3 times its last reported book operating/invested capital, respectively. Figure 8.15 shows the EV/BEV multiples of the peers plotted against the expected return on operating/invested capital as presented in Table 8.8.

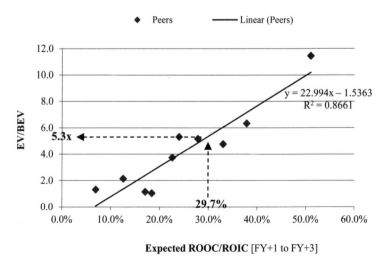

Figure 8.15   EV/BEV – derivation of the applicable value multiple using expected return on operating/invested capital

As seen in Figure 8.15, the relationship is quite clear: the higher the expected return on operating/invested capital, the higher the EV/BEV multiple. The relationship is, as in the case of EV/Sales vs. expected operating margin earlier, logical as investors are likely willing to pay more per dollar of operating/invested capital, the higher the expected return on that dollar of operating/invested capital (even though, in reality, it most likely is not specifically book assets, but rather the hidden, i.e. not accounted for in the balance sheet, built-up non-book intangible assets, such as customer relationships, brand name, structure capital, work processes, etc., that should be credited with the high expected return and, consequently, that investors are willing to pay a premium for).

We can then conclude that Engineering Corp, at an expected average return on operating/invested capital for the coming three years of 29.7 percent, and all else being equal, is justified at a valuation at about 5.3 times its last reported (i.e. its book) operating/invested capital.

We are thus provided with the following data:

Derived EV/BEV multiple (at given ROOC/ROIC):   **5.3x**
Book operating/invested capital of Engineering Corp – BEV ($ millions): **761**

Consequently, applying this "return on operating/invested capital adjusted" EV/BEV multiple to Engineering Corp, we arrive at the following value (market value of operating/invested capital):

$$5.3 \times \$761 \text{ million} = \$4,033 \text{ million}$$

The enterprise value of Engineering Corp (i.e. the market value of its operating/invested capital) is thus, by way of a "return on operating/invested capital adjusted" EV/BEV multiple, calculated at $4,033 million.

Had we valued the company using the unrevised 4.3x multiple (i.e. the median peer group multiple), without regard to the expected return on operating/invested capital value driver, all else being equal, we would thus have underestimated the value of Engineering Corp's invested capital by $761 million (i.e. $4,033 million less $3,272 million).

EV/BEV therefore has one prime value driver: – expected return on operating/invested capital (i.e. ROOC or, alternatively, ROIC), disregarding risk, which we will return to later.[17] However, ROIC has two underlying value drivers: operating margin and capital turnover. A high return on operating/invested

---

[17] The multiple is, first and foremost, driven by expected return on invested capital (ROIC) and secondarily by growth. However, in contrast to the EV/Sales multiple (as displayed in our operating margin regression previously) which is also secondarily driven by growth, significant parts of this growth are captured by expected ROIC as a value driver. In other words, an increased capital turnover (thus an increased sales volume on the basis of existing assets) will manifest itself as higher expected ROIC. Should, however, the subject company in question, additionally, have higher expected value-creating growth relative to the average peer, that is, an additional expected growth in terms of value-creating net investments (thus investment opportunities expected to generate a higher return than its corresponding cost of capital), there might be reason to slightly shift the regression line using the previously reported technique. For a description of the variables and relationships that drive the EV/BEV multiple, see the Appendix.

capital may thus be a result of either a high operating margin or a high capital turnover or, alternatively, some combination of the two. Both these parameters are therefore captured in the expected return on operating/invested capital value driver.

It is finally worth noting that the regression has, in this case, a very high coefficient of determination at 0.8661. That means over 86 percent of the changes in the dependent variable (i.e. EV/BEV) are explained by changes in the independent variable (i.e. by expected return on operating/invested capital). The relationship may thus be considered very reliable.

8.1.4   Some closing remarks

As a final point to make in this section, it should be stressed that the individual key value driver(s) of each individual value multiple, and the resulting individual level of that value multiple, is purely individual. For example, we concluded that the key value driver of the EV/Sales multiple was operating margin (in our Engineering Corp case study, we chose to apply the EBIT margin) and so a high level of expected operating margin justified a high level of EV/Sales multiple.

The value multiple EV/EBIT, on the other hand, has growth in operating profit (i.e. EBIT growth) as its chief value driver. Accordingly, a high level of expected EBIT growth will justify a high level for the EV/EBIT multiple. Growth in EBIT may, in accordance with the previous reasoning, be created on existing revenues and assets, respectively, either by an improved margin or improved capital turnover or, alternatively, by expected return on future investments. A high operating margin may but will not necessarily have to result in good EBIT growth.

If we for a moment focus on growth expected by future investments, i.e. if we assume that the company in question can change neither its current operating margin nor its existing capital turnover, we can conclude that this (i.e. the expected growth) in its entirety is a product of future investments (if any). Hence any expected growth in EBIT will, in its entirety, be a product of operating profit of future net investments/capital expenditures and nothing else. Expected return on future investments is, like expected return on existing assets, dependent upon expected margin and capital turnover.

Suppose that we have two comparable companies: Low Margin Corp and High Margin Corp.[18] Figure 8.16, i.e. the well-known DuPont formula, illustrates the expected pre-tax return on operating/invested capital (i.e. pre-tax ROOC or, alternatively, ROIC, see Chapter 7 for further details on this subject)

---

[18] In order to simplify the example, return on invested capital is calculated pre-tax.

of Low Margin Corp (the expected return is the result of a 10 percent operating margin at a 1.5 capital turnover rate (10% × 1.5 = 15%)).[19]

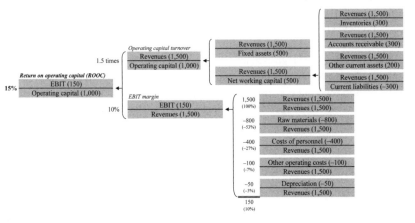

Figure 8.16   Return on operating/invested capital (i.e. ROOC/ROIC) – Low Margin Corp

Figure 8.17 illustrates the expected return on operating/invested capital of High Margin Corp (the expected return is the result of a 15 percent operating margin at a 1.0 capital turnover rate (15% × 1.0 = 15%)).

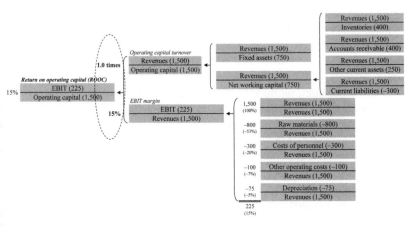

Figure 8.17   Return on operating/invested capital (i.e. ROOC/ROIC) – High Margin Corp

---

[19] Return on operating capital (ROOC) may be defined as either operating profit in relation to (i.e. operating profit divided by) operating capital, or as operating margin multiplied by capital turnover. Accordingly, these two alternatives correspond to one another, i.e., whichever methodology is applied, the result will be exactly the same (as illustrated in the example, the ROOC can be calculated as either operating income, EBIT, divided by operating capital, which is 150/1000 = 15%, or as operating margin, EBIT%, multiplied by capital turnover, which is 10% × 1.5 = 15%).

Low Margin Corp and High Margin Corp are thus expected to produce exactly the same return on invested capital, i.e. 15 percent, though as a result of two totally different combinations of operating margin and capital turnover. Thus, and in accordance with previous discussion, a company whose business model (i.e. future investments) comprises a low margin at a high capital turnover, i.e. Low Margin Corp in the above example, will generate exactly the same future EBIT growth as a company whose business model (i.e. future investments) comprises a high margin at a low capital turnover, i.e. High Margin Corp in the above example, assuming that both reinvest exactly the same proportional share of operating profit (i.e. EBIT) after tax, all else being equal:

$$g = NIR \times ROIC$$

where:

g   = growth in EBIT
NIR = net investment ratio (i.e. gross investments in fixed assets, less depreciation, and net working capital in relation to EBIT after tax)
ROIC = return on invested capital (that is, in this case, return on reinvested capital, i.e. reinvested EBIT after tax as per above)

High Margin Corp will therefore not produce a higher EBIT growth than Low Margin Corp, even though it operates at a 50 percent higher margin than Low Margin Corp (it will in fact, in accordance with the above reasoning, produce exactly the same EBIT growth) or a greater free cash flow (as, due to the same expected level of ROOC/ROIC and g, and all else being equal, it is expected to have exactly the same reinvestment ratio, according to the equation above). In the same way, they are also justified with a valuation at exactly the same EV/EBIT multiple.

If two companies, on the other hand, expect to have identical capital turnover, the company with the highest expected margin will also have the highest expected growth (due to a higher expected return on future reinvestments), all else being equal. If that should be the case, the margin will drive the EV/EBIT multiple (i.e. the company with the highest margin, all else being equal, will also have the highest expected growth and, consequently, the highest EV/EBIT multiple). However, it could as easily be the other way around. That is, if these two companies instead expect to have exactly the same operating margin, the company with the highest capital turnover will instead have the highest expected growth (and thus also the highest EV/EBIT multiple), all else being equal.

In accordance with the previous statement, however, these two companies will most likely, owing to the all-encompassing forces of the market (i.e. as a result of their choice of business model), be forced to show only either/or, i.e. either a high margin at a low capital turnover (the company will sell few but very profitable/expensive goods) or vice versa (the company will sell less profitable/expensive goods, but at quite large volumes), not both. Therefore, neither the margin nor the capital turnover will, on their own (i.e. in isolation), drive the EV/EBIT multiple. Only the end product, i.e. the resulting return on investment (the resulting ROOC/ROIC) will be of value; in other words, be of EV/EBIT multiple driving status (just as in our High Margin Corp/Low Margin Corp case above).[20]

It follows that one should not use operating margin as the prime explanatory variable (i.e. value driver) of the EV/EBIT multiple. Should someone state, without further analysis, that a company should be valued at a premium on the basis of the EV/EBIT multiple owing to a higher operating margin than the corresponding peer(s), then he or she may be skating on very thin ice.[21]

This implies that a given company may, as a result of a high expected operating margin, be justified a high valuation, i.e. a high value multiple, in terms of EV/Sales, for example, and at the same time, as a result of a relatively modest expected earnings growth (in consequence of a somewhat moderate capital turnover in contrast to the high expected margin), be justified a low valuation, i.e. a low value multiple, in terms of EV/EBIT, for example, or vice versa if that should be the case. In accordance with the previous reasoning however, the resulting value(s) for the valuation subject in question will be the same irrespective of the applied multiple(s), otherwise one has, again, made a mistake somewhere.

We can illustrate the problem above using a simple concrete example: suppose we have two companies, Company A and Company B, with an identical capital base in absolute terms (i.e. an identical asset base in absolute U.S. dollars). We assume that to be $500 million. Company A has a turnover (i.e. sales) of $1,000 million, whereas Company B has a mere $500 million in overall sales. However, Company B has twice the operating margin of Company A (20 percent vs. 10 percent). Suppose further that a comparable companies analysis justifies a 1.00x EV/Sales valuation for Company A (that is, we assume that a 1.00x EV/Sales multiple has been derived from comparable companies with a 10 percent expected operating margin), whereas a corresponding 2.00x EV/

---

[20] One could also possibly argue that a high operating margin, compared with a corresponding low one, could, all else being equal (i.e. given exactly the same capital turnover), also reduce the risk of the company in question. Based on this, a high margin would, all else being equal, imply a lower risk exposure and, in consequence, justify a higher multiple. However, one could just as easily (as in the example above) argue that a high capital turnover, all else being equal (i.e. given exactly the same operating margin), would give exactly the same effect. Hence it makes no difference whether the higher overall returns (which, in fact, is what is to be accredited for the lower risk exposure) originates from a high margin or a high capital turnover, all else being equal, the end result will be the same.

[21] Anyone wishing for physical evidence of this may establish an EV/EBIT vs. operating margin regression for just about any group of comparable companies. There is a very high probability that the graph will show more or less no correlation at all, i.e. it will most likely look like a "shower of hail."

Sales valuation is justified for Company B (that is, we assume that a 2.00x EV/ Sales multiple has been derived from comparable companies with a 20 percent expected operating margin), all else being equal (which, among other things, also presupposes the valuation subject and its peers have an equal risk profile).

As regards growth in EBIT, Company A and Company B are both expected to reach a level of about 5 percent. Certainly, Company B is expected to reach twice the operating margin of Company A. On the other hand, Company A is expected to have twice the capital turnover of Company B (as given by its $1,000 million turnover in relation to its $500 million capital base versus $500 million turnover in relation to its $500 million capital base for Company B). Under these conditions their return on future investments will be exactly the same. All else being equal (i.e. essentially assuming their net investment ratios are similar), their future growth in EBIT will also be exactly the same. As they are expected to show exactly the same growth in EBIT, all else being equal, they are also justified as valued with exactly the same EV/EBIT multiple (we assume a 10.0x EV/EBIT multiple, derived from comparable companies with 5 percent expected growth in EBIT) (Table 8.9).

Table 8.9   Company A and Company B – calculated value on the basis of EV/Sales and EV/EBIT, respectively

Valuation of Company A & Company B, respectively ($ millions)	Company A	Company B
Sales	1,000	500
EBIT margin	*10%*	*20%*
EBIT	100	100
Applicable EV/EBIT multiple (as per discussion above)	10.0x	10.0x
Calculated value (applicable EV/EBIT multiple times EBIT)	**1,000**	**1,000**
Applicable EV/Sales multiple (as per discussion above)	1.00x	2.00x
Calculated value (applicable EV/Sales multiple times Sales)	**1,000**	**1,000**

The calculated value of both Company A and Company B is therefore $1,000 million using the EV/EBIT multiple. Consequently, exactly the same $100 million expected cash flow before tax (in simplified terms EBIT), and the exact same expected growth rate of that cash flow, all else being equal, will merit exactly the same valuation result, i.e. $1,000 million.

As noted, the calculated value using the EV/Sales multiple is for both Company A and Company B also $1,000 million. It is logical that the calculated value is exactly the same for both using the EV/Sales multiple as that calculated using the EV/EBIT multiple, as their expected cash flow before tax (in simplified terms, their EBIT), i.e. the $100 million, and the expected growth rate of that EBIT, as above, is exactly the same, all else being equal. Thus the fact that Company B has twice the justified EV/Sales multiple due to it having twice the expected operating margin of Company A is therefore offset by its having half the expected sales of Company A; that is, half the capital turnover. The reverse applies to Company A.

The justified level of the respective value multiple is thus (as illustrated in the example above) dependent on the level of individual value driver(s) associated with that particular multiple and nothing else. One must therefore not be led to believe that a company that, for example, is valued at a very high level of EV/Sales as a result of a very high expected operating margin (such as Company B above) should also automatically be valued at a high level for all other value multiples (which indeed Company B was not).[22]

It is thus not the sales themselves that justify the resulting value from the EV/Sales multiple, but instead the result, or the cash flow, of the expected sales (hence the influence of the operating margin on the EV/Sales multiple). As a result, it is logical that companies with exactly the same level of earnings capacity, irrespective of their accompanying level of sales (such as Company A and Company B in the case above), also are valued at exactly the same amount whether this value has been derived using the EV/Sales multiple or the EV/EBIT multiple (or any other multiple, for that matter), all else being equal.

Note also that a DCF valuation of Company A and Company B in accordance with terms and conditions above would look exactly the same. That is, the expected gross cash flow before tax (in simplified terms, EBIT) of Company A and Company B would be exactly the same, i.e. $100 million (even though the expected turnover would differ significantly), and the expected growth of that cash flow is also forecasted as the same, i.e. 5 percent. In addition, we have, in accordance with the statement above, also assumed that peers and Company A and Company B have exactly the same risk profile (i.e. exactly the same cost of capital). Hence, as the assumptions in our cash flow valuations are exactly the same as in our market approach valuations, the resulting values must then therefore also be exactly the same. If we have carried it out correctly, our cash flow valuations of Company A and Company B will therefore give the exact same value as that given by the corresponding market approach valuations, i.e. $1,000 million.

---

[22] However, even though the multiples are not automatically driven by exactly the same underlying variables, some multiples may, under certain circumstances, be influenced by the same underlying variables and changes. For example, the EV/Sales multiple is primarily driven by operating margin and revenue growth. The EV/EBIT multiple, on the other hand, is, for the reasons above, driven by (on existing sales and assets) improvements in operating margin or capital turnover, or on expected return on future net investments. Thus, should the company in question improve its capital turnover through increased sales (i.e. should it manage to earn more revenues from its current asset base), the EV/Sales multiple and the EV/EBIT multiple will be driven by the same factor. The message, however, is that no relationship can be taken for granted and an individual analysis has to be carried out on each multiple.

As both the DCF approach and the market approach are based on the same foundations (i.e. are each other's mirror image), in accordance with the given reasoning, they must logically also, given exactly the same valuation purpose and underlying assumptions, provide exactly the same value. Regardless of the applied multiple (e.g. EV/Sales, EV/EBIT, or anything else, for that matter) or methodology (e.g. DCF, the market approach, or any other method, for that matter), the calculated value of a given company, as performed by the same analyst under the same valuation purpose, must be exactly the same. Should this not be the case, one has either:

1. made a technical mistake (i.e. been the victim of miscalculation); or
2. (directly or indirectly) applied different assumptions in different models and multiples, which would not, accordingly, be a correct course of action. You need to either stand by your analysis and assessment of the concerned company's most likely development, as regards all multiples and methodologies, or implement exactly the same changes to all methodologies and multiples. You cannot, whether directly or indirectly (i.e. at random and without cause or justification), change your view on the expected risks and prospects of the concerned company depending just on what methodology or multiple you happen to be using at the time.

8.2 RISK

When we analyzed the EV/Sales multiple at the beginning of this chapter (and all other subsequent value multiples for that matter), we stated the all-important value drivers *in addition to or besides* risk. Now it is time to investigate the impact of risk on our appropriate multiple analysis.

As outlined initially in this book, there are three generally accepted valuation methods:

- *Method 1 – The DCF approach:* The discounted cash flow approach aims to net present value a cash flow generating asset (e.g. a company) by discounting its future expected returns with an appropriate rate of return for the asset in question.
- *Method 2 – The market approach:* The market approach aims to derive a company's value based on how similar firms are priced on the stock market or via transactions.
- *Method 3 – The net asset approach:* The net asset approach aims to value a company on the basis of its balance sheet statement.

First, a clarification: a net asset valuation concerns the calculation of a company's value with reference to its balance sheet statement. However, as the basic foundation of such a valuation is generally "business as usual," i.e. going concern (unless we are about to value a liquidation subject), the individual assets should be valued accordingly. This means that all assets should be valued on the basis of the returns they can expect to generate under present use (i.e. not just to the values they currently carry at book or can be sold or replaced at). Consequently, in order to capture these values *and* the values of intangible assets not carried on the balance sheet, including expected synergies among all these assets, most individual assets need, in practice, to be cash flow valued (with the exception of more or less liquid assets, such as cash, marketable securities, accounts receivables, etc.).

Hence, if the net asset valuation has been executed correctly (i.e. not a simplified version in which only adjusted values of effortlessly identified tangible assets, such as machinery and equipment, office buildings, etc., have been reported at market value equivalents), the calculated value of the company should, in theory as well as in practice, be identical to that arrived at using Method 1, the discounted cash flow approach (as the expected free cash flow of the DCF represents/reflects the real earnings capacity of all these assets, whether recorded on the balance sheet or not). However, as the methodology is extremely difficult as well as extremely time-consuming to implement in real life, and as it is founded on the same theoretical basis as the DCF approach, it is justifiable to restrict oneself to using only the market approach and the DCF approach.

The primary target of this book is not to dwell on the cash flow valuation approach, but the market approach and the DCF approach are two sides of the same coin in the same way as the net asset approach and the DCF approach are (i.e. all three methods are, theoretically, linked with one another). To create an understanding of how the risk of a stock or a business enterprise affects the derivation of an applicable value multiple for the company in question, an overview of the function and derivation of a cash flow valuation and a risk-adjusted discount rate is required. The purpose of this is not to teach the cash flow valuation method, but instead to illustrate the importance of risk when calculating equity or enterprise values using value multiples derived from comparable companies. One need not be able to apply the discounted cash flow methodology in practice, but one does need to grasp and embrace the reasoning and conclusions (and its importance for derivation of applicable value multiples) that the review is aimed at.

8.2.1   The discounted cash flow approach (DCF)

The discounted cash flow approach aims to estimate the value of an asset or investment by:

1. projecting its future expected cash flows; and
2. discounting these to a present value with an appropriate rate of return for the asset or investment in question.

Consequently, the concepts of required rate of return (alternatively, discount rate or cost of capital), present value, and future value are all important matters to be familiar with when working with cash flow valuations. To exemplify: if we as individuals deposit $100 in our bank for a period of one year, we will demand a certain return (interest) for this (that is, compensation from the bank for them borrowing the $100 from us for a year). Let us assume the going market rate for this is 5.0 percent, i.e. the average bank in the market is expected to offer 5.0 percent interest on an annual basis for such a deposit. This means that we require a 5.0 percent return over the next year to deposit $100 in a bank selected at random. Should a bank offer only 3.0 percent, we would not deposit our $100 with them since the return falls short of our, or the market's (in accordance with above), 5.0 percent "required rate of return."

In a year we will therefore be handed our $100 deposit plus $5 in interest, meaning we receive a total of $105 from our bank (the future value is thus $100 × 1.05 = $105). This means that $100 today is equivalent to $105 in one year. Correspondingly, the same thinking applies to present value of future payments. In other words, to receive $105 from the bank in one year is equivalent to having $100 today (present value is thus $105/1.05 = $100) as we can deposit our $100 in the bank, as illustrated above, and let that sum "grow" to $105 in a year. Consequently, given the above prerequisites and assumptions, $100 today is worth exactly the same as $105 in a year (and vice versa), or to put it in other words, we are indifferent, i.e. equally happy, to receive $100 today as to receive $105 in one year (and vice versa).

The general formula for cash flow valuation of a given asset is as follows:

$$PV = \sum_{i=1}^{n} \frac{CF_i}{(1+k)^i}$$

where:

PV = Present value
$\sum$ = Sum of
i = The period in the future in which a prospective cash flow is expected to be received
CF_i = Expected cash flow in the ith period in the future
k = Discount rate
n = The last period in the future in which a cash flow is expected to be received. If we are dealing with an asset that is expected to generate cash flows for an infinite time, such as a company under the assumption of going concern, n is equal to infinity: ∞.

The above formula may at first glance look complicated. In principle, however, one merely needs to replace the symbols with numbers and summarize the product. The formula may be expanded as follows to show each period individually:

$$PV = \frac{CF_1}{(1+k)} + \frac{CF_2}{(1+k)^2} + \frac{CF_3}{(1+k)^3} + \ldots + \frac{CF_n}{(1+k)^n}$$

where:

PV   = Present value
$CF_{1\ldots n}$ = Expected cash flow in each of the periods 1 through n, n being the last period in which a cash flow is expected to be received
k   = Discount rate

We illustrate this using a simple example: suppose you have won the top prize in a state-run lottery. The prize consists of the state paying you $100,000 per year for a period of five years. What then is this win worth? Cash flow (CF) is $100,000 and is assumed to be payable at the end of each year. Duration (n) is five years. How then do we determine the rate of return, or the discount rate (k), for such a cash flow stream? The likelihood that the state would go bankrupt is virtually non-existent. Furthermore, the cash flows will not vary, i.e. they will be exactly $100,000 a year, meaning we have a risk-free cash flow stream. The corresponding rates of returns should thus reflect zero risk at maturities corresponding to the payments in question (i.e. 1–5 years), in consequence matching government bonds of equivalent maturities. We assume for simplicity's sake that the rate of returns (i.e. the interest rates) on government bonds with maturities of 1, 2, 3, 4, and 5 years, as at the valuation date, are alike at 5.0 percent (i.e. we assume a flat yield curve). We can thus calculate the present value of the winnings by inserting given numbers into the formula:

$$PV = \frac{CF_1}{(1+k)} + \frac{CF_2}{(1+k)^2} + \frac{CF_3}{(1+k)^3} + \frac{CF_4}{(1+k)^4} + \frac{CF_5}{(1+k)^5}$$

$$PV = \frac{100,000}{(1+0.05)} + \frac{100,000}{(1+0.05)^2} + \frac{100,000}{(1+0.05)^3} + \frac{100,000}{(1+0.05)^4} + \frac{100,000}{(1+0.05)^5}$$

$$PV = 95,238 + 90,703 + 86,384 + 82,270 + 78,353$$

$$PV = 432,948$$

The present value to receive a total of $500,000 over a period of five years, on basis of conditions and distribution as presented above, is therefore $432,948. Similarly, the future value, i.e. the value at the end of year 5 to receive $78,353 today, $82,270 in one year, $86,384 in two years, etc., as cited, is $500,000:

$$FV = CF_1(1+k)^5 + CF_2(1+k)^4 + CF_3(1+k)^3 + CF_4(1+k)^2 + CF_5(1+k)$$

$$FV = 78,353\ (1.05)^5 + 82,270\ (1.05)^4 + 86,384\ (1.05)^3 + 90,703\ (1.05)^2 \\ + 95,238\ (1.05)$$

$$FV = 100,000 + 100,000 + 100,000 + 100,000 + 100,000$$

$$FV = 500,000$$

Now let us widen the above example: suppose in the same lottery we had the alternative of winning $100,000 for infinity, i.e. that we would receive $100,000 every 12 months from the state on a never-ending basis. What would be the present value of such winnings? The so-called Gordon's formula provides the answer:

$$PV = \frac{CF_1}{k-g}$$

where:

PV   =   Present value
CF_1 =   Expected cash flow in period 1, i.e. the period immediately following
            the valuation date
k   =   Discount rate
g   =   Expected cash flow growth rate compounded in perpetuity

The payments are not expected to grow with time, i.e. we will receive exactly $100,000 annually for an indefinite period (g thus equals zero). Furthermore, for the sake of simplicity we assume that the yield curve is flat, i.e. the annual government bond yield for all maturities from one year to infinity is assumed to be 5.0 percent. We can thereby calculate the present value of such a winning using the Gordon's formula:[23]

$$PV = \frac{CF_1}{k-g}$$

$$PV = \frac{100,000}{0.05 - 0.00}$$

---

[23] This is exactly the same as forecasting and present value calculating the payments above (i.e. the $100,000) by hand year by year through all eternity. In other words, if we enter $100,000 per year (in accordance with the originally presented formula) into a spreadsheet, at a 5 percent discount rate, on a never-ending basis (that is, we create a 100,000-year forecast period rather than the applied 5 years above), the present value (PV) of this cash flow stream would be identical to that reported by Gordon's formula, i.e. $2 million.

$$PV = 2,000,000$$

The present value to receive $100,000 annually, in accordance with conditions and assumptions above, is thus $2 million. One could also say we are equally happy to receive $2 million in a lump sum today as to receive $100,000 per year forever if we had the choice of these two options, all else being equal.

Gordon's formula, however, presupposes a constant growth factor (g). Should growth be expected to fluctuate over the period concerned, we will be forced to use a combination of the initially presented formula and Gordon's formula. To give an example: let us say that in the lottery example we would instead have won $100,000 per year at an annual 10 percent increase over a period of five years, and then 2 percent per year forever, all else being equal; how would we calculate the present value of such winnings? We would be forced to compute the value of the winnings using a combination of the two formulas above, i.e. the total value of the winnings have to be estimated in two steps. Step one, we estimate the present value of each of the expected cash flows over the five-year period constituting the super-growth phase (i.e. the explicit forecast period). Step two, when growth has reached a constant sustainable stage, we calculate the value of all cash flows expected to be received as of year 6 and onwards (i.e. the residual, or the terminal, value). The technique is shown below as a formula:[24]

$$PV = \frac{CF_1}{(1+k)} + \frac{CF_2}{(1+k)^2} + \frac{CF_3}{(1+k)^3} + \ldots + \frac{CF_n}{(1+k)^n} + \frac{\left(\dfrac{CF_n(1+g)}{k-g}\right)}{(1+k)^n}$$

where:

PV $\quad$ = Present value
$CF_{1\ldots n}$ = Expected cash flow in each of the periods 1 through n, n being the last period in the discrete forecast period
k $\quad$ = Discount rate
g $\quad$ = Expected cash flow growth rate compounded in perpetuity, starting with the last period of the discrete forecast period as base year

We may now use this formula above to calculate the present value of the lottery winnings at hand:

---

[24] Note that the formula in brackets (i.e. at the top right of the equation) is "Gordon's formula". That is, directly following last year's cash flow, in the originally presented formula, we now find Gordon's formula.

$$PV = \frac{CF_1}{(1+k)} + \frac{CF_2}{(1+k)^2} + \frac{CF_3}{(1+k)^3} + \frac{CF_4}{(1+k)^4} + \frac{CF_5}{(1+k)^5} + \frac{\left(\dfrac{CF_5(1+g)}{k-g}\right)}{(1+k)^5}$$

$$PV = \frac{110,000}{(1+0.05)} + \frac{121,000}{(1+0.05)^2} + \frac{133,100}{(1+0.05)^3} + \frac{146,410}{(1+0.05)^4} + \frac{161,051}{(1+0.05)^5}$$

$$+ \frac{\left(\dfrac{161,051(1+0.02)}{0.05-0.02}\right)}{(1+0.05)^5}$$

$$PV = 104,762 + 109,751 + 114,977 + 120,452 + 126,188 + 4,290,381$$

$$PV = 4,866,510$$

The present value of the lottery winnings is thus $4,866,510. If we had wanted to, we could have varied the growth rate as well as the extent of the explicit forecast period. We would therefore have experimented with a variable growth rate across individual years in the explicit forecast period rather than using the steady 10 percent applied in the example above. We could also have increased or decreased the duration of the explicit forecast period. However, to calculate the residual value of the asset after the explicit forecast period (i.e. to value an infinite cash flow stream using Gordon's formula), we must be in a stage of steady growth, i.e. the explicit forecast period must be made long enough so that by the end of it we have reached a constant growth stage.

The exercises above refer to simple state lottery winnings. Since there was no uncertainty about either the amount or the time of payment, we were able to calculate present as well as future values using prevailing risk-free rates. The examples may seem simple but the concept remains the same for all types of cash flow generating assets. However, different assets/investments carry different risks. The required rate of return (i.e. the discount rate) should reflect the risk associated with the asset or investment in question. Should we calculate the value of an asset or investment that is substantially riskier than the lottery winnings in our exercises (i.e. where we do not beforehand know either the exact amount of cash flows to be received or the exact point in time when they will be received, in contrast to our lottery winning examples), we would require a substantially higher rate of return. In other words, we would estimate the present value of such an asset or investment (i.e. discount the expected cash flows of the asset in question) by a rate of return substantially higher than the 5.0 percent risk-free rate used above. This discussion therefore brings us straight to the subject of business valuation. If we invest funds in a stock or a business, we will not know in advance what return is to be received.

On this basis, we will demand a long-term annual rate of return significantly above that of corresponding risk-free assets.[25]

The generic cash flow valuation formula (as presented initially in this chapter) is:

$$PV = \sum_{i=1}^{n} \frac{CF_i}{(1+k)^i}$$

where:

PV $=$ Present value
$\sum$ $=$ Sum of
i $=$ The period in the future in which a prospective cash flow is expected to be received
CF_i $=$ Expected cash flow in the ith period in the future
k $=$ Discount rate
n $=$ The last period in the future in which a cash flow is expected to be received. If we are dealing with an asset that is expected to generate cash flows for an infinite time, such as a company that is assumed to be going concern, n is equal to infinity – ∞.

Had we been dealing with a business valuation, the term CF above would have been equivalent to the subject company's expected cash flows instead of annual lottery payments, as above. The discount rate (k) would have been tantamount to an investor's expected return of such an investment (i.e. the investor's required rate of return on investments with this type of risk exposure) rather than the risk-free rate of return as above.

Furthermore, making use of this formula for business valuation, we face the same choices as with the multiples earlier, i.e. should we wish to derive the equity value of a given company, for example, one may either calculate the value of the business enterprise and adjust for, i.e. subtract, the existing net debt balance or one may calculate the value of the equity via a direct approach. If one chooses the former, the formula above is adapted as follows (i.e. one starts off with a derivation of firm value or EV):

$$PVF(EV) = \sum_{i=1}^{\infty} \frac{FCFF_i}{(1+WACC)^i}$$

where:

---

[25] It is important to note that we are referring to expected returns. Actual returns (i.e. realized capital gains and dividends over the concerned period) may thus prove to be completely different.

PVF   = Present value firm (i.e. enterprise value – EV)
$\sum$ = Sum of
FCFF$_i$ = Expected free cash flow to firm in the ith period in the future
i   = The period in the future in which a prospective cash flow is expected to be received
WACC = Weighted average cost of capital
∞ = Infinity

It follows that the equity value, or the value of 100 percent of the shares, is given by the firm or enterprise value as presented, less the interest-bearing net debt balance.

The equity cash flow value may also be estimated directly, i.e. without passing through the enterprise value. Cash flow valuation of equity capital (equity value or P):

$$PVE(P) = \sum_{i=1}^{\infty} \frac{FCFE_i}{\left(1+K_e\right)^i}$$

where:

PVE   = Present value equity (i.e. price – P)
$\sum$ = Sum of
FCFE$_i$ = Expected free cash flow to equity in the ith period in the future
i   = The period in the future in which a prospective cash flow is expected to be received
K_e = Cost of equity
∞ = Infinity

This routine provides the equity value directly, with no adjustment (i.e. no deduction) of interest-bearing liabilities to derive equity value (P) since lender claims on the business enterprise, as opposed to the corresponding valuation of the firm (EV), are already reflected as reductions in cash flows (in the form of interest payments, etc.). Should you for any reason wish to calculate the value of the business enterprise using this approach, it is given by the market value of equity as presented with the addition of interest-bearing net debt.

It is additionally vital that the numerator and the denominator, as in the case of the value multiples earlier, go hand in hand. Should the numerator cash flows be solely in favor of the company's equity holders (i.e. free cash flows to equity – FCFE), the denominator rate of return should reflect proceeds solely to the shareholders' favor (i.e. a cost of equity – K_e). Should the numerator cash flows, on the other hand, be available to all business enterprise investors (i.e. free cash flows to firm – FCFF), the denominator rate of return should reflect proceeds available to all financiers of the firm (i.e. a weighted average cost of capital – WACC) (Figure 8.18).

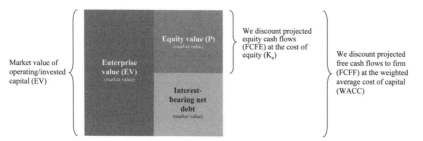

Figure 8.18   Enterprise value (i.e. market value of operating/invested capital) vs. shareholder value (i.e. market value of equity) – the cash flow and the discount rate must go hand in hand

One can therefore calculate the DCF value of any business enterprise (EV) as well as the corresponding value of the equity (P) using a direct approach as well as an indirect approach. The calculated EV or P, respectively, as given by either of these two approaches, should prove exactly the same, no matter which method is used. To be precise, the equity value of the subject company in question as given by the indirect approach, i.e. the equity value as derived using cash flows to firm (adjusted by its interest-bearing net debt) must be identical to that derived using the direct approach, i.e. the equity value of the subject company as derived via cash flows to equity, otherwise you have made a mistake somewhere.

8.2.2   Forecasted cash flows

When performing business valuations, one would normally, as in our lottery winnings examples earlier, forecast explicit cash flows for a well-defined time period (often in the range of 5–10 years). Then a normalized sustainable level ("Normal") is set as the basis for the residual value calculation.

(a) Free cash flow to firm (FCFF)

Earnings before interest and tax (EBIT)
− Taxes on EBIT[26]
+ Non-cash charges (depreciation)
− Capital expenditures
− Investments in net working capital
= **Free cash flow to firm (FCFF)**

(b) Free cash flow to equity (FCFE)

Earnings before interest and tax (EBIT)
− Net financial expense/income
− Taxes on EBT[27]
+ Non-cash charges (depreciation)
− Capital expenditures
− Investments in net working capital
+ Increase in interest-bearing debt
= **Free cash flow to equity (FCFE)**

The forecasted cash flows presented above should then (in addition to the question of the right discount rate to the right cash flow above) be discounted at a *risk-adjusted* rate of return, i.e. the discount rate should reflect the risk associated with the subject company in question. So, how do you assess the risk or required rate of return (K_e and WACC, respectively) of a given company?

8.2.3   Cost of capital (discount rate)

The most fundamental relationship of the capital markets is that between risk and return – the higher the risk, the higher the required return. The risk of financial instruments is generally defined by volatility, i.e. variance up or down around an expected estimate. Generally speaking, a stock that, over a given time period, fluctuates greatly in price is considered volatile, whereas a stock that, during the same period, is stagnant is considered non-volatile.

It is, moreover, important to note that from a strict financial risk point of view it normally does not matter whether the asset in question, in effect, actually has/is moved or is moving up or down in value. Thus it is the variance

---

[26] Non-deductible depreciations should not be allowed to affect taxable income, i.e. if the company in question has non-deductible depreciations, e.g. non-deductible amortizations, then taxes should be calculated on EBITA.

[27] As the cost of equity (K_e) computation, unlike the weighted average cost of capital (WACC) calculation, contains no debt component, tax effects (i.e. the fact that interest is tax deductible) cannot be modeled in the discount rate (hence, the tax effect needs to be accounted for in the cash flows). Thus, tax should be calculated on an income measure after interest payments (EBT instead of EBIT).

in itself that governs the applicable risk score, not the direction of the actual motion. Following that, high expected volatility, i.e. a high expected risk exposure, will require a high expected return, i.e. a high cost of capital (discount rate). The higher the cost of capital, the lower the value (i.e. the lower the appropriate value multiple), all else being equal.

Here I run through, step by step, the practice of constructing a risk-adjusted required rate of return on (i) equity capital (hence the cost of equity – K_e) and (ii) operating/invested capital (hence the weighted average cost of capital – WACC). To illustrate the relevant technique and variables, I will draw on our valuation subject Engineering Corp as a reference point.

8.2.4   Cost of equity (K_e)

When performing a cash flow valuation of a company, a key issue is the equity holder's required rate of return (or cost of capital). The required return on equity represents the return or the "interest" that shareholders would demand (or expect) in order to invest in the company. The return refers to total annual compensation (i.e. dividends and capital gains) exclusively available to common equity holders.

According to modern financial theory, the capital asset pricing model (CAPM)[28] is one of the models that may be used to derive the shareholder's required rate of return.[29] Using CAPM, one starts off with a risk-free asset and adds an equity risk premium.

8.2.5   The capital asset pricing model (CAPM)

$$K_e = R_f + \beta \times EMRP$$

where:

K_e = Cost of equity
R_f = Risk-free rate
β = Equity beta
EMRP = Equity market risk premium

---

[28] Sharpe (1964), Lintner (1965), Mossin (1966).

[29] Another model often discussed, but hardly ever used in practice (as it is, relative to the CAPM, more complex to apply), is the arbitrage pricing model – APM (Stephen Ross). CAPM is a single-factor model (i.e. the proper level of risk, or the required rate of return, of the share/ company in question is dictated by its covariance with only one factor – the market portfolio), whereas the APM is a multi-factor model (i.e. the proper level of risk, or the required rate of return, of the share/company in question is dictated by its covariance with multiple factors – the general level of interest rates, inflation, GDP, etc.).

(a) Risk-free rate (R_f)

The risk-free rate may roughly be broken down into two main components. The first seeks to compensate the investor for expected inflation and the second to compensate the investor for deferred consumption (i.e. that investors would request for "lending" their funds to another party rather than using it themselves). The risk-free rate will thus form the expected equity return "floor," i.e. our investor will always have the opportunity to invest his or her funds in a risk-free government bond instead of in a stock unit.

In a perfect world, all future company cash flows, like in our lottery winnings examples, should be discounted by a rate of return in accordance with its duration. Thus, when performing a business valuation, the first year's cash flow is to be discounted at a rate of return based on a risk-free rate with a maturity of one year, the second year's cash flow should be discounted at a rate of return based on a risk-free rate with a maturity of two years, etc. As a business enterprise is normally considered to have an infinite lifetime (given a "going concern" assumption) this procedure may easily become complex (and may in the long run add only marginal worth). It may therefore be appropriate, when performing business valuations, to approximate average risk-free rate on a never-ending basis using a long-term government bond.[30]

As regards our case company, Engineering Corp, I have selected a risk-free interest rate corresponding to a time period of 20 years. This risk-free base rate is approximated with a government bond of similar maturity. To illustrate a proper required rate of return for Engineering Corp, we assume that this base rate carries an annual interest rate of 3.3 percent at the valuation date.

(b) Equity market risk premium (EMRP)

The EMRP refers to the extra return that investors generally require in addition to the risk-free rate in order to invest in the more risky (i.e. more volatile) shares asset class. EMRP is defined as total market return (return on market – R_m) less the risk-free rate (risk-free rate – R_f). It is important to note that we, like all other variables on which CAPM is based, refer to expected returns.

The reason for investors demanding this extra return on top of the risk-free rate is equity return volatility. If one invests in a government bond, for example, one will know beforehand the exact annual return over the period in

---

[30] One could, of course, also argue in favor of a short-term rate as investors (i.e. the people actually buying and selling the concerned shares) are unlikely to apply an infinite time basis to their holdings. However, the value of a share/company is the result of its expected future cash flows, which are forecasted on a never-ending basis, which is why they may logically be argued discounted by a matching rate of return as regards the issue of timing. In addition, the equity market risk premium (i.e. the EMRP) is usually derived with reference to a long-term government bond. Consequently, if the technique above of discounting each year's expected cash flow by a cost of capital based on a risk-free rate of a similar duration is effectively going to work, an equivalent derivation of the equity market risk premium is required.

question (provided, of course, that you hold the security until its maturity). On the other hand, should you invest the same amount of money in shares, you will not know in advance the exact annual rate of return (i.e. the actual return received may be higher or lower than expected). Moreover, in the worst case an equity investor will lose money on his or her investment. To compensate for this extra risk exposure, the shareholder will require a premium (i.e. an extra return) beyond that given by the risk-free rate.

To illustrate an appropriate rate of return for Engineering Corp, we assume that the equity market risk premium (EMRP) at the time of our valuation, based on analysis of historical records as well as empirical forward-looking surveys, has been estimated at 5.0 percent.[31] Put simply, this means that if we invest our funds in the general stock market index, rather than in an analogous risk-free government bond, we expect to be compensated for this in the long term with a 5.0 percentage point additional annual return (i.e. in addition to the 3.3 percentage points set by the risk-free rate, as above).

(c) Beta (β)

CAPM divides a company's risk (i.e. volatility) into systematic and unsystematic risk (the sum of systematic and unsystematic risk equals total risk). Systematic risk represents the portion of the asset's total risk that is correlated with overall market movements (simplified, the stock market in general). Systematic risk affects all shares/businesses in unison (however, different businesses and industries allow themselves to be more or less affected by systematic risk factors) and can therefore not be diversified away (i.e. cannot be avoided). Such types of risk factors relate to unexpected changes in inflation, the general level of interest rates, economic outlook, etc.

Unsystematic risk represents the portion of the asset's total risk that is not correlated with general market movements. This risk thus relates to company-specific factors, such as success/failure of unique projects, (un)successful product launches, (un)successful acquisitions, etc. These factors have, in themselves, no direct link with the stock market as such, but instead they affect separate companies on an individual basis (i.e. no obvious correlation with general stock market ups and downs). Such risks may thus be diversified away (i.e. avoided) by holding a large portfolio of similar companies (shares). If one company drops in value as a result of unique company-specific factors, this may accordingly be counteracted by another company in the portfolio increasing in value for likewise unique company-specific factors.

Beta aims to quantify systematic risk exposure (i.e. risk that cannot be diversified away in a portfolio). Specifically, this risk (i.e. this volatility) cannot

---

[31] Among others, please refer to the writing of Aswath Damodaran at NYU Stern School of Business; Pablo Fernandez, Javier Aguirreamalloa, and Luis Corres from IESE Business School; the Duff & Phelps Risk Premium Report; and the Morningstar/Ibbotson SBBI Valuation Yearbook.

be avoided even if the investor was to spread their funds across a large number of similar companies or shares (note again, however, that the beta may very well vary widely among different industries and companies). The stock market as such (i.e. the stock market index) has by definition a beta of 1.0. Hence, at a 5.0 percent EMRP, as above, a beta of 1.0 indicates a risk premium in addition to the prevailing risk-free rate at about 5.0 percent (i.e. a 1.0 beta times a 5.0 percent equity market risk premium equals 5.0 percent). Thus, if a certain stock has the same expected risk exposure (i.e. volatility) as the stock market as a whole, its expected return will also be on a par with the stock market as a whole. Put simply, this means that we can expect a total annual return of 8.3 percent in the long run if we put our funds in a stock (or index) as outlined/ given above (or, this stock's required rate of return is estimated at 8.3 percent), but only 3.3 percent per year if we put an equivalent amount of funds in a risk-free government bond, all else being equal.

Accordingly, a beta above 1.0 would indicate that the share in question is more risky (volatile) than the overall market (i.e. than the stock market index). A beta below 1.0 would consequently indicate that the share in question is less risky than the market as a whole. A beta of 1.3, for example, would imply that a stock market upturn of 1.0 percent would result in a corresponding 1.3 percent increase for the stock in question. The same applies in the event of a downturn: if the overall market declines 1.0 percent, the stock in question will, accordingly, go down by 1.3 percent. This means that the company concerned is justified as charged with a total equity risk premium add-on of about 6.5 percent in addition to the risk-free rate (i.e. a 1.3 beta times a 5.0 percent equity market risk premium as above equals 6.5 percent). This means that if we invest in a stock in accordance with the above, we can expect a total annual return of 9.8 percent in the long term (i.e. a 6.5 percent equity market risk premium as outlined above plus a 3.3 percent risk-free rate of return), i.e. the cost of equity of this stock is estimated at 9.8 percent.

We can conclude this discussion by emphasizing that beta measures a given stock's covariance with the overall market (i.e. with the stock market index). If a given share swings sharply in value from day to day, then its individual risk, or total risk (i.e. its total volatility), is high. However, if these fluctuations are not correlated with the stock market as a whole, then its risk/volatility toward the stock market will be low too (and therefore its systematic risk, or beta, will also be low). Consequently, its unsystematic risk is high (overall risk is thus equal to the sum of systematic and unsystematic risk). In accordance with CAPM, unsystematic risk can be diversified away (i.e. avoided) by holding a broad portfolio of similar shares or companies. As a result, the only risk the investor then bears is systematic risk. The implication of this is that a well-diversified investor, in theory, under CAPM, does not necessarily prefer to invest in such shares, at a given expected return, that have the lowest overall risk (i.e. the lowest total volatility). For a well-diversified investor, only the respective stock's covariance relative to index (i.e. its systematic risk exposure), at a given expected return, will increase or decrease the investor's total risk exposure (and thus also its required rate of return).

Should the valuation subject be listed on a public market, its beta could be observed (i.e. estimated) based on its historical correlation with the stock market index:[32]

$$\beta_{l(i)} = \frac{Cov(R_i, R_m)}{\sigma^2(R_m)}$$

where:

$\beta_{l(i)}$ = Beta levered (equity beta) of security i
R_i = Return on security i
R_m = Return on market
$Cov(R_i, R_m)$ = The covariance between security i's return and the market return
$\sigma^2(R_m)$ = The variance of the market return

However, should the company in question be unlisted, one will be forced to estimate a proper beta. One suggestion is that this may be carried out on the basis of (or with the assistance of) a peer group of comparable companies in accordance with the following mode of procedure.

Beta as derived of traded shares refers to the systematic risk of the company's shares, and is therefore called equity beta (or levered beta). Equity beta thus captures both operating risk and financial risk as the risk of shares is dependent on operating *as well as* financial risk. Consequently, the higher the debt, the higher the financial risk. The equity beta of a geared company is thus, all else being equal, higher than the corresponding equity beta of an ungeared company. That said, to estimate only industry or operating risk, i.e. to equate companies irrespective of their funding decisions (i.e. to strip the equity beta of its financial risk component), a restatement of each company's leveraged beta into a similar unlevered beta is applicable. This free-from-debt beta will then reflect solely the operating risks, or the risk of the company's assets, and is thus labeled asset beta (or unlevered beta).

The unlevered beta (i.e. the asset beta) will thus portray a company's beta as if it were financed solely by equity, i.e. the additional risk component added to a share as the company takes on debt (i.e. the effect of financial leverage) is eliminated. Taking on debt or not is an individual strategic choice of a company; it may by itself, by increasing or decreasing its borrowings, raise or

---

[32] Note that beta, in accordance with the formula, refers to historical volatility. Historical volatility need not necessarily be the same as future volatility.

lower its equity beta. The asset beta (i.e. the unlevered beta) is, on the other hand, assigned as given by the industry or the business model of the respective companies. This is preset and cannot be influenced by the companies concerned (unless, of course, they choose to modify their business offering). The formula below shows how to calculate an asset beta (i.e. an unlevered beta) using a given equity beta (i.e. a levered beta):[33]

$$\beta_u = \frac{\beta_l}{(1 + D/E)}$$

where:

β_u = Beta unlevered (asset beta)
β_l = Beta levered (equity beta)
D = Interest-bearing net debt (at market value)
E = Equity capital (at market value)

When one has, from recorded equity betas of public comparable companies, identified the appropriate applicable asset beta for the valuation subject in question (i.e. identified the relevant operating risks of the subject company), one may adjust (i.e. convert or recalculate) this unlevered beta to an equivalent levered beta. Following this adjustment, the beta in question will then reflect the level of gearing deemed proper for the subject company in question. The asset beta is thus adjusted to reflect the level of gearing, or put another way, the level of financial risk, deemed proper for the valuation subject at issue. By doing so, we have once again arrived at an equity beta, but now at an equity beta that reflects the unique conditions, in terms of financial risk/capital structure, of our valuation subject. The formula below shows how to calculate an equity beta from a set asset beta:

$$\beta_l = \beta_u (1 + D/E)$$

where:

β_l = Beta levered (equity beta)
β_u = Beta unlevered (asset beta)
D = Interest-bearing net debt (at market value)
E = Equity capital (at market value)

---

[33] The formula describes the handling of beta under the assumption of an unchanged capital structure, i.e. debt and equity is expected to increase proportionately in line with growth. If one were to assume, in absolute terms, a constant debt, the formula would additionally encompass a tax component.

Table 8.10 presents the beta values of the peer group companies at the valuation date (based on 5 years of historical monthly data, i.e. 60 observations) so as to illustrate an appropriate cost of equity calculation for our valuation subject, Engineering Corp.[34]

Table 8.10   Peer group key ratios – debt/equity ratios and beta values

Company	D/E (at market values) LFY	D/(D+E) (at market values) LFY	Equity beta (levered beta) Valuation date	Asset beta (unlevered beta) Valuation date
Peer 1	0.04	0.04	0.88	0.84
Peer 2	0.01	0.02	0.88	0.88
Peer 3	0.37	0.27	1.53	1.11
Peer 4	0.04	0.04	0.68	0.65
Peer 5	0.01	0.01	0.64	0.64
Peer 6	0.00	0.00	0.60	0.60
Peer 7	0.61	0.38	0.94	0.58
Peer 8	0.12	0.11	0.78	0.70
Peer 9	0.02	0.01	1.33	1.31
Peer 10	0.34	0.25	1.48	1.10
Mean	0.16	0.11	0.97	0.84
Median	0.04	0.04	0.88	0.77

As noted in Table 8.10, the median equity beta (i.e. the median levered beta) of the peer group is calculated at 0.88. Adjusted for gearing, the corresponding median asset beta (i.e. the median unlevered beta) is calculated at 0.77. Given the assessed 0.11 debt equity ratio of Engineering Corp (see section 8.2.8 "Capital structure" for further details), its resulting equity beta can, in accordance with the formula above, be calculated at 0.86:

$$\beta_l = \beta_u \left(1 + D/E\right)$$

$$\beta_l = 0.77 \left(1 + 0.11\right)$$

$$\beta_l = 0.86$$

---

[34] In addition to calculating beta values in accordance with the formula above, they may also be obtained from several independent suppliers such as Bloomberg, FactSet, S&P Capital IQ, Thomson Reuters, etc.

Engineering Corp's cost of equity, in accordance with CAPM, can thus be estimated at 7.6 percent:

$$K_e = R_f + \beta \times EMRP$$

$$K_e = 3.3\% + 0.86 \times 5.0\%$$

$$K_e = 7.6\%$$

8.2.6   Adjusted CAPM

CAPM presupposes a perfectly diversified portfolio, which is not always the case in real life, especially for unlisted companies. It is considerably more difficult and expensive to form a diversified portfolio of shares in private companies than a similar diversified portfolio of shares in listed companies.

On the stock exchange it is possible to spread risk over a large number of companies at a low cost. The effects of any random company-specific factors, such as success/failure of unique projects, can be diversified away (i.e. avoided). Therefore, if a certain company in a given portfolio were, for unique and company-specific factors, to perform worse than the corresponding portfolio average, it is, if not likely, at least possible for any other company in the same portfolio, for likewise company-specific factors, to perform better than the portfolio average. As a result, the portfolio's total risk exposure, or total volatility, will be driven solely by systematic risk, i.e. risk factors that affect all companies in unison.[35]

Company-specific risk factors, i.e. unsystematic risk, may thus be diversified away on the stock exchange. However, buyers and sellers of privately held companies cannot diversify away these risks, at least not to the same extent and low cost. Company-specific factors and events (i.e. unsystematic risk which should, in theory, be possible to diversify away) can therefore significantly affect the returns that investors/owners of these companies can be expected to realize. They may therefore require compensation (i.e. return) even for unsystematic risk/volatility. As a consequence, at times you might want to supplement CAPM with: (i) a small stock premium; and (ii) one or a few extra company-specific premiums.

---

[35] This, in accordance with the previous statement, refers to factors like unexpected inflation, changes in interest rates, economic outlook, etc.

(a) Small stock premium (SSP)

Studies have shown that smaller listed companies have generated higher historical returns over time than equivalent larger listed companies.[36] This indicates that investors assign smaller companies a higher risk premium (i.e. a higher required rate of return) than corresponding larger companies. The higher rate of return can be split in two parts:

1. Smaller companies have historically been shown to have higher betas than equivalent larger companies, all else being equal.
2. In addition, these companies have, in an equal historical perspective, generated a return in excess of that justified by their higher betas.

If the beta used to estimate a small listed company's cost of capital is its own observed, or derived from a group of comparable companies of the same size class, a good portion of the higher risk stemming from small cap effects (i.e. that part of the small cap effect attributed to the beta in accordance with point 1 above) should be seized in that company's (or that group of companies') actual observed beta. Should, however, the beta have been derived from a group of equivalent listed larger companies, there is a risk that the applied systematic risk premium will fall short of the appropriate one.[37]

In addition, these small cap companies have, in accordance with point 2 above, shown historical returns above that justified solely by their higher betas (i.e. a size premium/small stock premium has been identified). Although such types of unsystematic risks should, according to CAPM, be fully diversifiable, these studies indicate that this does not always ring true in real life.

As a result, the derived/applied beta may not fully reflect the risk of the concerned investment (i.e. may not fully reflect the appropriate risk exposure of the valuation subject in question). Table 8.11 shows U.S. small cap premiums as estimated by Ibbotson/Morningstar.

---

[36] For example, the Morningstar/Ibbotson SBBI Valuation Yearbook, and the Duff & Phelps Risk Premium Report.

[37] This issue is of particular importance when valuing privately held companies. To calculate the beta of a given company, in accordance with the formula above, one must be able to observe its share price movements on a regular basis (i.e. the concerned company has to be listed). If the subject company is unlisted, we will be forced to use the previously stated technique (i.e. we will be forced to use listed comparable companies) to derive its applicable beta. As private companies are often considerably smaller than corresponding listed ones, we may underestimate the risk, i.e. the proper cost of capital, of the valuation subject in question if not considering the problem at hand.

Table 8.11   Small cap premiums – Ibbotson/Morningstar

Stratification of companies by market cap Decile ($ millions)		Smallest company	Largest company	Beta	Size premium (return in excess of CAPM)
1 – Largest		15,485 –	354,352	0.91	−0.38%
2		6,928 –	15,408	1.04	0.78%
3		3,597 –	6,896	1.10	0.94%
4		2,366 –	3,578	1.13	1.17%
5		1,621 –	2,363	1.16	1.74%
6		1,091 –	1,621	1.19	1.75%
7		683 –	1,091	1.24	1.77%
8		423 –	683	1.30	2.51%
9		207 –	423	1.35	2.80%
10 – Smallest		1 –	207	1.41	6.10%
Breakdown of the 10th decile					
10a		129 –	207	n.a.	4.34%
	10w	171 –	207	n.a.	3.80%
	10x	129 –	171	n.a.	4.75%
10b		1 –	129	n.a.	9.81%
	10y	87 –	129	n.a.	8.93%
	10z	1 –	87	n.a.	11.77%

Source: Stocks, Bonds, Bills, and Inflation® 2012 Ibbotson® SBBI® Risk Premia Over Time Report, Estimates for 1926–2011, © 2012 Morningstar Inc. All rights reserved. Used with permission.

(b) Company-specific premium (CSP)

Moreover, should the valuation subject in question hold additional unique risk factors not picked up by either the applied beta or the warranted size premium as outlined above, there may be cause to add one or a few premiums in addition to those solely provided by CAPM and the SSP.

Company-specific unique factors that may justify additional risk premium supplements can include inexperienced management, lack of customer loyalty, great dependence on one or only a few customers, suppliers, key personnel, etc. For this reason it is important to carefully analyze the companies that form the peer group used. Even though the beta would be derived from companies of a similar size (which can potentially already be presumed to be affected by the types of issues and factors listed above, in relation to an equivalent large company), it is, however, not certain that the unique risk factors of the valuation subject in question are fully captured by (or consistent with) those factors embodied in this particular derivative beta.

These risk premium supplements may, moreover, not generally (not in a simple way anyway) be estimated mathematically, nor may they be derived from independent studies (such as the small stock premium above), but may instead be the subject of a subjective assessment by the analyst in question.

Taking into account the above-mentioned supplements (i.e. the small stock premium and the company-specific premium), CAPM takes the following appearance:

$$K_e = R_f + \beta \times EMRP + SSP + CSP$$

where:

K_e = Cost of equity
R_f = Risk-free rate
β = Equity beta
EMRP = Equity market risk premium
SSP = Small stock premium
CSP = Company-specific premium

So, how will this reasoning impact the appropriate cost of equity for Engineering Corp? The listed peers of Engineering Corp, from which the 0.77 unlevered beta has been derived, are somewhat larger than Engineering Corp. The difference, as regards the size of beta provided by the 4th decile (i.e. the decile in which we would put our $3 billion subject company, Engineering Corp) versus the betas of the top deciles, is marginal (roughly 0.1 as presented in Table 8.11). As the data is not in any way scientifically exact and as it also reflects U.S. companies in general (i.e. not specifically companies in the engineering sector), we judge that difference to be negligible. However, the size premium in excess of CAPM (as indicated in Table 8.11) for companies of Engineering Corp's size, i.e. of a market cap of about $3 billion, is approximately one percentage point. Engineering Corp is therefore deemed to be burdened with a small stock premium of about 1.0 percentage point.

In addition, an analysis of Engineering Corp's operations reveals that 15 percent of its total sales relate to one sole customer (that is, we assume for the sake of the argument that we have identified this additional company-specific risk factor of Engineering Corp). This client is, moreover, presumed not to be locked in to Engineering Corp with a long-term contract. This additional risk factor is captured in neither the beta nor the small stock premium (that is, neither the larger nor the smaller companies in our peer group face the same dependence on a single customer as our valuation subject). As a result,

Engineering Corp is deemed to be burdened with a company-specific risk premium at about 1.0 percentage point.[38]

From that Engineering Corp's cost of equity can be estimated at 9.6 percent:

$$K_e = R_f + \beta \times EMRP + SSP + CSP$$

$$K_e = 3.3\% + 0.86 \times 5.0\% + 1.0\% + 1.0\%$$

$$K_e = 9.6\%$$

8.2.7   Cost of debt (K_d)

Corporations can finance their operations via equity as well as loan capital. Both of these capital sources come at a cost: shareholders require a return for the capital they have invested in the business in the form of dividends or value appreciation (the cost of equity we have just worked out as per CAPM above) and lenders require a return on the capital they have invested in the business (i.e. the loans) in the form of interest.

Should a company finance its assets (i.e. its operating/invested capital) solely via equity, its cost of capital will equal its cost of equity. However, as interest is tax deductible, shareholders can gain value by funding a given business with a certain part of borrowed capital. This will enable the overall cost of capital to be reduced, which in turn anticipates an overall company market value uplift and, consequently, a corresponding equity market value boost.[39]

---

[38] One may also argue in favor of the higher risk being reflected in the subject company's cash flow rather than in its required rate of return (that is, in the numerator rather than in the denominator). Should the company in question lose this one customer, this would result in lower future cash flows. An alternative approach, and maybe even a better one, would be to remove the impact of that customer from the company's expected cash flows, without burdening the company's required rate of return with an extra risk premium, and to calculate the resulting value effect (i.e. the resulting value decrease), and then to adjust the calculated value effect (i.e. the value decrease) upwards on the basis of an assessed probability of customer loss (thus, taking out the full value effect, one will assume a 100 percent probability of customer loss, which is obviously not reasonable as the customer in question is still active). Whichever approach is taken, the end result should be the same. The risk premium addition should not, for example, lead to a value decrease in excess of that given by a total customer wipe-out (in our case study, the 1 percentage point extra risk premium equals a 50 percent probability of customer loss).

[39] The WACC is therefore first and foremost reduced as a result of taxes being deductible, not because borrowed capital in any way is "cheaper" than equity capital. In accordance with the Modigliani-Miller theorem (see Modigliani F. and Miller M. (1958), *The Cost of Capital, Corporation Finance and the Theory of Investment*, American Economic Review, Vol. 48) the risk (i.e. the cost of capital) of any business is given/set. Specifically, a company's risk is determined by its business risk (that is, by its business model/offerings, its clients, competitors, technical status, general business environment, etc.), not its financing decisions (i.e. not by its choice of capital structure). Given a number of (indeed quite stringent) assumptions and no taxes, the lower

Therefore, besides the derivation of a relevant cost of equity, a company's proper cost of capital calculation also often includes an estimate of a reasonable cost of debt.

The cost of debt calculation starts with a long-term risk-free base rate. We add a premium to this base rate to reflect the proposed bank's assessment of the company's credit risk. The estimated cost of debt is then adjusted for taxes:

$$K_d = K_{d,\text{pre-tax}} \times (1 - T)$$

where:

K_d = Cost of debt
$K_{d,\text{pre-tax}}$ = Cost of debt pre-tax
T = Tax rate

To illustrate a proper level of debt capital cost for Engineering Corp, we apply the previously given 3.3 percent risk-free base rate with a 2.0 percent debt margin addition. The tax effect is calculated with reference to U.S. corporate tax rates (approximated at 40 percent). Engineering Corp's post-tax cost of debt can then be estimated at 3.2 percent:

$$K_d = K_{d,\text{pre-tax}} \times (1 - T)$$

$$K_d = 5.3\% \times (1 - 40.0\%)$$

$$K_d = 3.2\%$$

8.2.8   Capital structure

The weighted required return is dependent on the capital structure that is implemented. Estimates are based on what proportion of overall invested capital is assumed to be financed by debt capital (i.e. interest-bearing loans) and equity capital. When deriving a reasonable level of debt finance it is, moreover, the market value of equity point of reference that is of interest, which is why

---

cost of capital, as a result of borrowed capital having a lower required rate of return than equity capital, that is, a lower risk (as a result of its fixed coupon rate payments and higher priority in case of default; hence a lower expected volatility), will be perfectly offset by the now instead increased equity risk (thus, as the leverage increases, equity capital will face higher financial risk/volatility, and so the cost of equity will increase accordingly). Technically, this is given by an increased leveraged beta (see section 8.2.5(c) "Beta (β)" for more information). As a result, the weighted average cost of capital disregarding the tax shield and potential bankruptcy costs will, across all combinations of equity and loan capital (i.e. throughout the 0–100 percent gearing range), in theory remain unaffected by its financing mix.

this type of benchmarking is normally limited to listed companies.[40] The debt/equity ratio put in practice should, furthermore, be appropriate in a sustainable long-term perspective, and should not be based on temporary fluctuations that are in progress (such as interim acquisition financing, bridge financing, etc.).

To illustrate this for our study subject Engineering Corp we assume a long-term sustainable capital structure, at market values, comprising interest-bearing debt equivalent to 10 percent of its total invested capital (note: a D/(D+E) ratio of 0.10 corresponds to a 0.11 D/E ratio). The applied debt/equity ratio is derived from our reference group of comparable listed companies. The resulting debt equity ratio is, furthermore, not only in line with the average peer, but also with Engineering Corp's current level of gearing.

8.2.9   Weighted average cost of capital (WACC)

The weighted required rate of return, or WACC (weighted average cost of capital) takes into account the cost of capital of both equity investors (i.e. shareholders) and debt holders (i.e. the bank or other external funders).

The WACC thus reflects a reasonable cost of capital, at market values, for the company's entire capital structure at a given mix of equity and borrowed capital (Figure 8.19).

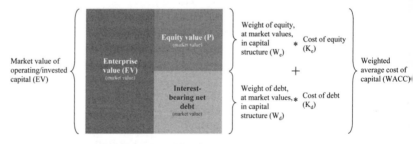

Figure 8.19   Enterprise value (i.e. market value of operating/invested capital) – weighted average cost of capital (WACC)

$$WACC = \left(K_e \times W_e\right) + \left(K_d \times W_d\right)$$

where:

---

[40] The market value represents the funds that shareholders de facto have tied up in the company, and for which they consequently would require a market rate of return. In other words, investors can at all times, if they so wish, realize their holdings at current market value and then invest these funds in an alternate asset, which can be expected to generate a normal market rate of return.

WACC = Weighted average cost of capital
K_e = Cost of equity
K_d = Cost of debt
W_e = Weight of equity in capital structure (at market values)
W_d = Weight of debt in capital structure (at market values)

Based on the above given conditions and assumptions, Engineering Corp's WACC is calculated at 9.0 percent (Figure 8.20):

$$WACC = (K_e \times W_e) + (K_d \times W_d)$$

$$WACC = (9.6\% \times 0.90) + (3.2\% \times 0.10)$$

$$WACC = 9.0\%$$

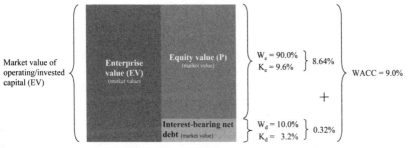

Figure 8.20   Enterprise value (i.e. market value of operating/invested capital) – Engineering Corp's weighted average cost of capital (WACC)

How will this affect the appropriate value multiples of Engineering Corp? To find out, we return to our analysis of the EV/Sales multiple and its premier value drivers, operating margin and revenue growth. Initially, by using value multiples derived from a reference group of listed U.S. engineering companies, we determined Engineering Corp's market value of invested capital without taking into account relevant value drivers (the derived 1.33x median EV/Sales multiple thus resulted in an estimated enterprise value of $1,995 million). Then we adjusted the above-mentioned value multiple for value driver no. 1, expected operating margin (the post adjustment derived 2.37x EV/Sales multiple resulted in an estimated $3,555 million enterprise value). Finally, this multiple was adjusted for value driver no. 2, expected revenue growth (the derived 2.75x EV/Sales multiple then resulted in an estimated $4,125 million enterprise value) (Figure 8.21).

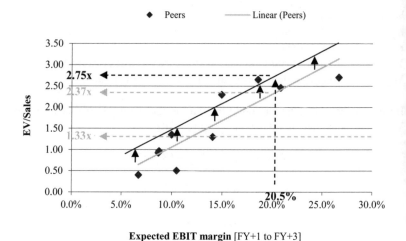

Figure 8.21   EV/Sales vs. operating margin – derivation of an appropriate value multiple using a revenue growth adjusted regression line

The appropriate EV/Sales multiple for valuing Engineering Corp was thus finally deemed to be 2.75x. However, you may remember that we presented the EV/Sales multiple in question, versus both operating margin and revenue growth, with the proviso "all else being equal" – and the calculation of Engineering Corp's cost of capital, in accordance with the above review, has shown differences in risk profile between the valuation subject and the average peer.

The comparable companies from which the value multiples in question have been derived are, in general, large caps and do not share Engineering Corp's large customer dependence. Engineering Corp was thus deemed to be burdened with two percentage points of total risk premium addition on top of that given by a pure implementation of CAPM (in terms of a one percentage point small stock risk premium and a one percentage point company-specific risk premium). Hence, the epithet "all else being equal" no longer applies. As a result, we have to adjust for value driver no. 3: risk.

The above-mentioned 2.75x EV/Sales multiple must therefore be adjusted in relation to the comparable companies from which the multiple in question has been derived, so that it finally reflects the individual risk profile of our valuation subject. This means that we are forced to adjust the EV/Sales vs. operating margin regression line above a third time (this time downwards as Engineering Corp has a higher risk profile than its average peer).

How much then should the regression line be shifted due to this additional risk adjustment? Like other supplementary value drivers, such as expected sales growth (i.e. the most recent adjustment of the regression line EV/Sales vs. operating margin due to divergent revenue growth expectations), this is quite a challenging task. If using only the comparable companies' price quotations, the same type of approach as applied previously has to be utilized. That is, an analysis of the constituent companies' valuations, in relation to each other, on the basis of their relative size and risk profile. To illustrate, we implement such an analysis and its impact on the applicable value multiple conclusion for Engineering Corp with the help of our (untouched original) regression EV/Sales vs. operating margin (Figure 8.22).

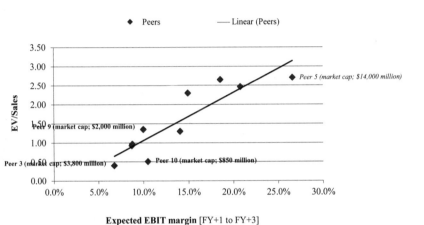

Figure 8.22   EV/Sales vs. operating margin – detected peer group small caps

Peers 3, 9, and 10 have market caps significantly below $15 billion, which we have established, as before (see Table 8.11 for further details), gives rise to a small stock premium. The remaining peers have market caps above $15 billion.[41]

In Figure 8.22 we note that Peers 3 and 10 are positioned substantially below the regression line, whereas Peer 9 sits above the line. However, an analysis reveals that Peer 9 has more than twice the expected sales growth of the average peer (16.7 percent versus the peer mean and median of 7.9 percent and 6.5 percent, respectively), which justifies a valuation substantially above that given by the pure regression line, all else being equal.[42] As regards Peer 9 in the regression EV/Sales vs. operating margin, we thus have two opposing supplementary value drivers, i.e. a revenue growth that justifies a position far above the regression line and a risk profile that justifies a position slightly

---

[41] See Table 8.2, "Selected value multiples – EV and P," for further information.
[42] See Table 8.3, "Selected key ratios – value drivers," for further information.

below the same regression line. Furthermore, Peers 3 and 10 may also be considered slightly affected by a non-standard revenue growth versus the average peer. These companies' expected revenue growth (at about 4 to 4.5 percent) is a few percentage points lower than the average peer (i.e. that given by the regression line). A tiny part of these two companies' position below the regression line could thus, in addition to the risk factor, be due to somewhat lower expected revenue growth. The other companies' position above or below the regression line is principally due to differing revenue growth expectations versus the average peer as on the whole they are significantly larger than the $15 billion hurdle, giving rise to the size premium. We note, however, that in Peer 5 we have a so-called "outlier," as it has a relatively high market capitalization (i.e. it should not be burdened by a size premium) and an expected revenue growth (7.9 percent) in line with the average peer, but is nonetheless positioned well below the regression line.

Consequently, Peer 3 (with a market capitalization of approximately $3,800 million) is justified (with reference to the previously discussed risk premium study by Ibbotson/Morningstar) as being burdened with a size premium of about 1.0 percentage points, whereas Peer 10 (with a market capitalization of approximately $850 million) is justified as being burdened with a size premium of about 2.0 percentage points. Engineering Corp, with an equity market value in line with (or slightly below, to be exact) Peer 3, is thus justified owing solely to size effects to be valued on a par with (or slightly below, to be exact) Peer 3. However, should we include the company-specific risk premium of 1.0 percentage point identified for Engineering Corp to the above-mentioned 1.0 percentage point size premium (i.e. a total risk premium addition comprising size effects as well as company-specific premiums), we can treat Engineering Corp in Figure 8.22 as if it would have been subject to a small stock premium of a total of 2.0 percentage points, which in turn should result in a position somewhere in line with Peer 10.

On the basis of this analysis, we can feel comfortable in shifting the regression line to a level in line with Peer 10, corresponding to an EV/Sales multiple reduction of about 0.65x (Figure 8.23).

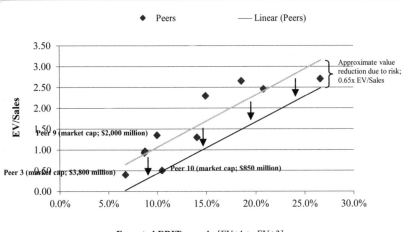

Figure 8.23   EV/Sales vs. operating margin – the derived applicable risk discount for Engineering Corp due to a deviating risk profile versus the average peer

As noted above, the analysis is complicated by the fact that the EV/Sales vs. operating margin regression is influenced by two additional primary value drivers, revenue growth and risk profile, which can work together or oppose one another. That said, let us wrap up our appropriate EV/Sales multiple analysis of Engineering Corp. We therefore downward adjust our previously derived growth and operating margin adjusted 2.75x EV/Sales multiple with the 0.65x EV/Sales risk discount derived above (Figure 8.24).

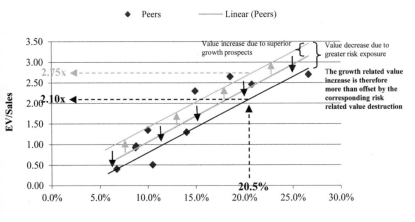

Figure 8.24   EV/Sales vs. operating margin – illustration of the net effect (on Engineering Corp) of a higher expected revenue growth versus the average peer at a simultaneously higher risk exposure (hence the graph is a combination of data from Figures 8.21 and 8.23, i.e. the 0.65x EV/Sales downward value adjustment derived in Figure 8.23, due to risk, has been incorporated into Figure 8.21)

We note then that Engineering Corp's value addition due to its higher expected revenue growth versus the average peer is more than offset by its higher risk profile versus a large cap peer. Consequently, a tailor-made EV/ Sales multiple for valuing Engineering Corp, at any given level of operating margin including the impact of its unique specific level of value driver no. 2, expected revenue growth, and its individual level of risk profile, is set by this "new" adjusted regression line.

Thus, given its unique risk profile, 20.5 percent expected operating margin, and 11.5 percent expected revenue growth, we can conclude that Engineering Corp is justified a valuation at about 2.10 times its last reported sales. In summary (the previously derived EV/Sales multiple, i.e. the position non-reflective of risk, is presented in brackets):

Derived (at given margin, revenue growth and risk)
EV/Sales multiple: **2.10x**   (2.75x)
Engineering Corp's turnover – Sales ($ millions):   **1,500**   (1,500)

Applying this "operating margin, revenue growth, and risk-adjusted" EV/ Sales multiple to Engineering Corp, we arrive at the following estimated value (market value of operating/invested capital):

$$2.10 \times \$1,500 \text{ million} = \$3,150 \text{ million}$$
$$(2.75 \times \$1,500 \text{ million} = \$4,125 \text{ million})$$

The estimated value of Engineering Corp's invested capital thus *decreases* by $975 million ($3,150 million less $4,125 million). In other words, had we used the EV/Sales multiple and valued Engineering Corp taking into account the operating margin value driver as well as the revenue growth value driver, but not its relevant risk profile, we would have overestimated the value of its invested capital by $975 million, or approximately 25 percent.

This relationship is true for *all* calculated multiples. The unique risk profile of the valuation subject versus the comparables (from which we have derived the value multiples in question) thus affects all derived (applicable) multiples alike. Therefore, as long as the unique risk position of the valuation subject does not match that of the average peer, we need to carry out these adjustments.

Notwithstanding the above, it should, however, be noted for the sake of order that the relationship may very well exhibit the reverse. In other words, should we value a very large privately held company using value multiples derived from listed (or acquired/divested) smaller comparables, there may be reason to believe the risk of the larger valuation subject is lower than that given by the corresponding peers. As opposed to our example above, the relevant regression line shift may then be upwards rather than downwards.[43]

Whether the valuation subject in question is listed or not thus does not determine its operational risk exposure. Companies in any given industry are affected by exactly the same external factors and risks whether they are listed or not. Therefore, there could be listed companies that are both small and risky in the same way as there may be privately held companies that are large as well as less risky. Notwithstanding that, it is very important to note that an investor, all else being equal, is given greater opportunities to diversify should the subject company be listed. Figure 8.25 shows Engineering Corp's risk-adjusted EV/EBIT multiple.

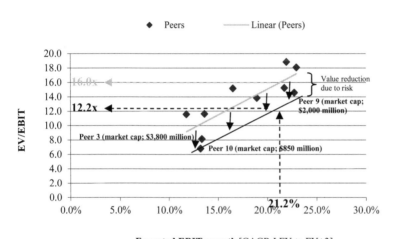

Figure 8.25   EV/EBIT vs. EBIT growth – derivation of the relevant value multiple using a risk-adjusted regression line

In Figure 8.25 we note that Peer 9, like the other two small cap companies, now ranks somewhat below the regression line (and not above the line as in

---

[43] Were we to value the privately held global furniture giant IKEA, for example, using value multiples derived from publicly listed local furniture companies, or, alternatively, using multiples derived from transactions of privately held small furniture companies, there may be reason to believe that the relationship could be the reverse: IKEA is more diversified than the comparable companies in terms of operations as well as geography, and so its risk profile may be considered lower than that of the corresponding peers. As a consequence, the regression line would then shift upwards instead (i.e. the appropriate risk-adjusted value multiple for IKEA may then be higher than that suggested by the comparables, all else being equal).

the case of EV/Sales earlier). This is because, unlike the EV/Sales multiple, the EV/EBIT multiple does not have two key value drivers. Disregarding risk, the EV/EBIT multiple is primarily driven by EBIT growth, whereas the EV/Sales multiple is driven by operating margin as well as revenue growth.[44] Therefore, under normal conditions, any obvious prime "counteractive" forces to the risk factor (such as sales growth in the EV/Sales vs. operating margin graph before) are not present with the EV/EBIT vs. expected growth in EBIT regression (note, however, the NIR discussion previously). As a consequence, the higher risk exposure (i.e. the small cap premium) of Peer 9, as illustrated in the graph above, will push its justified value multiple a little below that given by its expected growth in EBIT, i.e. somewhat below that suggested by the regression line.

Given its unique risk profile and its 21.2 percent expected EBIT growth, Engineering Corp is therefore justified a valuation at about 12.2 times its last reported EBIT. In summary (the previously derived EV/EBIT multiple, i.e. the position non-reflective of risk, is presented in brackets):

Derived (at given expected EBIT growth and risk)
EV/EBIT multiple: **12.2x** (16.0x)
Engineering Corp's operating profit – EBIT ($ millions):   **255**   (255)

Consequently, applying this "EBIT growth and risk-adjusted" EV/EBIT multiple to Engineering Corp, we arrive at the following estimated value (market value of operating/invested capital):

$$12.2 \times \$255 \text{ million} = \$3,111 \text{ million}$$
$$(16.0 \times \$255 \text{ million} = \$4,080 \text{ million})$$

In Figure 8.26 we show Engineering Corp's adjusted EV/BEV multiple as a result of its unique risk profile.

---

[44] EBIT growth may, as stated earlier, be driven either by an increased return on existing resources (by either an increased margin on existing sales, or an increased capital turnover on existing assets) or, alternatively, by expected return on new net investments. The EV/EBIT multiple and its primary value driver, growth in EBIT, are thus able to capture all these factors as one single regression (in contrast to the EV/Sales multiple previously, which also had more than one key value driver, operating margin and revenue growth). Hence, the one-dimensional regression EV/EBIT vs. expected growth in EBIT is able to capture multiple underlying value drivers at the same time. The EV/Sales regressions (at least our one-dimensional regressions), on the other hand, are only able to capture one value driver, expected revenue growth or expected operating margin, at a time.

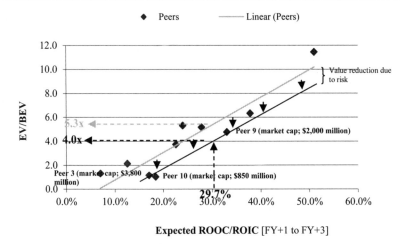

Figure 8.26   EV/BEV vs. ROOC (or, alternatively, ROIC) – derivation of the relevant value multiple using a risk-adjusted regression line

Given its unique risk profile and its 29.7 percent expected ROIC, Engineering Corp is justified a valuation at about 4.0 times its last reported book operating/invested capital (i.e. book enterprise value – BEV). In summary (the previously derived EV/BEV multiple, i.e. the position non-reflective of risk, is presented in brackets):

Derived (at given expected ROIC and risk) EV/BEV multiple: **4.0x** (5.3x)
Engineering Corp's book enterprise value – BEV ($ millions):   **761** (761)

Consequently, applying this "return on operating/invested capital and risk-adjusted" EV/BEV multiple to Engineering Corp, we arrive at the following estimated value (market value of operating/invested capital):

4.0 × $761 million = $3,044 million
(5.3 × $761 million = $4,033 million)

Apparently, it can be complicated to find the appropriate level of value adjustment to be applied to the subject company, owing to the differing risk profiles of the subject company and its peers, solely by means of value multiples derived from comparable companies. In the case above, the reference group happened to contain three small cap companies from which we could derive the appropriate level of deduction. However, should our reference group have consisted only of large cap companies, the opportunity would not have been available. This is not, however, synonymous with saying it is preferable to mix small and large cap companies in the peer group. In an ideal world you would find all peers to be of more or less exactly the same size and risk as the subject company. Derived multiples would then include the market's current assessment of the prevailing relevant risk exposure (i.e. these companies would be priced by the stock market with respect to small cap effects, etc.) and the above-mentioned adjustments should thus be obsolete. However, should we be given an assignment to value a company of a highly specific size or risk class, such as a significantly smaller company than our subject company, Engineering Corp, that opportunity might not be available (i.e. such specific listed small cap companies might not exist). In the next section we show how, should you only have access to a peer group of large cap public companies, you can derive the appropriate risk discounts by way of a DCF approach.

If valuing a large cap company using value multiples derived from other large cap companies (or for that matter, with respect to the small cap premium, a small cap company using value multiples derived from other small cap companies), one can normally assume that the risk profile (and consequently the required rate of return, i.e. the relevant cost of capital) of the valuation subject and its peer(s), with regard to size effects, are basically the same. As a result, no adjustment is necessary.[45] Put even more simply, multiples derived from listed companies, with the purpose of valuing another listed company of reasonably similar size and operations, typically require no substantial adjustments due to risk.

8.3   SUMMARY OF CALCULATED VALUES

Summarizing the conclusions from our appropriate value multiple analysis of Engineering Corp, we reach the following results.

8.3.1   EV multiples

The enterprise value (i.e. the market value of operating/invested capital) of Engineering Corp is estimated at about \$3,100 million (Table 8.12).

Table 8.12   Estimated shareholders' values (i.e. market value of equity) – Engineering Corp on the basis of EV multiples

Engineering Corp (\$ millions)	EV/Sales LFY	EV/EBIT LFY	EV/BEV LFY
Derived/applicable value multiple	2.10x	12.2x	4.0x
Base metric of Engineering Corp (i.e. Sales, EBIT, BEV)	1,500	255	761
Market value of operating/invested capital (EV)	**3,150**	**3,111**	**3,044**
Interest-bearing net debt of Engineering Corp	–251	–251	–251
Market value of equity (P)	**2,899**	**2,860**	**2,793**

---

[45] Possible differences as regards company-specific premiums and relevant/justified beta will remain, however.

Adjusted for Engineering Corp's $251 million interest-bearing net debt, the market value of all outstanding shares (i.e. the market value of equity) in Engineering Corp is calculated at approximately $2,850 million (Figure 8.27).

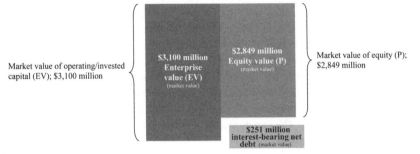

Market value of operating/invested capital (EV); $3,100 million

$3,100 million Enterprise value (EV) (market value)

$2,849 million Equity value (P) (market value)

Market value of equity (P); $2,849 million

$251 million interest-bearing net debt (market value)

Figure 8.27   Enterprise value (i.e. market value of operating/invested capital) vs. shareholders' value (i.e. market value of equity) – the equity value of Engineering Corp

As a closing point, it should be noted that the estimated equity value needs additionally to be adjusted for minority ownership interests (if any). In other words, if we have valued the company (should it be a corporate group) on a consolidated basis (i.e. should the derived multiples have been applied to operating earnings figures comprising 100 percent of Group subsidiaries), we need to adjust for (i.e. deduct) that portion of total estimated Group value that belongs to the minority interest holders. We should therefore calculate the market value of each of the Group's subsidiaries in which a minority ownership is present and adjust the resulting Group equity value by that portion of value that belongs to the minority interest holders.

Moreover, the derived value presupposes the valuation subject to have, if not exactly the same, then at least the proper level of invested capital tied up compared with those companies from which the multiples in question have been derived. Any deficit or surplus of, for example, working capital or fixed assets (this could be extraordinarily high or low level of inventory, accounts receivable, recently accomplished or neglected capital expenditures, etc.) may give rise to a reduction or a supplement of value relative to that estimated using just the derived multiples.

8.3.2   Price multiples – short tuning

In accordance with our earlier reasoning, it is also possible to use the multiples and value drivers for price to estimate the value of equity directly, i.e. without having to go through the EV. However, this methodology typically requires a greater work effort as regards: (i) identification of the appropriate level of multiple; as well as (ii) adjustments of relevant input data.

As regards (i) – the choice of the appropriate level of multiple – significant capital structure differences between the valuation subject and the peers may complicate the identification of a suitable multiple.

An equity multiple, such as P/E, of a given company could be significantly affected if that company, for some reason, were to hold a disproportionately higher amount of cash than its peers (or vice versa if that should be the case). The value of that cash reserve would then increase the value of the shares (i.e. P) dollar by dollar, whereas the earnings, or the yield (i.e. the relatively low level of interest income), associated with this cash reserve would not affect net income (i.e. E) correspondingly. The effect would thus be that two companies with basically exactly the same operating earnings capacity are given significantly different P/E ratios.

We illustrate the problem with a simple example: suppose we have a listed company with a market value of $100 per share and a corresponding net profit of $10. This company's P/E ratio is thus calculated at 10.0x. Now let us assume that that company's cash balance accounts for 50 percent of its estimated shareholder value (i.e. $50 of that company's share value consists of cash). Assuming this cash yields 2.5 percent per year in interest after tax, then of the company's total earnings per share of $10, as above, $1.25 will consist of interest income and $8.75 will consist of operating net profit. Consequently, the cash P/E ratio is calculated at 40.0x ($50/$1.25), whereas the P/E ratio of the operating activities can be calculated at 5.7x ($50/$8.75). The estimated P/E ratio of 10.0x as above is therefore strongly influenced by the low-yielding cash balance (hence, the P/E of 10.0x = P/E 40.0x × ($1.25/$10.0) + P/E 5.7x × ($8.75/$10.0)). The high P/E ratio is thus explained by an inefficient capital structure (unless, of course, the 50 percent cash reserve is for some reason deemed to be of an operational nature) and not by high expected earnings growth, which would typically be the commonsensical conclusion.[46]

The unadjusted 10.0x P/E ratio as above would thus not be appropriate for derivation of a target/subject company's value unless that cash balance, for both the company and the peer, is for any reason deemed operationally necessary (it would instead be more appropriate to derive the value of the company using the, in accordance with above, "operating" 5.7x multiple, i.e. giving an approximately 40 percent lower valuation).

Analogous with this, the multiple will be affected by the opposite relationship, i.e. should the peer(s) hold a high proportion of debt in relation to the subject company in question rather than a high proportion of cash, as in the case above. Shareholders can benefit from profits only after lenders have had their prioritized portion (i.e. the interest payments). As interest payments are

---

[46] Strictly speaking, the high P/E ratio is explained by cash being a low risk asset, i.e. by cash having an exceptionally low required rate of return.

typically more or less fixed, the residual amount, i.e. the shareholder's profit after interest payments, will, at varying income and with leverage (and all else being equal), fluctuate in line with gearing. Thus the higher the gearing, the higher the shareholder's risk (that is, the higher the required return on equity), which, all else being equal, will require a discount. All else being equal, it may therefore be inappropriate to apply a P multiple derived from a highly geared company to an otherwise equivalent all equity financed target.

Were we as an alternative to calculate the equity value using EV multiples, we would, on the whole, avoid this problem. In accordance with the previously mentioned Modigliani-Miller theorem (see footnote 39 for additional information), the operating risks of a business enterprise are unaffected by its financing structure (or, to tie with the above paragraph, the operating profit will not, in contrast to the residual allocated to the shareholders, i.e. the net profit, fluctuate as a result of leverage as payment of interest only occurs at shareholder level). Consequently, if the EV multiples are defined correctly, i.e. if the numerator (in other words, the EV) is put in relation to an approved base metric, i.e. a measure of performance before financing activities (in other words, EBITDA, EBITA, EBIT, etc.), neither the multiples nor the outcome will be affected by each company's unique level of gearing.[47] Any existing difference in leverage between the valuation subject and its peer(s) will thus rather, at shareholder level, be reflected in the net debt adjustment. Hence, if the subject company's capital structure were to be significantly different from that of its peers, it may be recommended to use EV instead of P even though we are targeting the equity value.

As regards (ii) – adjustments of relevant input data – the calculated value multiples as well as the target company's reported earnings may, additionally, be influenced by non-representative items, in a sustainable earnings perspective. If this is the case, one should adjust for any differences between the valuation subject and its peer(s). Relevant adjustments may include taxes paid, tax loss carry forward, extraordinary income and expenses (note, however, that operating profits too may include items considered as one-offs even though, from a strict accounting perspective, they are not classified as "extraordinary"), amortization of goodwill, inaccurate net financial income/expense figures, appropriations, etc.

If all necessary adjustments have been executed and, as regards our unique valuation subject, and in accordance with (i) above, the appropriate level of the price multiple has been identified, the estimated equity value as derived using price multiples should be identical to that derived using EV multiples, otherwise one has, once again, made a mistake somewhere. To be exact, the estimated equity value, as calculated by the same analyst under the same valuation purpose, should, both in theory *and* in practice, be the same regardless of

---

[47] Disregarding (i) tax effects and (ii) implied (potential) bankruptcy costs expected to surface as leverage increases.

applied multiple, i.e. P/E, P/BV, EV/Sales, EV/EBIT, etc. (or methodology for that matter, i.e. market approach, DCF, etc.) – if not, a mistake has been made somewhere.

Figure 8.28 illustrates the P/E multiple of the peers plotted against the expected average annual earnings growth LFY to FY+3 value driver.[48]

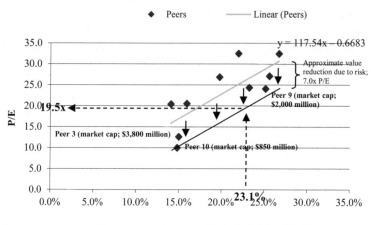

Figure 8.28   P/E vs. net earnings growth – derivation of relevant value multiple using a risk-adjusted regression line

Thus, adjusted for its unique risk profile (i.e. its individual cost of capital), in accordance with previous reasoning and methodology, we assign Engineering Corp a valuation at about 19.5 times its last reported earnings after tax.[49] In summary:

Derived (at given expected earnings growth and risk) P/E multiple: **19.5x**
Engineering Corp's earnings after tax – E ($ millions):   **146**

---

[48] Here we have the same type of reasoning as we had with the EV/EBIT multiple and its primary value driver, expected EBIT growth, previously (though in this case the variables are return on equity, ROE, and reinvested earnings after tax, rather than return on operating capital, ROIC, and reinvested operating profit after tax). Hence, the derivation of an appropriate P/E multiple for the valuation subject using expected growth in earnings requires the payout ratio of the subject company and its peers, at given growth, to be largely the same.

[49] We have previously noted that Engineering Corp and the average peer are expected to operate on a similar capital structure (see section 8.2.8 for further information). Any additional risk adjustment, as a result of gearing differences between the valuation subject and the average peer, is thus not required in our Engineering Corp case study.

Consequently, applying this "earnings growth and risk-adjusted" P/E multiple to our valuation subject, Engineering Corp, we arrive at the following estimated value (market value of equity):

$$19.5 \times \$146 \text{ million} = \$2,847 \text{ million}$$

Figure 8.29 shows the P/BV multiple of the peers plotted against the expected average annual return on equity (ROE) FY+1 to FY+3 value driver.[50]

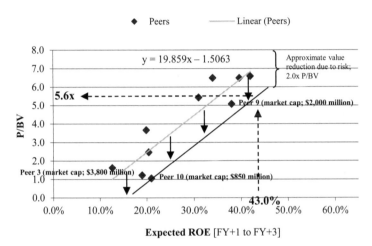

Figure 8.29   P/BV vs. ROE – derivation of relevant value multiple using a risk-adjusted regression line

Adjusted for its unique risk profile (i.e. its individual cost of capital), in accordance with previous reasoning and methodology, we assign Engineering Corp a valuation at about 5.6 times its last reported equity book value.[51,52] In summary:

---

[50] Expected return on book equity is calculated on the assumption of an unchanged equity/asset ratio.

[51] Note that, if that should be the case, the multiple is impacted by the same capital structure issues as the P/E multiple. Were the company in question, for example, to hold a disproportionately high amount of cash, the P/BV multiple would be affected in the same way as the P/E multiple; that is, its return on operating equity (i.e. its operating earnings) would possibly be significantly higher than its corresponding return on non-operating equity (i.e. its interest income), all else being equal.

[52] In addition, the multiple is (like the EV/BEV multiple) also affected by growth, in addition to its primary value driver expected return on equity (ROE). Parts of this growth (i.e. any part that is due to a more efficient capital utilization) will be captured by value driver expected ROE. However, were the subject company to have a higher expected growth in terms of upcoming value-creating investments than its peers, there may be reason to shift the regression line somewhat using the previously reported technique. For a description of the variables and relationships that drive the P/BV multiple, see appendix.

Derived (at given expected return on equity and risk) P/BV multiple: **5.6x**
Engineering Corp's book value of equity – BV ($ millions):   **510**

Consequently, applying this "return on equity and risk-adjusted" P/BV multiple to Engineering Corp, we arrive at the following estimated value (market value of equity):

$$5.6 \times \$510 \text{ million} = \$2,856 \text{ million}$$

The market value of Engineering Corp's equity capital (or, alternatively, the market value of all outstanding common shares) is therefore given directly by the respective P multiples. Any cost of debt financing is already reflected in the multiples, i.e. in the numerator, P, as the market value of equity, i.e. the market capitalization, reflects the sum of the shareholder's claims on the company's future cash flows – the allocated residual to the shareholders after payment of interest and suchlike financing costs, and so no deduction of financial liabilities need be carried out. An additional net debt deduction would thus result in double counting. It follows that the relevant base metric, i.e. the denominator, should go hand in hand with the relevant value metric, i.e. the numerator (Figure 8.30). Hence, the base metric of the P multiples should, in accordance with the reasoning in this as well as in other chapters of this book (see Chapter 6 for further details) be set after financial items (i.e. plus/less interest income/interest expenses, etc.).

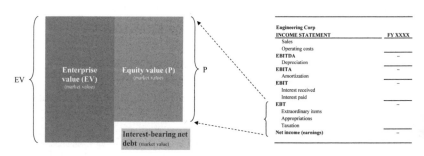

Figure 8.30   Shareholder value (i.e. market value of equity) – no net debt deduction when shareholder value is calculated using equity multiples, and the value (i.e. the numerator) must go hand in hand with the base metric (i.e. the denominator)

To conclude on the appropriate value multiple analysis of Engineering Corp, we reach the results shown in Table 8.13.

Table 8.13 Estimated shareholder values (i.e. market value of equity) – Engineering Corp on the basis of EV as well as P multiples

Engineering Corp ($ millions)	EV/Sales LFY	EV/EBIT LFY	EV/BEV LFY	P/E LFY	P/BV LFY
Derived/applicable value multiple	2.10x	12.2x	4.0x	19.5x	5.6x
Base metric of Engineering Corp (Sales, EBIT, BEV, E, BV)	1,500	255	761	146	510
Market value of operating/invested capital (EV)	**3,150**	**3,111**	**3,044**	**n.a.***	**n.a.***
Interest-bearing net debt of Engineering Corp	–251	–251	–251	n.a.	n.a.
Market value of equity (P)	**2,899**	**2,860**	**2,793**	**2,847**	**2,856**

*The enterprise value, using P multiples, will be given by the market value of equity plus interest-bearing net debt.

We note that all multiples, whether based on EV or P, indicate an estimated market value of equity at about $2,850 million for Engineering Corp. As a result, the market value of Engineering Corp's equity capital (i.e. the market value of all outstanding shares) is assessed to be in the range of $2,565 million to $3,135 million, with a target value of approximately $2,850 million. The value range is given by the $2,850 million target value ± 10 percent.

8.3.3   Concluding remarks

Based on the analysis above, we can feel comfortable concluding that the market value of equity in Engineering Corp is approximately $2,850 million. At this stage, to calculate the value of Engineering Corp with the addition of further value multiples would offer more or less no added value. We derive the value of the company using several value multiples so as to minimize the risk of error in the analysis, *not* to obtain a trustworthy mean or median value. If you aim to produce a "statistically safe" target value using a large number of average or median multiples (as is the case when one rolls the dice a sufficient number of times), you end up skating on very thin ice. The concluding value is given by the individual prospects and risks (and thus by the expected level of value driver(s)) of the subject company in question and nothing else. The concluding value is therefore not a statistic random variable, i.e. the values, as given by the unrevised average or median peer group multiples, are not by definition normally distributed around the true and fair value of the target company. If our analysis above is correct, the estimated equity value will thus be approximately $2,850 million regardless of whether we derive that value using 1, 3, 5, 10 or 150 different multiples (and also irrespective of what the mean or the median of those different ranges of multiples happen to be).

Explicitly, the calculated market approach value of any given company, if calculated by the same analyst with the same valuation purpose, should (i.e. must) be the same irrespective of the applied multiple(s) (that is, no matter which multiple(s), out of all the possible and impossible ones that have been developed or will be developed in the future, are applied), otherwise we have, again, made a mistake somewhere.[53]

At times, the estimated value is also, apart from the more traditional equal weighting (i.e. as opposed to a straight average), stated as a weighted value per respective multiple, often on the basis of a pure subjectively assessed relevance or quality. In other words, if the respective multiples were to produce different outcomes (i.e. different values) for the valuation subject, the most divergent results (i.e. those multiples judged to be of "inferior" quality) are given less weight when settling the concluding value of the company. This is *not* a viable approach either. As indicated earlier, the resulting divergent values as given by the respective multiples in such cases are thus due to inadequate adjustments of the respective multiples (or, put another way, an incomplete analysis has been performed), and not any specific multiple(s) being of better or worse "quality" than any other. *Accordingly, you cannot avoid this problem by assigning various multiples and methodologies with arbitrary (or any!) weights.*

On the same theme, nor should one be deceived by a perfectly centered peer group. For example, were all peers to be valued at EV/EBIT in the very tight range of 10.5x to 11.5x, it does *not* necessarily mean that this group of peers is better as a basis for direct derivation of the subject company's value than an equivalent group of peers with a wider spread. The only thing that clustered peers indicate is that they probably have similar levels of value drivers and risk among themselves, not necessarily that they have similar levels of value drivers and risk compared with the valuation subject. That is, as long as our valuation subject has divergent levels of value drivers and risk versus the corresponding average peer, its justified value multiple *will* differ from that of the peer group average no matter how perfectly centered that average may now be.

As a result, one cannot enhance the value of the subject company by "massaging" the peer group if one carries out the analysis correctly. In other words, the prospective value increase, or the premium, of the subject company reached when removing "low-value" companies from the peer group will be more or less perfectly offset by the equivalent discount then justified as the level of value driver "gap" between the valuation subject and its peers instead increases. That is, if the subject company were a "poor performer," i.e. a company with modest future expectations, and one selects for the peer group

---

[53] The discrepancies as reported above, i.e. in the range of one or a few percent of the target value, are in this respect so small that they can be considered as rounding errors. Should we want to, we could, theoretically, keep calibrating our analysis until the above multiples produce exactly the same result (value) to the dollar.

solely "top performers," i.e. companies with excellent future prospects (who then, of course, will also be highly valued) in order to "enhance" the value of the subject company, this will be exposed in the regression analysis. In other words, high-value companies have a high valuation because they are expected to develop very well (i.e. their value drivers, such as expected earnings growth, are projected at high levels). If the valuation subject is not expected to show the same high level of value driver, its position (i.e. its valuation) in the regression (i.e. high above the regression line) cannot be justified, and so neither can its high value. To put this in other words, the value of our company is, again, given by its individual conditions and prospects. These individual conditions and prospects do not, evidently, change just because we reshuffle the peer group. Consequently, its value should not change either.

Carried to its extreme, this reasoning in theory implies that one can value any company (for example, a truck manufacturer) by means of any other company (for example, a pharmaceutical company). The effect that is seen (i.e. the problem it will bring) is, however, that it will force you to make more adjustments than would otherwise have been the case. The value multiple of the peer (i.e. the value multiple of our pharmaceutical company in this case) should therefore be adjusted (in line with the technique presented in this chapter) on the basis of its expected level of value driver(s) to the extent that it reflects, in every possible way, the conditions of our valuation subject (i.e. our truck manufacturer in this case) instead. Hence, in our standard approach, we choose "comparable" companies for the simple reason that we want to minimize the need for adjustments as far as possible.

One may also reverse this reasoning; rather than (as for our truck manufacturer above) make a series of adjustments to "back out" an appropriate multiple from a less comparable peer, one may instead consider searching the population, from a broad portfolio of listed companies and disregarding its industrial affiliation (e.g. airlines, engineering companies, consultants, investment companies, mining companies, telecom operators, etc.), for comparable peers to the valuation subject in terms of all relevant points. The resulting multiple may then be applied directly (i.e. it does not need to be "adjusted" in any way as it already reflects the exact same conditions and prospects as our valuation subject) to the target company in question (for example, our truck manufacturer as in the case above). This reasoning stems from the first rule of finance: the inviolable relationship of risk and return. If two investments, no matter how different they may appear on the surface (an airline and a hospital operator, for example), are expected to carry exactly the same risk and return to its owner, they will also bear exactly the same price, otherwise there is, in theory at least, opportunity for arbitrage. In other words, you may sell the expensive (i.e. overvalued) asset from a risk and return perspective and accordingly use the funds to buy the cheap (i.e. undervalued) asset with the same risk and return, and thus make a "risk-free" profit; that is, you may benefit from high returns without taking the corresponding accompanying risk.

In practice, however, such a technique is difficult to both apply and put into words, i.e. it is challenging to identify the industries and companies expected to have exactly the same future development and risk exposure as the valuation subject, and it is not the simplest of tasks to convince others that that is really the case. Notwithstanding this, what one may, however, conclude from this discussion is that it is, as emphasized in Chapter 4, more important when putting together a reference group to think in terms of value driver(s) than in terms of what appear, at least on the surface, to be similar products and services.

Figure 8.31 summarizes in chart form the calculated equity values of Engineering Corp discussed above.

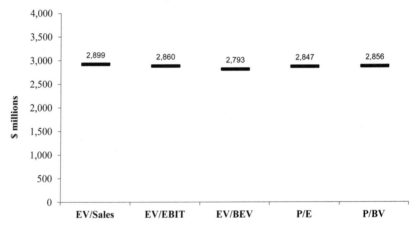

Figure 8.31   Estimated shareholder values (i.e. market value of equity) – Engineering Corp on the basis of EV as well as P multiples

We thus close this chapter by stating that an unadjusted average peer group multiple is only applicable when the specific level of value driver(s) (i.e. expected growth, margins, risk, etc.) of the subject company perfectly matches that of the average peer. Unfortunately, it is, if not impossible then at least exceptionally difficult, to find peers that are entirely (or even to a significant degree) in accordance with the above specification of requirements. All companies, even within the same industry, are individual and thus have different business models. They therefore also have different expected outcomes for future growth, profitability, capital formation, risk, etc. Hence, even though it is straightforward as well as convenient to estimate the value of a given company using an unadjusted/unanalyzed peer group average or median multiple, this calculated value brings with it a *very* high probability of substantial fault.

9

Using the Market Approach for Reconciliation

The attentive reader has by now realized that it can be quite a challenging task to estimate the value of a company using only value multiples. Many assumptions need to be made, and to find the absolute level of adjustments required in terms of the relationship value driver(s) and risk differences between the valuation subject and its peers in order to uncover the true and fair value of the subject company is challenging. It may consequently be advantageous to use the market approach alongside the discounted cash flow (DCF) approach.

The purpose of using the DCF approach in conjunction with the market approach is *not,* however, to calculate two diverse values based on two diverse methods and then to apply a straight or weighted average. Instead, the aim is to minimize the risk of miscalculations and misjudgments in terms of the underlying assumptions and computations. Once again, bear in mind that the two approaches represent "two sides of the same coin." Should you, under a well-defined valuation purpose, estimate the value of a given company using both the market approach and the DCF approach and arrive at two fundamentally different values, you have either made a mistake in the market approach or, alternatively, in the DCF approach (or, in the worst case, you have made a mistake in both).

It may therefore be easier as well as safer to use the market approach for reconciliation rather than direct value derivation. In this chapter, we will review how to carry out such a procedure.

9.1 THE DISCOUNTED CASH FLOW VALUE OF ENGINEERING CORP

We now close the loop on our cash flow valuation of Engineering Corp.

We opt to calculate the market value of Engineering Corp's equity capital (i.e. its P) by first calculating the market value of its operating/invested capital (i.e. its EV). This is given by the discounted cash flow to firm formula previously presented:[1]

---

[1] This is the most common approach when valuing standard companies. Exceptions typically include banks and other financial institutions, as their business concept is to work the interest rate differential between lending and deposits. Accordingly, taking on debt is a commercial act for them, not a financial one. The equity value of such companies is therefore generally calculated using a direct approach (using the dividend discount model), without going through the EV first.

$$PVF(EV) = \sum_{i=1}^{\infty} \frac{FCFF_i}{(1+WACC)^i}$$

where:

PVF = Present value firm (i.e. Enterprise value – EV)
$\sum$ = Sum of
$FCFF_i$ = Expected free cash flow to firm in the ith period in the future
i = The period in the future in which a prospective cash flow is expected to be received
WACC = Weighted average cost of capital
∞ = Infinity

The formula above tells us to forecast and discount the subject company's future expected free cash flows to firm (i.e. free cash flows to operating/invested capital) year by year in infinite time. In practice, however, one will, in accordance with previous reasoning, rarely forecast individual years further than 5–10 years; one will then calculate a residual value (i.e. the value of all expected cash flows after the explicit forecast period). The formula above then takes the following form:[2]

$$PVF(EV) = \frac{FCFF_1}{(1+WACC)^{0.5}} + \frac{FCFF_2}{(1+WACC)^{1.5}} + ... + \frac{FCFF_n}{(1+WACC)^{n-0.5}}$$

$$+ \frac{\left(\dfrac{FCFF_n(1+g)}{WACC-g} \right)}{(1+WACC)^{n-0.5}}$$

where:

---

[2] This is the same formula as set out earlier, but adjusted in accordance with the so-called "mid-year convention"; that is, the cash flows are assumed to be evenly distributed over the fiscal year (rather than to come as a lump sum at the end of each year). This formula may, mathematically, also be expressed as:

$$PVF(EV) = \frac{FCFF_1}{(1+WACC)^{0.5}} + \frac{FCFF_2}{(1+WACC)^{1.5}} + ... + \frac{FCFF_n}{(1+WACC)^{n-0.5}} + \frac{\left(\dfrac{FCFF_n(1+g)(1+WACC)^{0.5}}{WACC-g} \right)}{(1+WACC)^n}$$

PVF   = Present value firm (i.e. Enterprise value – EV)
$FCFF_{1...n}$ = Expected free cash flow to firm in each of the periods 1 through n, n being the last period in the discrete forecast period
WACC   = Weighted average cost of capital
g   = Expected free cash flow to firm growth rate compounded in perpetuity, starting with the last period of the discrete forecast period as base year

Below we present the assumptions underpinning our cash flow valuation of Engineering Corp:

- For FY+1 to FY+3 we assume a development in line with that of our market approach; that is, a development in accordance with the existing company forecast. *In other words, the input to our DCF valuation must be identical to our market approach valuation – or put another way – us moving from one valuation model spreadsheet to another will neither impact the performance nor the risk of the subject company at issue.*
- For FY+4 and onwards we assume an annual revenue growth rate in line with expected long-term U.S. inflation, i.e. approximately 2 percent.
- For FY+4 and onwards we assume an operating margin (EBIT) of 17.7 percent. This is equivalent to the average operating margin of Engineering Corp over a full business cycle (i.e. three historical and three future years as represented by the period FY–2 to FY+3, under the simplified assumption that as at LFY we are in the middle of the business cycle and that this in the U.S. engineering industry typically runs in 6-year periods).
- Capital expenditures for FY+1 and onwards are assumed at 3.7 percent of sales (as represented by the historical levels of Engineering Corp as of FY–2 to LFY), corresponding to 105 percent of depreciation allowances.
- Net working capital for FY+1 and onwards are assumed at 10 percent of sales (i.e. on a par with that of last fiscal year).
- The standard tax rate is set at 40 percent.

Table 9.1 shows the projected cash flows to firm of Engineering Corp for a period of five years including the normalized or terminal year. The discount rate (i.e. the WACC) has, in accordance with the description in the previous chapter, been estimated at 9.0 percent. Based on this information, and in compliance with the cash flow formula above, the market value of invested capital (EV) in Engineering Corp is calculated at $3,092 million.

Table 9.1 The discounted cash flow value of Engineering Corp (enterprise value or market value of operating/invested capital)

ENGINEERING CORP ($ millions)	LFY	FY+1	FY+2	FY+3	FY+4	FY+5	Terminal year (TY)
Sales	1,500	1,748	1,957	2,081	2,123	2,165	2,165
Operating costs	−1,193	−1,353	−1,485	−1,555	−1,673	−1,706	−1,706
Depreciation & amortization	−53	−61	−68	−73	−74	−76	−76
EBIT	**255**	**334**	**403**	**454**	**376**	**383**	**383**
Add: depreciation & amortization	53	61	68	73	74	76	76
EBITDA	**308**	**395**	**472**	**526**	**450**	**459**	**459**
Investment in net working capital	−26	−25	−21	−12	−4	−4	−4
Capital expenditures	−58	−64	−72	−76	−78	−80	−80
Taxes on EBIT*	−102	−134	−161	−181	−150	−153	−153
Free cash flow to firm (FCFF)	**122**	**172**	**218**	**256**	**218**	**222**	**222**

Terminal value = FCFF TY × (1+g)/ (WACC−g)		↓	↓	↓	↓	↓	$\dfrac{222 \times 1.02}{0.09 - 0.02}$
							↓
Free cash flow to firm (FCFF)		172	218	256	218	222	3,259
Discount factor = 1/ (1+WACC)$^{n-0.5}$		95.8%	87.9%	80.7%	74.1%	68.0%	68.0%
		↓	↓	↓	↓	↓	↓
ENTERPRISE VALUE (EV)	**3,092** =	165 +	191 +	207 +	161 +	151 +	2,217

IMPLIED MULTIPLES

EV/Sales	**2.06x**
EV/EBITDA	**10.1x**
EV/EBIT	**12.1x**
EV/BEV	**4.1x**

Key ratios

Revenue growth (year-on-year)	*20.6%*	*16.5%*	*12.0%*	*6.3%*	*2.0%*	*2.0%*	*2.0%*
EBITDA margin	*20.5%*	*22.6%*	*24.1%*	*25.3%*	*21.2%*	*21.2%*	*21.2%*
EBIT margin	*17.0%*	*19.1%*	*20.6%*	*21.8%*	*17.7%*	*17.7%*	*17.7%*

*Any non-deductible depreciations/amortizations to be added back to EBIT

Note again that we have calculated the market value of Engineering Corp using projected free cash flows to firm; that is, cash flows before financial income and expenses (i.e. before interest payments, etc.). These cash flows should therefore benefit all financiers of the company's assets (i.e. shareholders as well as lenders). Consequently, to attain the equity value of Engineering Corp, we must adjust for (i.e. deduct) interest-bearing net debt as we did for the enterprise value multiples earlier (i.e. EV/Sales, EV/EBIT, etc.) (Figure 9.1).

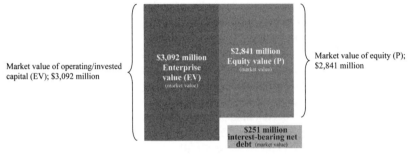

Figure 9.1   Enterprise value (i.e. market value of operating/invested capital) vs. shareholders' value (i.e. market value of equity) – the calculated equity value of Engineering Corp

Thus the market value of equity in Engineering Corp is calculated at $2,841 million ($3,092 million less $251 million).

We return to the invested capital of Engineering Corp. The market value of its invested capital (EV) as per our cash flow valuation above was $3,092 million. Based on this value we can compute the resulting value multiples:

EV/Sales   **2.06x** (i.e. Engineering Corp's $3,092 million EV as above divided by its $1,500 million Sales)

EV/EBIT   **12.1x** (i.e. Engineering Corp's $3,092 million EV as above divided by its $255 million EBIT)

EV/BEV   **4.1x** (i.e. Engineering Corp's $3,092 million EV as above divided by its $761 million BEV)

Following this we revisit the previous graphs in which we plotted the value multiples of the peers against their relevant value drivers. The approach now, however, will not be to derive an applicable value multiple for our valuation subject from the graph of plotted peers, but instead to position the resulting value multiples, as given by our discounted cash flow valuation, in the graphs and then analyze their consequent positions relative to the regression line.

9.1.1   EV/Sales

We start off with the EV/Sales multiple. When, in Chapter 8, we derived the value of Engineering Corp using value multiples and their accompanying value drivers, we had to remind ourselves that the regressions, and thus also the derived value multiple (and by that, of course, also the resulting value), only reflected one specific dimension or value driver at a time. For example, the derived value of Engineering Corp using EV/Sales and its premier value driver, expected operating margin, was built upon the assumption that the valuation subject had an expected revenue growth and risk exposure exactly in line with the average peer. If this expected growth and/or risk exposure were to deviate from the peer group average, we had to adjust the multiple step by step, upwards or downwards, depending on the valuation subject's specific conditions and circumstances versus its peers.

In our cash flow valuation of Engineering Corp, we created a detailed forecast of its expected future financial performance. As in this model we entered Engineering Corp's expected financial performance (i.e. its expected free cash flow) and its unique risk profile (i.e. its individual risk-adjusted required rate of return), we captured and adjusted for all of Engineering Corp's company-specific conditions and prospects in the same model.

Expected growth, operating margin, capital requirements, individual risk profile, etc., have thus in the cash flow model been "tailored" to fit Engineering Corp's unique state of affairs and prospects. In the cash flow model we have therefore, in contrast to value derivation using value multiples and their accompanying value drivers (i.e. what we presented in the previous chapter), simultaneously taken into account *all* of Engineering Corp's unique and company-specific variables versus the peer group average in the same model (i.e. the 11.5 percent expected average growth rate versus the peers' 7.9 percent, the 20.5 percent expected average operating margin versus the comparative companies' 14.0 percent, the expected higher risk exposure, i.e. the higher required rate of return, versus the comparable companies' similar average, etc.).

In other words, Engineering Corp's unique company-specific conditions and prospects versus the corresponding average peer, which in the previous chapter required step-by-step adjustments of the derived multiples, are now reflected as input data in Engineering Corp's cash flow model. Accordingly, the resulting (implied by the DCF valuation) value multiples (i.e. the 2.06x EV/Sales, the 12.1x EV/EBIT and the 4.1x EV/BEV, as above) will, without fault, mirror all of Engineering Corp's unique company-specific conditions and prospects. It follows that the value multiples derived from the cash flow valuation above do not need to be "adjusted" in any way.

Consequently, rather than to derive an applicable EV/Sales multiple for Engineering Corp from the corresponding multiples and value drivers of the peers, as in the previous chapter, we instead reverse this and put Engineering Corp's calculated EV/Sales multiple provided by our "tailor-made" cash flow valuation above (i.e. the 2.06x) into our previously presented (i.e. in the first and unadjusted) regression graph, EV/Sales vs. operating margin. As noted below, the estimated EV/Sales multiple based on our cash flow valuation will place Engineering Corp a little way up on the right and slightly below the regression line (Figure 9.2).

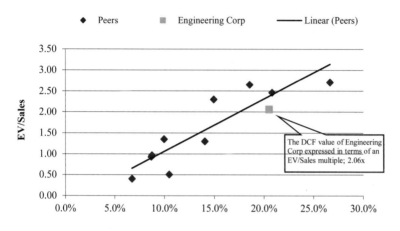

Figure 9.2   EV/Sales vs. operating margin – Engineering Corp's discounted cash flow value expressed in terms of an EV/Sales multiple

Instead of adjusting the value multiple in question by the level of identified value driver(s) difference(s) between the subject company and the average peer, as in the method of direct valuation using derived peer group multiples, we instead now apply the cash flow approach as the main method and use the market approach for "fine tuning." Our task here is to analyze, explain, and possibly adjust Engineering Corp's position in the regression graph as given by the input data fed into the DCF model. We thus need to put these assumptions in relation to the corresponding assumptions for the comparables, as given by the stock market, implicitly, by each and every peer's unique position in the regression graph.

It is therefore important to note that each comparable company's unique position in the regression graph above is based on the same reasoning we just applied to Engineering Corp. That is, each of the peers' resulting EV/Sales multiples is in the graph above "tailored" by *its* individual state of affairs and prospects, i.e. each and every peer is, by the stock market (this time), priced on the basis of its individual risk profile and future prospects in the same way as Engineering Corp's 2.06x EV/Sales multiple was (by us as at that time) tailored to its individual state of affairs and prospects. The reason why the peers are scattered above or below the regression line in the graph above is consequently in essence that they are, by the stock market, assigned different growth expectations and/or risk profiles (i.e. the supplementary value drivers sales growth and risk are, by the stock market participants, for each and every peer group company, expected at different levels). Should all companies be attributed exactly the same risk and growth expectations, the value would be solely driven by operating margin, all else being equal. If this were the case, the spread above/below the regression line EV/Sales vs. operating margin would cease to exist. In other words, all companies would be *at* the regression line and only expected operating margin would drive each company's value up or down.

Should one then encounter a peer group showing a tight spread about the trend line with regard to the regression EV/Sales vs. operating margin, this would thus indicate small discrepancies among the peers' individual growth expectations and risk profiles, all else being equal. However, to be on the safe side, an analysis of each value multiple's (i.e. each peer's) specific level of value driver should nonetheless be undertaken to identify any potential counteractive effects. A company may, for example, possess strong growth prospects, but at a high risk level, leading to these effects offsetting each other (i.e. the growth prospects will push the value upwards, but the accompanying risk exposure will simultaneously pull the value downwards, as in the case of Peer 9 in Chapter 8). The company in question may then appear to be fully representative of the average peer in terms of both growth and risk owing to its position on the regression line, but this is in fact not the case.

Hence, we find our cash flow valuation generating a "tailor-made" EV/Sales multiple of 2.06x for Engineering Corp. The principal value drivers (operating margin, revenue growth, and risk) are still the same. The regression we have chosen as the basis for analysis, EV/Sales vs. operating margin, picks up operating margin as the key explanatory value driver. Therefore expected revenue growth and individual risk profile are left to explain Engineering Corp's position in the graph above. If one so wishes, one can, of course, instead choose a regression graph showing revenue growth as the chief value driver. The supplementary explanatory variables would then be operating margin and individual risk profile.

Our cash flow valuation of Engineering Corp provides us with endless opportunities to test and simulate various levels of EV/Sales output as per various changes in input data.

We know that the peers are, on average, expected (based on analyst's projections) to grow in terms of sales by approximately 7.9 percent per annum. We have found the corresponding expectations for our valuation subject Engineering Corp to be approximately 11.5 percent. Engineering Corp's higher expected revenue growth than the peer group average thus indicates (all else being equal) a position *above* the regression line.

On the other hand, we also know from our previous calculation of Engineering Corp's individual cost of capital that the company has a higher risk profile than the corresponding average peer. This thus suggests that Engineering Corp (all else being equal) should position itself *below* the regression line.

To find out how much each of Engineering Corp's individual conditions and prospects, in relation to the corresponding average peer, affect its resulting EV/Sales multiple in the above regression, we "reset" Engineering Corp's individually set levels of supplementary value drivers, revenue growth and risk profile, in our discounted cash flow valuation.

(a) Revenue growth

We start with the value driver revenue growth. Recall that in the graph of EV/Sales vs. operating margin shown earlier (Figure 8.9) we identified three companies with an expected revenue growth in excess of that expected for the average peer. As these three companies had expected revenue growth reasonably well in line with that of Engineering Corp, we decided the regression line to shift up to a level alongside these three companies when deriving an applicable multiple for Engineering Corp. We now apply this reasoning to our cash flow model.

As step one we thus adjust Engineering Corp's expected sales growth from its current anticipated annual 11.5 percent level over the coming three-year period to the corresponding 7.9 percent of the average peer. For simplicity, we assume that Engineering Corp and the average peer have an expected growth rate as of FY+4 and onwards in line with anticipated long-term U.S. inflation, i.e. at about 2 percent per annum. Should this not be the case, however, nothing prevents us from extending the forecast period until we have reached the "normalized" stage. That is, the forecast period should be long enough to allow the valuation subject and its peers to converge at a long-term sustainable level, which normally comprises expected inflation (and perhaps, in highly specific cases, the addition of all or part of expected GDP growth[3]). Whether this period should be 0, 1, 5, 10 or 50 years is up to the analyst to assess and justify.

Table 9.2 shows the calculated value of Engineering Corp after adjustment for differing growth expectations as above. That is, we have now valued Engineering Corp as if it had had an expected growth rate in line with the average peer (i.e. 7.9 percent per year over the coming three-year period) instead of the growth rate it de facto expects to have (i.e. 11.5 percent per year over the coming three-year period).

---

[3] GDP growth is, to a great extent, driven by new innovations, new technological breakthroughs, and new industries and businesses. To give, in a never-ending perspective, full credit of expected GDP growth to an established and mature company, in an established and mature industry, could thus lead to a significant overestimation of that company's growth potential. Should the company in question, for a period longer than is normally expressed in the explicit forecast period (note: explicit forecast periods are rarely modeled longer than 10–15 years), have an expected growth rate above that deemed sustainable, it is preferable to increase the forecast period (i.e. beyond the customary 10–15 year maximum range) until an expected normalized sustainable mode is reached, rather than to apply a high perpetual growth rate to the terminal value calculation.

Table 9.2   The discounted cash flow value of Engineering Corp (enterprise value or market value of operating/invested capital) – given revenue growth in line with the average peer and with in other respects unchanged assumptions

ENGINEERING CORP ($ millions)	LFY	FY+1	FY+2	FY+3	FY+4	FY+5	Terminal year (TY)
Sales	1,500	1,619	1,746	1,884	1,922	1,960	1,960
Operating costs	−1,193	−1,253	−1,325	−1,408	−1,515	−1,545	−1,545
Depreciation & amortization	−53	−57	−61	−66	−67	−69	−69
EBIT	255	309	360	411	340	347	347
Add: depreciation & amortization	53	57	61	66	67	69	69
EBITDA	308	366	421	477	407	416	416
Investment in net working capital	−26	−12	−13	−14	−4	−4	−4
Capital expenditures	−58	−59	−64	−69	−71	−72	−72
Taxes on EBIT*	−102	−124	−144	−164	−136	−139	−139
Free cash flow to firm (FCFF)	122	171	200	229	197	201	201

Terminal value = FCFF
TY × (1+g)/(WACC–g)

$\downarrow \quad \downarrow \quad \downarrow \quad \downarrow \quad \downarrow \quad \dfrac{201 \times 1.02}{0.09 - 0.02}$
$\downarrow$

Free cash flow to firm (FCFF)		171	200	229	197	201	2,951
Discount factor = 1/ $(1+WACC)^{n-0.5}$		95.8%	87.9%	80.7%	74.1%	68.0%	68.0%
		$\downarrow$	$\downarrow$	$\downarrow$	$\downarrow$	$\downarrow$	$\downarrow$
ENTERPRISE VALUE (EV)	2,815 =	164 +	176 +	185 +	146 +	137 +	2,007

IMPLIED MULTIPLES	
EV/Sales	1.88x
EV/EBITDA	9.2x
EV/EBIT	11.0x
EV/BEV	3.7x

Key ratios

Revenue growth (year-on-year)	20.6%	7.9%	7.9%	7.9%	2.0%	2.0%	2.0%
EBITDA margin	20.5%	22.6%	24.1%	25.3%	21.2%	21.2%	21.2%
EBIT margin	17.0%	19.1%	20.6%	21.8%	17.7%	17.7%	17.7%

*Any non-deductible depreciations/amortizations to be added back to EBIT

As a result of this adjustment, the calculated value of Engineering Corp decreases by $277 million (from $3,092 million to $2,815 million), and the resulting EV/Sales multiple declines by 0.18x (from 2.06x to 1.88x), which is analogous with a 10 percent discount. The higher expected revenue growth of Engineering Corp versus the average peer is thus, given the above presented prerequisites and assumptions, worth about 0.18x EV/Sales in a regression line *uplift* (or, alternatively, a $277 million value *addition*).

(b) Discount rate (i.e. risk)

We now perform a sensitivity analysis in which we "zero out" the identified 1.0 percentage point size premium as well as the identified 1.0 percentage point company-specific risk premium from the required return on equity (however, before we do so we reverse the above-mentioned revenue growth adjustment).

These risk factors are, in comparison with the average peer, unique for Engineering Corp. Hence, by "zeroing out" these risk premiums we can get an indication of how much the value of Engineering Corp is affected, compared with the well-diversified large cap companies that primarily constitute the peer group, by its smaller size and extra company-specific risk. That is, we now value Engineering Corp as if it was on a par with its large cap peers in size terms as well as not being burdened with a large customer dependency (Table 9.3).

Table 9.3   The discounted cash flow value of Engineering Corp (enterprise value or market value of operating/invested capital) – given risk exposure (i.e. cost of capital) in line with a large cap peer and with in other respects unchanged assumptions

ENGINEERING CORP ($ millions)	LFY	FY+1	FY+2	FY+3	FY+4	FY+5	Terminal year (TY)
Sales	1,500	1,748	1,957	2,081	2,123	2,165	2,165
Operating costs	–1,193	–1,353	–1,485	–1,555	–1,673	–1,706	–1,706
Depreciation & amortization	–53	–61	–68	–73	–74	–76	–76
EBIT	**255**	**334**	**403**	**454**	**376**	**383**	**383**
Add: depreciation & amortization	53	61	68	73	74	76	76
EBITDA	**308**	**395**	**472**	**526**	**450**	**459**	**459**
Investment in net working capital	–26	–25	–21	–12	–4	–4	–4
Capital expenditures	–58	–64	–72	–76	–78	–80	–80
Taxes on EBIT*	–102	–134	–161	–181	–150	–153	–153
Free cash flow to firm (FCFF)	**122**	**172**	**218**	**256**	**218**	**222**	**222**

Terminal value =
FCFF TY × (1+g)/
(WACC–g)

↓ ↓ ↓ ↓ ↓

$$\frac{222 \times 1.02}{0.072 - 0.02}$$

↓

Free cash flow to firm (FCFF)		172	218	256	218	222	4,399
Discount factor = 1/ (1+WACC)$^{n-0.5}$		96.6%	90.2%	84.2%	78.5%	73.3%	73.3%

↓ ↓ ↓ ↓ ↓ ↓

ENTERPRISE VALUE (EV)	**4,137** =	167 +	196 +	216 +	171 +	163 +	3,225

IMPLIED MULTIPLES	
EV/Sales	**2.76x**
EV/EBITDA	**13.5x**
EV/EBIT	**16.2x**
EV/BEV	**5.4x**

Key ratios

Revenue growth (year-on-year)	*20.6%*	*16.5%*	*12.0%*	*6.3%*	*2.0%*	*2.0%*	*2.0%*
EBITDA margin	*20.5%*	*22.6%*	*24.1%*	*25.3%*	*21.2%*	*21.2%*	*21.2%*
EBIT margin	*17.0%*	*19.1%*	*20.6%*	*21.8%*	*17.7%*	*17.7%*	*17.7%*

*Any non-deductible depreciations/amortizations to be added back to EBIT

The calculated value of Engineering Corp hence increases by $1,045 million (from $3,092 million to $4,137 million). Putting this "new" adjusted DCF value of Engineering Corp in relation to its $1,500 million turnover, the resulting EV/Sales multiple is calculated at 2.76x, compared with the 2.06x we initially calculated in this chapter. This is analogous with a 30 percent premium. The higher expected risk profile of Engineering Corp versus the corresponding large cap peers is thus, given the prerequisites and assumptions above, worth about 0.70x EV/Sales in a regression line *downward* adjustment (or, alternatively, a $1,045 million value *reduction*).

Let us now return to the note we made at the end of the previous chapter. We have now used our cash flow valuation to identify the level of EV/Sales adjustment (i.e. the 0.70x as per above) applicable to Engineering Corp in relation to a corresponding large cap peer as a result of its total two percentage points higher required rate of return (i.e. higher risk profile). Anyone with a good memory will recall that this is very close to the adjustment, as a result of risk, that we carried out in Chapter 8 by "free hand," i.e. the adjustment using the smaller companies' position in relation to the corresponding larger companies that we made in the previous chapter in the EV/Sales vs. operating margin regression graph (that is, from 2.75x EV/Sales to 2.10x EV/Sales, or about minus 0.65x EV/Sales[4] – see Figure 8.24). Had we not had access to a reference group containing a number of small cap companies from which we could directly derive the relevant small cap discount of Engineering Corp (and in which we also included the company-specific discount due to its large

---

[4] Note that the value effect (i.e. the value reduction) is dependent on the starting point of the sensitivity analysis. In the sensitivity analysis above, we started from Engineering Corp's individual level of expected revenue growth, i.e. 11.5 percent. If we instead were to perform a similar analysis and "zero out" Engineering Corp's two percentage points of higher required rate of return in our DCF at an expected revenue growth in line with the corresponding peer group average (i.e. 7.9 percent), we would arrive at an equivalent 0.63x EV/Sales reduction, more in line with the previously derived 0.65x using the market approach. The problem is, moreover, the same in our sensitivity analysis of expected revenue growth above. Hence, the 0.18x EV/Sales reduction from the discounted cash flow approach is calculated on the basis of Engineering Corp's individual risk profile (i.e. required rate of return). Should that sensitivity analysis have, on the other hand, been derived on the basis of the risk profile (i.e. the required rate of return) of the average large cap peer, the resulting value reduction would be calculated at 0.25x EV/Sales. A weakness of our manual regression line shifts when using the technique in the previous chapter is that in terms of the supplementary value drivers they are based on the comparable companies' individual circumstances and conditions, not on our subject company's individual circumstances and conditions. We thus avoid this problem when utilizing the discounted cash flow approach.

customer dependency), we could have derived the proper discount using a cash flow valuation.[5]

We move forward in our cash flow model and implement adjustment 1 (the revenue growth difference) and adjustment 2 (the required rate of return difference) simultaneously. That is, we now replace the real expected revenue growth of Engineering Corp in our cash flow valuation with the corresponding growth of the average peer (i.e. we replace the 11.5 percent average expected revenue growth of Engineering Corp for the coming three years with the corresponding 7.9 percent peer group average). At the same time, we "zero out" the unique risk factors of Engineering Corp (i.e. the one plus one size and company-specific premiums) from its required rate of return.

When executing both of these adjustments, we will see an aggregated net effect in relation to the initially estimated $3,092 million value at about $668 million or, alternatively, 0.45x EV/Sales[6] (Table 9.4).

---

[5] Even if our peer group were to provide us with an opportunity to derive appropriate discounts and premiums, this methodology is still preferable. As we also noted in the previous chapter, the effects are difficult to quantify (and often pull in opposite directions) and the quality of the adjustments is far greater when we carry them out in a cash flow valuation than when we derive them from the comparable companies' relative positions in the regression graphs. In addition, as is also evident from the note above, the analysis is severely limited by the comparable companies' present/actual level of supplementary value driver(s).

[6] Note hence that the aggregated value of the two adjustments in a single model does not equal the sum of the individual adjustments as presented previously (i.e. whether or not they are allowed to influence one another has a bearing on the outcome).

Table 9.4   The discounted cash flow value of Engineering Corp (enterprise value or market value of operating/invested capital) – given revenue growth in line with the average peer and risk exposure (i.e. cost of capital) in line with a large cap peer, and with in other respects unchanged assumptions

ENGINEERING CORP ($ millions)	LFY	FY+1	FY+2	FY+3	FY+4	FY+5	Terminal year (TY)
Sales	1,500	1,619	1,746	1,884	1,922	1,960	1,960
Operating costs	−1,193	−1,253	−1,325	−1,408	−1,515	−1,545	−1,545
Depreciation & amortization	−53	−57	−61	−66	−67	−69	−69
EBIT	**255**	**309**	**360**	**411**	**340**	**347**	**347**
Add: depreciation & amortization	53	57	61	66	67	69	69
EBITDA	**308**	**366**	**421**	**477**	**407**	**416**	**416**
Investment in net working capital	−26	−12	−13	−14	−4	−4	−4
Capital expenditures	−58	−59	−64	−69	−71	−72	−72
Taxes on EBIT*	−102	−124	−144	−164	−136	−139	−139
Free cash flow to firm (FCFF)	**122**	**171**	**200**	**229**	**197**	**201**	**201**

Terminal value = FCFF TY × (1+g)/ (WACC–g)		↓	↓	↓	↓	↓	$\dfrac{201 \times 1.02}{0.072 - 0.02}$
							↓
Free cash flow to firm (FCFF)		171	200	229	197	201	3,983
Discount factor = 1/ $(1+\text{WACC})^{n-0.5}$		96.6%	90.2%	84.2%	78.5%	73.3%	73.3%
		↓	↓	↓	↓	↓	↓
ENTERPRISE VALUE (EV)	**3,760** =	165 +	180 +	193 +	155 +	147 +	2,920

IMPLIED MULTIPLES	
EV/Sales	**2.51x**
EV/EBITDA	**12.2x**
EV/EBIT	**14.7x**
EV/BEV	**4.9x**

Key ratios

Revenue growth (year-on-year)	20.6%	7.9%	7.9%	7.9%	2.0%	2.0%	2.0%
EBITDA margin	20.5%	22.6%	24.1%	25.3%	21.2%	21.2%	21.2%
EBIT margin	17.0%	19.1%	20.6%	21.8%	17.7%	17.7%	17.7%

*Any non-deductible depreciations/amortizations to be added back to EBIT

Now let us return to our EV/Sales vs. operating margin regression. We have now eliminated those unique factors (i.e. the sales growth and the risk exposure) in our cash flow valuation that separate Engineering Corp from an average large cap peer. Our "new" adjusted cash flow valuation of Engineering Corp thus portrays a company with an expected revenue growth and risk profile in line with an average large cap peer.

Accordingly, the only force now driving our value multiple in the EV/Sales vs. operating margin graph is expected operating margin, i.e. the regression line. Engineering Corp should now be located if not directly on, then at least very close to, the regression line. That is, if our sensitivity analysis eliminates both Engineering Corp's expected "super growth" and its higher risk exposure, then all of the prime supplementary factors that justify a deviation from the regression line have been eliminated. Thus, its resulting valuation should also be on a par with the regression line, all else being equal (Figure 9.3).

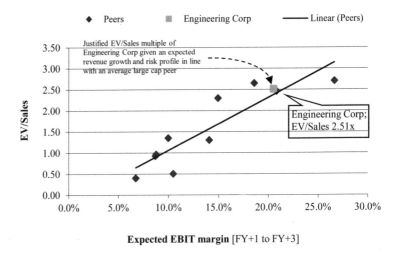

Expected EBIT margin [FY+1 to FY+3]

Figure 9.3   EV/Sales vs. operating margin – the discounted cash flow value of Engineering Corp expressed in terms of the EV/Sales multiple (given revenue growth in line with the average peer and a risk exposure, i.e. a cost of capital, in line with a large cap peer, and with in other respects unchanged assumptions)

As noted above, the EV/Sales multiple of Engineering Corp when stripped of the company's unique sales growth and risk profile ends up very close to the regression line. In this "synthetic" valuation Engineering Corp is thus given a position on the regression line at a level representative of its future expected 20.5 percent operating margin. In other words, if Engineering Corp were expected to produce a 7.9 percent annual average revenue growth rate for the coming three years, instead of its actual forecasted 11.5 percent, and, in addition, if it were to hold a minimum $15 billion market value as well as reduced large customer dependency, then the company would, all else being equal, be justified at a valuation of 2.51x EV/Sales.

That is not the case, however. In Figure 9.4 we illustrate in terms of the EV/Sales vs. operating margin regression the resulting value addition of Engineering Corp's higher expected revenue growth rate (vis-à-vis the average peer) as well as the resulting value reduction due to Engineering Corp's higher expected risk profile (vis-à-vis a large cap peer) as derived by our cash flow valuation (i.e. we have now repopulated the cash flow model with Engineering Corp's real expected revenue growth and required rate of return).

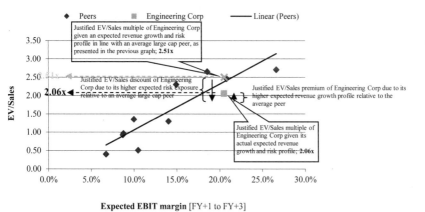

Figure 9.4 EV/Sales vs. operating margin – illustrated net effect of Engineering Corp's higher expected growth rate at a simultaneously higher expected risk (i.e. the net value of Engineering Corp's higher expected revenue growth and cost of capital versus an average large cap peer)

Engineering Corp's higher expected revenue growth rate versus the average peer is thus, given the above presented conditions and assumptions, worth $277 million (i.e. $3,092 million vs. $2,815 million) or, alternatively, 0.18x EV/Sales (i.e. 2.06x EV/Sales vs. 1.88x EV/Sales), and the corresponding loss of value, owing to Engineering Corp's higher risk profile compared to a large cap peer, given the above presented conditions and assumptions, is thus $1,045 million (i.e. $4,137 million vs. $3,092 million) or, alternatively, 0.70x EV/Sales (i.e. 2.76x EV/Sales vs. 2.06x EV/Sales) when derived separately.

The estimated value addition due to Engineering Corp's higher expected revenue growth than the average peer is therefore lower than the corresponding value decrease due to its higher expected risk compared to a large cap peer. The net of these effects, when allowed to influence one another, is thus negative at 0.45x EV/Sales (i.e. 2.06x EV/Sales minus 2.51x EV/Sales as above) or, alternatively, minus $668 million.

Thus, using the DCF analysis set out in this chapter, we can conclude that the resulting EV/Sales multiple, and accordingly, also the estimated enterprise value, is justified (or "correct"). However, should our cash flow valuation have generated a ratio inexplicably over or below the regression line, we would have been forced to revisit the model to identify and clarify the underlying reasons for the divergence.

9.1.2   EV/EBIT

The prime value driver of the EV/EBIT multiple, apart from the ever-present risk factor, is expected growth in EBIT. Returning to our cash flow valuation, we note that the $3,092 million enterprise value of Engineering Corp, in relation to its $255 million EBIT, results in a calculated EV/EBIT multiple of 12.1x.

Like the EV/Sales vs. operating margin regression, the EV/EBIT vs. expected growth in EBIT regression is only capable of capturing one dimension, i.e. one value driver, at a time. A prerequisite when deriving the value of a company using an EV/EBIT vs. expected growth in EBIT regression is thus that the subject company has more or less exactly the same risk profile as the average peer (as these companies form the basis of the regression line). If the subject company, or any of the peers for that matter, were to hold a risk profile noticeably different from that of the average peer, they would accordingly be located either above or below the regression line, and, in consequence, the greater the deviation, the greater the distance from the regression line.

If we plant the 12.1x EV/EBIT multiple of Engineering Corp, as provided by our cash flow valuation, in the EV/EBIT vs. expected growth in EBIT regression graph, the company should be positioned near the top right of the regression line as its value multiple as well as its level of value driver (its expected growth in EBIT) are well above that of the corresponding average peer. However, the company simultaneously has a higher expected risk exposure (i.e. the 1.0 percentage point size premium and the 1.0 percentage point company-specific premium as per above) than the average peer, thus implying a position somewhat below the same regression line.

Our sensitivity analysis (see the review on EV/Sales above for details) shows that the estimated value of Engineering Corp increases by about 4.1x EV/EBIT, or approximately 30 percent (i.e. 16.2x EV/EBIT/12.1x EV/EBIT = +30 percent) when "zeroing out" the extra two percentage points of risk premium additions from its required rate of return. The "adjusted" cash flow valuation of Engineering Corp, and the resulting EV/EBIT multiple, consequently now portray a company with a risk profile on a par with an average large cap peer, as was the case with the "adjusted" cash flow valuation and the resulting EV/Sales multiple previously. The only prime value driver of the EV/EBIT multiple of

Engineering Corp in the EV/EBIT vs. expected growth in EBIT regression is thus now expected growth in EBIT, i.e. the regression line. Therefore, Engineering Corp should now be positioned if not directly on, then at least very close to, the regression line (as is also indicated by the cross in Figure 9.5).

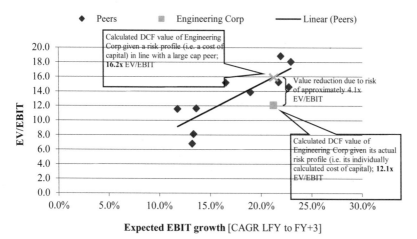

Figure 9.5   EV/EBIT vs. EBIT growth – illustrated value effect of Engineering Corp's higher expected risk profile (i.e. higher cost of capital) versus a corresponding large cap peer

Accordingly, we conclude that the position of Engineering Corp (at a negative 4.1x EV/EBIT) on the regression graph (Figure 9.5) is fully explained by its higher risk profile than a corresponding large cap peer.

At this point in time, it may be appropriate to elaborate more on the relationship between value and risk. Our valuation subject Engineering Corp experienced a value decrease of about 25 percent (i.e. 12.1x EV/EBIT/16.2x EV/EBIT = –25 percent as above, or as already concluded via the EV/Sales analysis earlier, 2.06x EV/Sales/2.76x EV/Sales = –25 percent) as an effect of its smaller size and extra company-specific risk versus an equivalent large cap peer. Hence, in relation to the large cap peers, which principally form the basis of our peer group, Engineering Corp was concluded to be a small cap company. Whilst this is true in reality, Engineering Corp is nonetheless worth several billion dollars. What if Engineering Corp were of no more than a tenth of that size (or even less than that)? How would this affect the resulting value, all else being equal?

To find out, we conduct a sensitivity analysis: let us assume that Engineering Corp is a very small privately held company with only one-twentieth of its original sales and earnings (to minimize the risk of misunderstandings, we will call this "new" company "Small Engineering Corp"). In other words, it has a \$75 million turnover (versus the original \$1,500 million for Engineering Corp) and a \$12.75 million operating profit (versus the original \$255 million for Engineering Corp), with all else being equal (i.e. no change in terms of expected growth, profitability, capital requirements, etc.).

Just its sheer size will now warrant a higher beta (as the 0.77 asset beta, i.e. the unlevered median peer group asset beta we used to calculate Engineering Corp's 0.86 equity/levered beta, was derived principally from large cap peers) as well as an additional size premium, in excess of that given by CAPM. Referring again to the Ibbotson/Morningstar study, we notice that companies of Small Engineering Corp's size are justified with a size premium addition of roughly six percentage points (compared with the mere one percentage point that we deemed reasonable for Engineering Corp) in excess of that given by CAPM. Moreover, as the 0.77 unlevered beta (as indicated above) applied to Engineering Corp was derived from large cap peers, we need to adjust for that abnormality. As noted in the Ibbotson/Morningstar table, companies of Small Engineering Corp's size are, on average, and irrespective of their industry affiliation, justified an approximately 40 percent higher beta. Hence, using the simplified assumption that that relationship also applies to the general engineering sector, Small Engineering Corp's new adjusted "small cap" equity beta can be calculated at approximately 1.2.

Let us furthermore, for the sake of argument, assume that Small Engineering Corp holds a plethora of extra company-specific factors not reflected in the small cap premium identified above. Let us assume that Small Engineering Corp is very dependent on a few key personnel, sees a full 30 percent of its sales stemming from a single customer, and is also especially dependent on a few large suppliers. Without entering into the details, we assume our analysis has given rise to a total of five percentage points in overall company-specific risk premium (compared with the mere one percentage point that we deemed reasonable for Engineering Corp). The required rate of return of Small Engineering Corp is then calculated at:

$$K_e = R_f + \beta \times EMRP + SSP + CSP$$

where:

K_e	=	Cost of equity
R_f	=	Risk-free rate
β	=	Equity beta
EMRP	=	Equity market risk premium
SSP	=	Small stock premium
CSP	=	Company-specific premium

$$K_e = R_f + \beta \times EMRP + SSP + CSP$$

$$K_e = 3.3\% + 1.2 \times 5.0\% + 6.0\% + 5.0\%$$

$$K_e = 20.3\%$$

$$WACC = (K_e \times W_e) + (K_d \times W_d)$$

where:

WACC	=	Weighted average cost of capital
K_e	=	Cost of equity
K_d	=	Cost of debt
W_e	=	Weight of equity in capital structure (at market values)
W_d	=	Weight of debt in capital structure (at market values)

$$WACC = (K_e \times W_e) + (K_d \times W_d)$$

$$WACC = (20.3\% \times 0.90) + (3.2\% \times 0.10)$$

$$WACC = 18.6\%$$

The weighted average cost of capital of Small Engineering Corp is thus estimated at 18.6 percent, compared with 9.0 percent for Engineering Corp. In addition, note that the corresponding cost of capital for an equivalent large cap corporation, where the small cap premium and the company-specific premiums have been wiped out, is calculated at 7.2 percent.[7]

Then what about the actual impact? We apply a 18.6 percent WACC, all else being equal, to our cash flow valuation of Engineering Corp and compute the resulting EV/EBIT multiple (i.e. to illustrate the resulting value effect of a higher required rate of return, we calculate the cash flow value of Engineering Corp using the cost of capital of Small Engineering Corp, all else being equal) (Table 9.5).

---

[7] $K_e = 3.3\% + 0.86 \times 5.0\% + 0.0\% + 0.0\% = 7.6\% \rightarrow WACC = (7.6\% \times 0.90) + (3.2\% \times 0.10)$ = 7.2%.

Table 9.5   The discounted cash flow value of Engineering Corp (enterprise value or market value of operating/invested capital) – given risk exposure (i.e. cost of capital) in line with Small Engineering Corp, and with in other respects unchanged assumptions

ENGINEERING CORP ($ millions)	LFY	FY+1	FY+2	FY+3	FY+4	FY+5	Terminal year (TY)
Sales	1,500	1,748	1,957	2,081	2,123	2,165	2,165
Operating costs	−1,193	−1,353	−1,485	−1,555	−1,673	−1,706	−1,706
Depreciation & amortization	−53	−61	−68	−73	−74	−76	−76
EBIT	**255**	**334**	**403**	**454**	**376**	**383**	**383**
Add: depreciation & amortization	53	61	68	73	74	76	76
EBITDA	**308**	**395**	**472**	**526**	**450**	**459**	**459**
Investment in net working capital	−26	−25	−21	−12	−4	−4	−4
Capital expenditures	−58	−64	−72	−76	−78	−80	−80
Taxes on EBIT*	−102	−134	−161	−181	−150	−153	−153
Free cash flow to firm (FCFF)	**122**	**172**	**218**	**256**	**218**	**222**	**222**

Terminal value = FCFF TY × (1+g)/ (WACC–g)	↓	↓	↓	↓	↓		$\dfrac{222 \times 1.02}{0.186 - 0.02}$ ↓
Free cash flow to firm (FCFF)		172	218	256	218	222	1,365
Discount factor = 1/ (1+WACC)^{n-0.5}		91.8%	77.4%	65.3%	55.1%	46.4%	46.4%
		↓	↓	↓	↓	↓	↓
ENTERPRISE VALUE (EV)	**1,351** =	158 +	168 +	167 +	120 +	103 +	634

IMPLIED MULTIPLES	**WACC**	WACC	WACC	
	18.6%	9.0%	7.2%	
EV/Sales	**0.90x**	2.06x	2.76x	All else being equal (i.e. no changes in expected cash flows), the higher the risk (i.e. the higher the discount rate), the lower the value (i.e. the lower the value multiple)
EV/EBITDA	4.4x	10.1x	13.5x	
EV/EBIT	5.3x	12.1x	16.2x	
EV/BEV	1.8x	4.1x	5.4x	

Key ratios

Revenue growth (year-on-year)	*20.6%*	*16.5%*	*12.0%*	*6.3%*	*2.0%*	*2.0%*	*2.0%*
EBITDA margin	*20.5%*	*22.6%*	*24.1%*	*25.3%*	*21.2%*	*21.2%*	*21.2%*
EBIT margin	*17.0%*	*19.1%*	*20.6%*	*21.8%*	*17.7%*	*17.7%*	*17.7%*

*Any non-deductible depreciations/amortizations to be added back to EBIT

As noted, the value of Engineering Corp more than halves (new value is $1,351 million compared with the originally calculated $3,092 million) when calculated using the required rate of return of Small Engineering Corp, i.e. when increasing the discount rate from 9.0 percent to 18.6 percent, all else being equal.

Owing to the higher required rate of return (i.e. discount rate) of Small Engineering Corp, its justified EV/EBIT multiple drops from 12.1x to 5.3x. All else being equal, Small Engineering Corp should, owing to its higher expected risk profile versus its significantly larger peer Engineering Corp, thus be valued at a 55–60 percent discount. As a result, the market value of invested capital in Small Engineering Corp can be calculated at $67.5 million (as given by its justified 5.3x EV/EBIT multiple, as per above, times its $12.75 million reported EBIT). It is also worth noting that the drop in value relative to a corresponding large cap company is even greater (from EV/EBIT 16.2x to EV/EBIT 5.3x). This is chiefly why small unlisted companies are typically valued at substantially lower value multiples than equivalent listed large cap companies, as illustrated in Figure 9.6.[8]

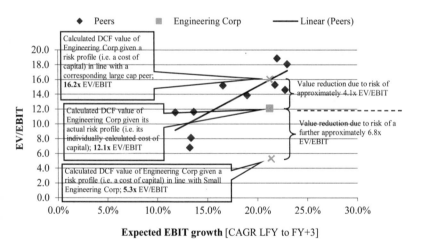

Figure 9.6   EV/EBIT vs. EBIT growth – illustrated value effect of Engineering Corp's divergent expected risk profile (i.e. divergent cost of capital) versus an equivalent large cap peer as well as Small Engineering Corp

---

[8] Note that this issue is not to be confused with the control/marketability problem addressed at the beginning of this book. In other words, should we be valuing a minority interest in Small Engineering Corp, for example, then a further discount for lack of marketability might very well be applicable. On the other hand, should we be valuing 100 percent of the shares, then a control premium as well as a marketability discount may be applicable. If the control premium is deemed to be of equal size to the marketability discount, then the equity value, as derived from the 5.3x EV/EBIT multiple above, is to be left unadjusted.

The lower valuation is therefore the result of a greater risk exposure (i.e. a higher required rate of return), and not that the subject company is inferior (i.e. having lower capital efficiency, lower margins, lower expected growth, etc.) to its listed large cap peers. A prerequisite of CAPM is that investors diversify away company-specific risks, as described above. As regards the small cap premium, studies have, in accordance with previous reasoning, shown the premium to exist regardless of the concerned company being listed or not (i.e. the small cap premium, as presented by Duff & Phelps and Ibbotson/Morningstar, for example, has in fact been derived from *listed* small cap companies). That part of the overall small cap premium stemming from the higher beta cannot be diversified away. The residual amount, however, may (in theory anyway) be fully diversifiable. However, the fact that the concerned premium has, according to the reasoning above, in reality been derived from publicly listed small cap companies indicates that that has not always been the case (that is, investors have not, historically, carried out the possible diversification benefits, or taken advantage of them in their entirety anyway).

In addition, investors aspiring to acquire a privately held company, such as Small Engineering Corp, will normally have extra difficulty in diversifying effectively. To diversify away both size premiums and company-specific premiums, the investor must acquire a very large portfolio of companies similar to Small Engineering Corp, which, in the real world, is not always feasible. Accordingly, to compensate for the higher risk exposure, they will require a higher rate of return (i.e. they will apply a higher cost of capital), which, all else being equal, will result in a lower value (that is, a lower value multiple).

In Table 9.6 we provide a sensitivity analysis of Engineering Corp's resulting change in value, given various levels of required rate of return (WACC) and all else being equal.

Table 9.6   The discounted cash flow value of
Engineering Corp (enterprise value or market value
of operating/invested capital) – given various levels
of risk exposure (i.e. cost of capital)

Engineering Corp WACC	EV $ millions	EV/EBIT LFY
7.0%	4,253	16.7x
8.0%	3,562	14.0x
9.0%	3,092	12.1x
10.0%	2,698	10.6x
11.0%	2,409	9.4x
12.0%	2,178	8.5x
13.0%	1,989	7.8x
14.0%	1,831	7.2x
15.0%	1,698	6.7x
16.0%	1,583	6.2x
17.0%	1,484	5.8x
18.0%	1,397	5.5x
19.0%	1,320	5.2x
20.0%	1,251	4.9x
21.0%	1,190	4.7x
22.0%	1,135	4.5x
23.0%	1,085	4.3x
24.0%	1,040	4.1x
25.0%	998	3.9x

9.1.3   EV/BEV

We also put Engineering Corp's calculated EV/BEV multiple (i.e. the market
value of invested capital in relation to the corresponding book value of invested capital) as given by the cash flow valuation into a graph plotted against
its key value driver, return on invested capital (ROIC or, alternatively, ROOC)
(Figure 9.7).

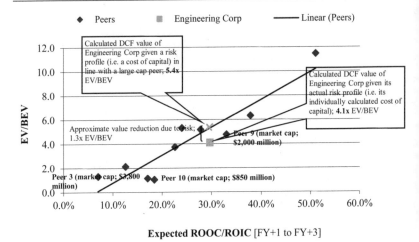

Figure 9.7   EV/BEV vs. ROOC/ROIC – illustrated value effect of Engineering Corp's higher expected risk profile (i.e. higher cost of capital) versus the average peer

Again, our calculated cash flow value of Engineering Corp, and the resulting EV/BEV multiple, may be deemed reasonable based on its individual level of value driver and risk. The resulting EV/BEV multiple from our cash flow valuation thus increases from 4.1x to 5.4x when we equate Engineering Corp's required rate of return with the corresponding average peer; that is, when we eliminate Engineering Corp's identified individual risk premium supplements of 1.0 plus 1.0 percentage points from its discount rate.

To conclude, we note that Engineering Corp's value as derived by the cash flow approach, like its value as derived using the market approach previously, results in a risk-adjusted justified valuation in line with that granted by its relevant level of value driver(s) and our three identified small caps.

9.1.4   Some closing remarks

As a point of order, it should be noted that there must be rhyme and reason for the underlying assumptions on which the cash flow valuation is based. One should always question whether the subject company is justified in having sharply divergent growth prospects, operating margin, risk profile, etc., versus the average peer.

As regards our valuation subject Engineering Corp, for example, and its higher expected operating margin, revenue growth, earnings growth, etc., relative to the corresponding average peer, it is essential to accurately substantiate the way in which it can expect to achieve this.

It is one thing to technically, as above, explain the position of the resulting value multiples in the graphs on the basis of the cash flow valuation. However, this is of little value if it is not combined with a very well-conducted analysis explaining and justifying why and how the subject company in question should and can have a significantly different level of value driver(s) in relation to its industry peers. Had our cash flow valuation assumed that Engineering Corp holds a 50 percent expected revenue growth for the coming three years, instead of the presumed 11.5 percent, it would have had positioned the company in terms of EV/Sales vs. operating margin, for example, substantially above the regression line. Technically, this would then be explained by Engineering Corp's dramatically higher expected revenue growth than the average peer. It would then, as in our original example above, be possible to calculate, to the dollar, the value of these strong growth expectations.

However, if the 50 percent growth forecast as per above is not accompanied by a thorough analysis of the underlying fundamentals, including a detailed association with the expected growth of its relevant industry peers, that explains and justifies, step by step, the way in which the company expects to achieve this success (taking market share, elimination of competitors, strong overall market growth in the company's specific niche, a new unique product launch, etc.), the value of these estimates is precisely zero. In a competitive market it is difficult, in the long run at any rate, to keep growth or return expectations greatly above the market average.[9] Competitors will inevitably fight to recover any lost ground, which most likely will (at least in the long run) negatively affect the growth and profitability of the companies we analyze and evaluate. As the comparable companies represent the subject company's established market, the link to, and any potential deviations from, the corresponding prospects of its closest peers needs to be properly documented as well as explained in a well-conducted analysis.

Incidentally, the same applies to a possible opposite position. Sometimes it is argued that if the market as such is "overvaluing" companies, i.e. if the stock market derived multiples of a particular company or sector were to be (or at least are argued to be) abnormally high, all other companies in this sector (for example, the unlisted companies whose values we target to derive from these listed "overvalued" peers) would therefore routinely also be overvalued when using the market approach. As the market approach, by definition, seeks to derive a company's value by reference to its publicly traded peers, an overvaluation of one type (such as the above-mentioned listed peers) would thus automatically provide an overvaluation of the second type (such as the corresponding unlisted companies that we aim to value). A cash flow valuation is argued then, compared with a corresponding market approach valuation,

---

[9] This is not, however, the same as saying that all companies of a given industry sooner or later converge at the same margin. Different companies, even within the same industry, may work with different business models. As regards the margin, in accordance with the previous reasoning, one strategy may be to work with a high margin at a low capital turnover (i.e. to sell few but pricey goods), while another (equally successful) strategy could be to work with a low margin at a high capital turnover (i.e. to sell low-priced goods in large volumes). Even in the long term, these companies are not expected to converge in terms of margin. Notwithstanding this, within each strategy segment the margin may, of course, converge in a long-term perspective.

to be a better or a "purer" type of valuation methodology (i.e. that it stands free of these market-derived "overvaluation" disorders). As an example, if we used average or median multiples derived from "overvalued" listed peers and calculated the value of a given company at $1,000 million, and simultaneously calculated the equivalent cash flow value at $500 million, according to the reasoning above the cash flow methodology would then be a "better" option (as we would not want to overestimate the market value of our subject company).

The above reasoning does falter though. Any potential "overvaluation" risk lies not in the methodology as such (explicitly, the cash flow valuation approach versus the market approach), but in the assumptions (direct or indirect) applied in each model. The reason for the peer/sector market upgrade (if any) is that its future growth and profitability and/or its corresponding risk exposure are perceived by the market participants to be highly favorable in a forward-looking perspective. Whether the market is right or not about these listed peers is a philosophical question; namely, we will find out soon enough if the market was right or not. The fundamentals are untouchable regardless – you do not pay more for an asset (unless it concerns things of sentimental value) than it is expected to return to its possessor. If the price of a given asset is high, one expects (or at least hopes for) a high return. That a share/sector is valued at a high level does not therefore automatically imply that it is overvalued. History shows a multitude of companies and sectors that have delivered in accordance with what their high valuation implies. Likewise, however, history shows many that do not. The problem is that at the relevant point in time you do not, on the whole, know which option is the winner.

Consequently, the value of any company is determined by its individual state of affairs and prospects and nothing else. In other words, if we enter our subject company's expected prospects (i.e. its expected cash flows) and its expected risk profile (i.e. its required rate of return) into a cash flow valuation and calculate the value at $500 million, in accordance with the example above, it is irrelevant that the market values other companies (i.e. those listed "overvalued" peers, as described above) with different expected prospects and risk exposures differently. As long as our valuation subject does not have exactly the same expected performance and risk profile as its peers, we cannot use their valuation, nor, consequently, their resulting multiples (i.e. we are forced to modify the multiples derived from the peers in accordance with the previously reported technique before they are applicable to our valuation subject).

Were we to use the unadjusted average or median multiples of the peers (i.e. those multiples that gave rise to the $1,000 million value in the example above), this would, of course, lead to "overvaluation." What we then do is that we, implicitly, assume that our valuation subject has exactly the same expected growth, profitability, and risk profile as the average peer, which is obviously an unreasonable assumption if we do not believe in such a development for our subject company. Correspondingly, this applies to cash flow valuations as well, i.e. if we enter prospects (i.e. cash flows) and risk assessments (i.e.

discount rates) we do not believe in into a cash flow valuation, this model will also lead to "overvaluation."

On the other hand, were our expectations of the target company's future prospects and risks in fact to be in line with the average peer's, as above, then the derived $1,000 million market approach value is the correct one. In that case, we have made some mistakes, i.e. we have applied too conservative assumptions, in our cash flow valuation. If we believe that the prospects and risks of our subject company are exactly the same as its peers', its valuation (i.e. its justified value multiple(s)) should also be exactly the same, all else being equal.

That said, when discussing these matters, it is important to note that valuation is not an exact science. Different analysts can apply totally different expectations for the one and the same company's future prospects and risks. In doing so, they may assign the one and the same company fundamentally different values. Nevertheless, the point is that the same analyst (under the same valuation purpose) cannot apply different assumptions, whether directly or indirectly, to the same valuation subject, depending just on which valuation methodology is applied (explicitly the market approach versus the discounted cash flow approach), as is the case if one values the subject company at $1,000 million using the market approach and at $500 million using the discounted cash flow approach, as above. Hence, we cannot value the subject company based on two fundamentally differing views (i.e. using two fundamentally different sets of forecasts and risk assessments) just depending on what type of valuation model we happen to use at the time.

In accordance with the reasoning above, the theory (i.e. the reality) is untouchable; that is, the value of any cash-generating asset will, by necessity, equal its future expected risk-adjusted returns, otherwise there will be opportunity for arbitrage (i.e. one can sell the (by risk and return) overvalued asset and use the resulting funds to buy the (by the same risk and return expectations) undervalued asset, and thereby make a risk-free profit). For this reason, this applies regardless of whether the value in question has been derived using the market approach or the discounted cash flow approach. It is, therefore, not the applied methodology (i.e. the cash flow valuation approach or the market approach) as such that determines whether or not we over- or undervalue a company; it is the assumptions (directly as in the case of the discounted cash flow approach and implied as in the case of the market approach) that we put into the models that determine whether or not we over- or undervalue companies.[10]

---

[10] We can, moreover, make exactly the same mistake when valuing other assets using the market approach. Were we, for example, to want to sell our 15-year-old Volvo, we would normally start trying to find its relevant/current market value by exploring what other 15-year-old Volvos are priced at/sold for. Hence, we would not put together a peer group consisting of more or less brand new Mercedes cars. Were we, moreover, to discover a dozen or so 15-year-old Volvo cars like ours, we would most likely not price our car right in the middle of the range. If our Volvo is completely rust-free and has only 1,500 miles on the odometer, we would likely put our car in the upper end of the range and vice versa if our car was a real wreck.

On the same theme, we can mention so-called "multiple expansion" (or "contraction" should that be the case). The general idea behind "multiple expansion" is that the expansion (i.e. the upward market adjustment of the peers' value multiples) will, by itself, "rub off" on the subject company at issue. Hence, if the market has revised upwards its valuation of the peers, thus giving rise to a "multiple expansion," our valuation subject is assumed to be affected accordingly. If the peer group companies have been selected correctly, that assumption is by and large correct.

However, the value effect (if any) of our subject company is not because the peer group multiples have, by some force of nature, "expanded." The reason why the comparable companies' multiples have increased (or expanded) is because the historical result, or the current forecast, which forms the basis of the multiple(s) in question, has not yet been updated by the changed conditions that underpin the corresponding value increase. Thus the changed conditions have been captured in the numerator, i.e. in the price, of the peers (as stock market prices adjust to new information instantaneously) but not in the denominator (i.e. the underlying result/base metric of the multiple in question). From this we can conclude two things:

1. At the point in time when the historical results – or the applied forecasts if that should be the case – have been updated, the "expansion" will disappear. The multiples will then revert to a "normal" level (apart from any unexpected changes in risk exposure, should that be the case).
2. If the comparable companies' changing conditions do not correspond with our valuation subject's corresponding conditions, we cannot expect to enjoy the effects. In other words, the value of our subject company is again dependent upon its individual circumstances and conditions and nothing else. Should none of these variables have changed for our valuation subject, the resulting value effect of the comparable companies' "multiple expansion" would thus be estimated at zero. Should our subject company, on the other hand, be expected to "tag along" with the positive development that is giving rise to the comparable companies' multiple expansion, then its value, like that of the comparable companies, can be assumed to be affected by the expansion in question, either by way of the expanding multiples applied to the "old" unadjusted result (i.e. that result or that forecast which has not yet been reflected by the now new updated conditions) or, in accordance with point 1 above, its re-adjusted "normal" multiple being applied to the "new" (i.e. according to the new conditions giving rise to the multiple expansion in question) updated higher level of earnings (but not both, i.e. it is not correct to apply the expanded multiple(s) to the revised higher results stemming from the changed conditions giving rise to the whole expansion – this would involve double counting).

To conclude, and at the obvious risk of being overly explicit, we should stress that only *new changed* circumstances justify an expansion. If the concerned companies "only" deliver in accordance with expectations, however good these expectations may now be, their multiples will not expand. In other words, these first-class results are already reflected in their current values, and thus in their current market capitalizations (i.e. in their discounted cash flow values as set by the market), and so, as discussed, also automatically in their current/ prevailing value multiples. Accordingly, we again state these companies' values, and thus also their justified multiples, as being a result of their individual conditions and prospects and nothing else. The increased (if that now should be the case) value for our valuation subject should hence be credited to the new and unexpectedly improved results, and *not* to "expanding" multiples.

Using the market approach for reconciliation rather than direct value derivation therefore has its advantages. Finding the level of adjustments required to directly calculate the value of a given company using only derived peer group multiples brings with it complexity. The discounted cash flow methodology gives us an opportunity to explicitly model assumptions and conditions specific to our target company and also to conduct a sensitivity analysis of changes as well as reasonableness of the data and assumptions in question. A positive side effect of these simulations is, moreover, that they will provide us with a better understanding of what variables are value creating or not value creating for the valuation subject.

We can thus use the discounted cash flow valuation approach to simulate value effects of various differences between the valuation subject and its peers with regard to any value driver whatsoever. Any difference in expected revenue growth, operating margin, earnings growth, capital tied up, tax rate, risk, etc., between the valuation subject and its peers, and, consequently, its impact on the subject company's plausible value multiples (i.e. how much the regression line, i.e. the value multiple, at stake should be adjusted as a result of these identified differences) can in the discounted cash flow model be simulated variable by variable. The final value conclusion, as given by either valuation approach (i.e. by either the discounted cash flow approach or the market approach) should not differ at the end, however. The value of any given company should thus again, and given no change in valuation purpose moving from one model to another, be exactly the same regardless of whether we calculate it using a discounted cash flow approach or a market approach, otherwise we have made a mistake somewhere.

On that same theme (or, explicitly, if we turn the reasoning above around), note that the implied multiples given by our DCF valuation in this chapter reconcile with those multiples we derived in the previous chapter using the direct market approach, i.e. EV/Sales 2.06x (vs. 2.10x), EV/EBIT 12.1x (vs. 12.2x), and EV/BEV 4.1x (vs. 4.0x). As we used exactly the same data in our market approach as in our DCF approach, the output of both models must, accordingly, also be the same (irrespective of that output being in the form of an absolute number, i.e. a company value, or absolute or implied value multiples).

We illustrate the reasoning above using the value chart we first presented as Figure 8.31, which is now supplemented in Figure 9.8 with Engineering Corp's calculated cash flow value as presented in this chapter.[11]

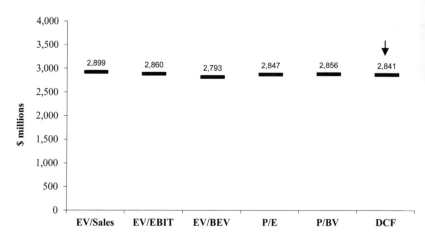

Figure 9.8 Estimated shareholder values (i.e. market value of equity) – Engineering Corp on the basis of the market approach as well as the discounted cash flow approach (DCF)

---

[11] In accordance with previous statement, different valuation methods/models and different input data to these methods/models can result in different types of output/values as regards the control/marketability issue. If based on value multiples derived from exchange-traded shares, the market approach will normally give a value on a marketable minority basis. Following that, if we assume that the expected cash flows of our DCF valuation are "neutral" or "non-biased," i.e. that the majority and minority shareholders can expect exactly the same economic benefits (i.e. that the majority interest holder has not "tampered" with the cash flows to benefit himself at the expense of the minority interest holders and therefore that minority and majority interest holders can expect fair cash flows proportional to their respective ownership), and that the discount rate reflects an unaltered capital structure (i.e. that any capital structure changes, which only a majority shareholder has the capacity to implement, have not been carried out), then the resulting DCF value may (also) be stated on a marketable minority basis. In accordance with Chapter 2, it is then possible to recalculate this value, using a premium for control and a corresponding discount for marketability, as a non-marketable majority interest (which is, accordingly, the value definition that we target in our case study, Engineering Corp). If we then in conclusion, and for simplicity's sake, assume the premium for control to be on a par with the discount for illiquidity, we may put the values of the above graph on equal footing (i.e. all values presented in the graph above, whether derived using value multiples or DCF, define the subject company on the basis of either a marketable minority interest or a non-marketable majority interest).

10

Forward-looking Value Multiples

A third methodology would be to compute value multiples in a forward-looking perspective and then use these to directly derive the value of the subject company in question. In other words, the forecasts we have of the comparable companies' expected development may be used to calculate value multiples on the basis of future results. These multiples are then applied directly to the corresponding data of the subject company.

If we revisit our table of peer group companies, we note that we have forecasts three years ahead. The value multiples we used in our regressions (i.e. on the basis of data of last fiscal year) were thus plotted against expected levels of the relevant value driver. Companies with high growth expectations, for example, were accordingly valued at high multiples. This was shown as a top right position in the graphs, on or near the regression line.

Value multiples are hence computed as the current value in relation to some adequate base metric, such as sales, operating profit, etc. Consequently, the higher the level of base metric, the lower the value multiple, all else being equal. Companies with strong expected growth will thus see their multiples reduced when calculated on future results (as the numerator, i.e. the current market value, is a constant, whereas the denominator, i.e. the expected earnings, is forecast to increase), whereas companies with low or no growth expectations will accordingly see their corresponding value multiples remaining relatively unchanged. The overall effect of this relationship is that multiples of different companies with different growth expectations will converge when put in a forward-looking perspective. That is, the high level of value driver, justifying the corresponding high level of current value multiple, is therefore, with this procedure, captured (i.e. accounted for) by the application of forward-looking multiples and, consequently, higher future base metric levels.

Let us take the EV/EBIT multiple as an illustration of this reasoning. Analyzing our table of comparable companies, we note that the EV/EBIT spread, on the basis of last fiscal year data (i.e. EBIT as of LFY), is within the range of 6.8x to 18.9x. In our earlier regressions we explained this large discrepancy by the individual companies being subject to radically different growth expectations. If we assume that these growth differences have an expected duration of three years (i.e. in line with our forecast) and that the comparable companies more or less converge after this period of time to an alike growth rate, the EV/EBIT multiples of the high-valued companies (those with a high expected growth rate) will then decline gradually for every utilized future annual EBIT estimate, whereas the corresponding multiples of the low-valued companies (those with a low expected growth rate) will accordingly be relatively constant, i.e. the multiples will converge in a forward-looking perspective.

Table 10.1   EV/EBIT – current EV (i.e. current market value of operating/invested capital) in relation to historical as well as forecast operating profit (i.e. EBIT)

Company	Enterprise value (EV) $ millions Valuation date	EV/EBIT FY–2	EV/EBIT FY–1	EV/EBIT LFY	EV/ expected EBIT FY+1	EV/ expected EBIT FY+2	EV/ expected EBIT FY+3
Peer 1	46,152	32.1x	33.5x	18.1x	13.5x	11.2x	9.7x
Peer 2	133,930	20.3x	14.5x	18.9x	13.5x	12.4x	10.4x
Peer 3	5,201	15.0x	13.6x	8.1x	5.9x	5.4x	5.6x
Peer 4	177,892	24.7x	20.8x	15.2x	11.6x	10.2x	9.6x
Peer 5	14,738	17.5x	13.4x	11.6x	9.6x	8.5x	7.9x
Peer 6	69,004	15.6x	13.4x	11.6x	9.3x	8.5x	8.3x
Peer 7	25,093	22.7x	15.5x	15.3x	12.6x	10.0x	8.5x
Peer 8	18,333	18.5x	34.9x	13.9x	11.9x	9.1x	8.2x
Peer 9	2,046	6.1x	5.1x	14.6x	12.8x	9.8x	7.9x
Peer 10	1,070	12.6x	8.5x	6.8x	4.7x	4.2x	4.7x
Mean	49,346	18.5x	17.3x	13.4x	10.5x	8.9x	8.1x
Median	21,713	18.0x	14.1x	14.2x	11.8x	9.5x	8.3x

As noted in Table 10.1, the EV/EBIT multiple and the dispersion of that multiple decrease in a forward-looking perspective. The expected growth in EBIT value driver has thus pushed the multiples of the high-valued companies downwards, whereas the multiples of the corresponding low-valued companies, without equivalent growth expectations, are accordingly relatively unchanged. If we now, in accordance with statement above, assume that the growth period of Engineering Corp and its peers at this point of time (i.e. at FY+4 and onwards) is, if not completely over, then at least alike, we can (disregarding risk, which we will return to shortly) derive the value of Engineering Corp using the unadjusted average EV/EBIT FY+3 peer group multiple. The value of Engineering Corp's invested capital is then calculated at $3,677 million (i.e. the forecasted FY+3 $454 million EBIT of Engineering Corp times the corresponding 8.1x FY+3 EV/EBIT multiple of the average peer as per Table 10.1).

It is important, however, to note that the methodology above only applies to multiples that have growth as their primary value driver. If, for example, we were to calculate forward-looking multiples of EV/Sales, we would most likely not capture the operating margin value driver (which we have previously found to be the multiple's most important value driver). The margin is dependent upon the business model of the company in question. Different business models, and thus also the resulting margins, do not, in accordance with previous reasoning, generally converge in a forward-looking perspective.[1] The forward-looking value multiple of EV/Sales would accordingly only capture most likely the weakest (that is, expected sales growth) of its three key value drivers (i.e. expected operating margin, sales growth, and risk). Should we wish to capture even the operating margin value driver, we would thus be forced (in accordance with the previously reported technique) to perform an EV/Sales vs. expected operating margin regression on the basis of the derived forward-looking EV/Sales multiple.

Note also that any difference between the valuation subject and the average peer in terms of risk is not reflected in the multiples above, irrespective of the applied time period. Recall that we earlier noted Peers 3, 9, and 10 were substantially smaller than the corresponding average peer, and that these companies were, as a result, deemed to be burdened with a higher required rate of return (that is, in effect, a lower value multiple). These differences therefore need to be considered. If we first strip the peer group of these three small cap companies, we arrive at an adjusted average FY+3 EV/EBIT multiple of 9.0x. Applying this adjusted multiple to the corresponding FY+3 $454 million expected EBIT of Engineering Corp, we reach an invested capital value of Engineering Corp of $4,086 million. This is very close to the corresponding $4,080 million we originally derived in Chapter 8 (the result we arrived at before we downward adjusted Engineering Corp's value as a result of its higher risk exposure relative to the average peer) by way of the LFY EV/EBIT multiple and the Expected growth in EBIT LFY to FY+3 value driver, and the corresponding $4,137 million that we later derived using the discounted cash flow approach.

A prerequisite of the estimated value of Engineering Corp above (i.e. the $4,086 million), in accordance with the reasoning above, is, however, a risk profile perfectly in line with a corresponding large cap peer. Thus, if we apply the percentage discount, as a result of Engineering Corp's higher expected required rate of return versus a corresponding large cap peer, as previously derived using the discounted cash flow approach (see Chapter 9 for further details), i.e. roughly a 25 percent discount, the resulting enterprise value of Engineering Corp is calculated at $3,065 million. If we finally deduct Engineering Corp's existing net interest-bearing debt (i.e. the $251 million), its resulting equity value is calculated at $2,814 million, i.e. in line with the $2,850 million concluding value in Chapter 8.

---

[1] In accordance with the reasoning in Chapter 8, different companies, even in exactly the same industry, may work with different business models. One strategy could thus be to work with a high margin at a low capital turnover (i.e. to sell few but pricey goods), while another (equally successful) strategy could be to work with a low margin at a high capital turnover (i.e. to instead sell low-priced goods in large volumes). These companies are therefore not expected to converge in terms of margin, even in the long term (within each strategy segment the margin may, of course, converge in the long term).

Note, however, that if after FY+3 there would still be great differences between the valuation subject and the corresponding peers in terms of growth expectations, exactly the same adjustments as before are required (although this also applies to the two previously presented methodologies used to perform the market approach).[2] In other words, we must in that case perform a regression analysis to plot the EV/EBIT multiple of FY+3 to EBIT growth expectations of FY+4 and thereafter, or we must continue to calculate forward-looking value multiples after FY+3.

When applying the approach above, one must thus act consistently and also be attentive to possible double counting. Hence, if calculating a value multiple of a comparable company on the basis of forecasted EBIT FY+3 (i.e. its current EV divided by expected EBIT FY+3), for example, one must apply that multiple to the corresponding base metric of the company in question, i.e. one must apply that multiple to the subject company's FY+3 expected EBIT. Moreover, one cannot, on the basis of that value multiple, run a regression against the Expected growth in EBIT LFY to FY+3 value driver. The expected EBIT growth of the valuation subject has already been captured by its FY+3 EBIT, i.e. the EBIT FY+3 base metric is therefore a product of the coming three years of growth. Or to put this in other words, one cannot be credited with the same growth twice. Hence, should you wish to make use of the Expected growth in EBIT LFY to FY+3 value driver, you must do so on the basis of EV/EBIT LFY and not EV/EBIT FY+3.

Should you, however, insist on an EV/EBIT FY+3 regression, you will be forced to run that against the Expected growth in EBIT FY+4 value driver (or any other combination of years starting with FY+3 as base year). Should we fail to do this, i.e. should we calculate the value of the target company using EV/EBIT FY+3, without the support of the Expected growth in EBIT FY+4 value driver (or any other period starting with FY+3 as base year), the calculated value based on the unadjusted (mean or median) FY+3 EV/EBIT multiple would still be more fair than that based on the unadjusted (mean or median) LFY EV/EBIT multiple, as by using the FY+3 EV/EBIT multiple, and the corresponding forecasted FY+3 EBIT of the subject company, we have at least captured the next three years of difference between the valuation subject and the average peer in terms of expected growth (even though we may have failed to account for any growth differences as of FY+4 and thereafter, should that be the case).[3]

---

[2] Which may explain why Peer 9 (whose especially high expected growth over the forecast period may consequently indicate a strong growth potential even after the concerned period) is, as noted in the table above, priced on a par with the average peer even though its size should justify a valuation in line with Peers 3 and 10.

[3] An alternative way to make use of projected results would be to apply an appropriate value multiple as of today, such as EV/EBIT as of last fiscal year (i.e. EV/EBIT LFY), to the corresponding base metric of the valuation subject for some future date (e.g. expected EBIT as of fiscal year +1, +2, +3, etc.). However, the values provided by this technique represent the

Let us illustrate the problem above by means of the FY+2 EV/EBIT multiple (i.e. current EV divided by expected EBIT FY+2). As the FY+2 EV/EBIT multiple, and accordingly also the resulting value, already reflects expected EBIT growth LFY to FY+2 (by way of the FY+2 EBIT component of the FY+2 EV/EBIT multiple and its accompanying applicable base metric, FY+2 EBIT), the appropriate value driver would thus be expected growth in EBIT *after* FY+2 (which in Figure 10.1 is just FY+3, but could just as well be expected growth of any period starting with FY+2 as base year).

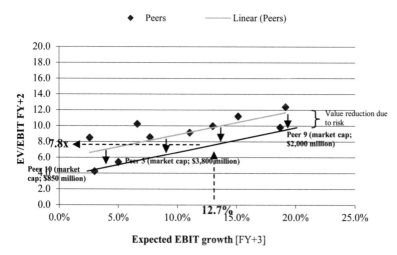

Figure 10.1   EV/EBIT FY+2 vs. expected growth in EBIT FY+3 – derivation of the relevant value multiple using a growth and risk-adjusted regression line

We can then conclude that Engineering Corp, adjusted for its unique risk profile in accordance with the previously reported technique and at an expected FY+3 EBIT growth (that is, *specifically* FY+3) of 12.7 percent,[4] is justified a valuation at approximately 7.8 times its *FY+2* expected operating profit (i.e. its FY+2 EBIT). This provides us with the following data (the calculated value

---

company's value at a future date, i.e. the company's expected value as at fiscal year +1, +2, +3, etc. If one wishes to know the company's value as of today one must thus discount (using a proper required rate of return) that future value to an equivalent present value. One must also be aware that last fiscal year multiples include a certain fixed (given) level of expected growth and risk. If the prospective date (i.e. if fiscal year +1, +2, +3, etc.) of the subject company does not accommodate exactly the same expected future growth and risk as the last fiscal year multiple, then the multiple of today (i.e. the EV/EBIT LFY multiple) will run the risk of being grossly misleading in a forward-looking perspective (i.e. as applied to the subject company's expected EBIT fiscal year +1, +2, +3, etc.).

[4] See Table 8.3, "Selected key ratios – value drivers", for further information.

of Engineering Corp, using the LFY EV/EBIT multiple and the Expected growth in EBIT LFY to FY+3 value driver, as given in section 8.2, is presented within brackets):

Derived (at given FY+3 EBIT growth and risk) EV/EBIT
FY+2 multiple: **7.8x** (12.2x)
Engineering Corp's FY+2 operating profit – EBIT FY+2
($ millions):   **403** (255)

Consequently, applying this "EBIT growth and risk-adjusted" FY+2 EV/EBIT multiple to Engineering Corp, we arrive at the following estimated value (market value of operating/invested capital):

$$\textbf{7.8} \times \textbf{\$403 million = \$3,144 million}$$
$$(12.2 \times \$255 \text{ million} = \$3,111 \text{ million})$$

Adjusted for Engineering Corp's $251 million net interest-bearing debt, the market value of all shares (i.e. the market value of equity) in Engineering Corp is accordingly calculated at $2,893 million ($2,860 million).

Irrespective of whether we apply the LFY EV/EBIT vs. expected growth in EBIT LFY to FY+3 regression, the EV/EBIT FY+2 vs. expected growth in EBIT FY+3 regression, or the EV/EBIT FY+3 multiple (or any other combination reflecting all relevant assumptions and value drivers, for that matter), the concluding value of the subject company as calculated by the same analyst under the same valuation purpose will therefore be exactly the same; otherwise we have made a mistake somewhere.

Consequently, the applied time period is of no real significance as long as we act consistently, i.e. as long as we handle time intervals correctly and capture all appropriate facts and value drivers for the calculation/analysis in question. Consequently, the three alternatives above contain exactly the same data, but just distributed in three different styles.

Given that we have not changed our opinion about the subject company's expected development and risk and, additionally, that we still have the same objective with our valuation, the estimated value should also, in accordance with the previous reasoning, be the same, irrespective of applied multiples or methodology. Again, it is not the model or the multiple as such that drives the value of a company, but the individual prospects and risks of that company – the model or the multiple is just a tool to help us identify that specific value. Thus the individual value of an individual company is driven by its individual level of value drivers and risk exposure and nothing else. As long as our opinion of the subject company's level of value drivers, that is, its expected performance (i.e. its expected cash flows) and its risk exposure (i.e. its discount rate), have not changed, neither has our perception of its value; or, put in other words, the justified value remains unaffected by, i.e. is *not* driven by, us moving from one spreadsheet, i.e. one valuation multiple or valuation approach, to another.

To conclude, we illustrate the relationship above using our previous value chart, which we have supplemented by the calculated equity values using EV/EBIT FY+2 and EV/EBIT FY+3 multiples as per the analysis presented in this chapter (note: all other value multiples in the chart below therefore refer to data as per last fiscal year, i.e. LFY) (Figure 10.2).

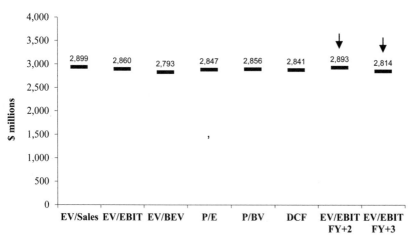

Figure 10.2   Estimated shareholder values (i.e. market value of equity) – Engineering Corp on the basis of LFY value multiples, discounted cash flow valuation, and forward-looking value multiples

11

Summary and Concluding Remarks

To tie this all together, and to conclude on the relationship between the DCF approach and the market approach, we will outline the link between these two approaches in a purely mathematical perspective. To do this, we apply the EV/FCFF multiple.

Suppose we have a British service company, Service Plc, with an expected free cash flow to firm (FCFF) next year of £10 million. Suppose further that we have calculated its proper cost of capital (i.e. its WACC) at 15 percent. Annual expected FCFF growth as from next year and in perpetuity is assumed at 2 percent.

As the expected growth of Service Plc is assumed to be constant, we need not compose an explicit forecast up until a "normalized" point of time, as was required with Engineering Corp. Recall that we created an explicit forecast for Engineering Corp as it was expected to have a cash flow growth significantly above that deemed sustainable, over the coming three years. Owing to the expected short-term "super growth" of Engineering Corp, we were forced to calculate its DCF value using a two-stage model in which we first estimated the net present value of the explicit forecast period and then estimated the net present value of all cash flows following that (i.e. the residual value). As we are in a position of sustainable growth with Service Plc from the start, we need not create an explicit forecast period as we had to with Engineering Corp. We can thus calculate the (total) enterprise value of Service Plc using just its year one expected cash flow.

The discounted cash flow value of Service Plc is then, as presented earlier, given by the steady growth cash flow valuation formula (i.e. the "Gordon's growth model"), as shown below:

$$PVF(EV) = \frac{FCFF_1}{WACC - g}$$

where:

PVF $\quad=\quad$ Present value firm (i.e. enterprise value – EV)
$FCFF_1 \quad=\quad$ Expected free cash flow to firm in period 1, the period immediately following the valuation date
WACC $\quad=\quad$ Weighted average cost of capital
g $\quad=\quad$ Expected FCFF growth rate compounded in perpetuity

If we enter the above set data of Service Plc into the model presented above, its discounted cash flow value (i.e. its DCF value) of operating/invested capital is calculated at:

$$PVF(EV) = \frac{FCFF_1}{WACC - g} \rightarrow \frac{10}{0.15 - 0.02} = 77$$

The above formula may mathematically be rewritten in many different ways. For example, by multiplying both sides by WACC – g, we can solve $FCFF_1$:

$$FCFF_1 = EV(WACC - g)$$

Should we have access to the EV, WACC, and g of Service Plc, we can then solve its expected $FCFF_1$:

$$FCFF_1 = EV(WACC - g) \rightarrow 77(0.15 - 0.02) = 10$$

If we rearrange the formula yet again, we get the following relationship:

$$\frac{EV}{FCFF_1} = \frac{1}{WACC - g}$$

If we have access to the WACC and g of Service Plc, we may then solve its $EV/FCFF_1$ (i.e. the value multiple $EV/FCFF_1$):

$$\frac{EV}{FCFF_1} = \frac{1}{WACC - g} \rightarrow \frac{1}{0.15 - 0.02} = 7.7$$

The value multiple $EV/FCFF_1$ is hence given by the inverse of the required return minus expected growth, which we can then relate in the more familiar definition:

$$\frac{EV}{FCFF_1} \rightarrow \frac{77}{10} = 7.7$$

If we rearrange the formula a final time, we arrive back at square one, i.e. with our cash flow model:

$$EV = \frac{FCFF_1}{WACC - g} \rightarrow \frac{10}{0.15 - 0.02} = 7.7$$

Given the expected cash flow (i.e. $FCFF_1$), the expected growth (i.e. g), and the estimated cost of capital (i.e. the WACC), Service Plc is (on a discounted cash flow basis) valued at £77 million. Based on exactly the same parameters, its $EV/FCFF_1$ multiple is calculated at 7.7x. However, should the expected cash flow (i.e. $FCFF_1$), the growth expectations (i.e. g), and the risk exposure (i.e. the WACC) of Service Plc change, so will its resulting cash flow value, and thus *also* its resulting $EV/FCFF_1$ multiple, change accordingly. All calculated or derived value multiples therefore include a number of set or implied assumptions for expected growth, profitability, risk, etc. Thus, if deriving the value of a given company by an unadjusted value multiple from a given peer or a given transaction, one will value the company in question on the assumption that it will have *exactly* the same future growth, profitability, risk, etc., as that given (thus implicitly given by way of the applied multiple) by this exact peer or transaction.

We may thus from discounted forecasted cash flows, i.e. from a DCF value, calculate the resulting (i.e. parallel/analogous) value multiple. Just as we can calculate a value multiple from a given company's discounted forecasted cash flows, i.e. from its DCF value, we can calculate a DCF value, i.e. derive forecasted cash flows, and an accompanying cost of capital, from a given value multiple. That is, any given value multiple may be broken up into a corresponding expected cash flow and an accompanying cost of capital (admittedly into a more or less infinite number of combinations of these two parameters, yet with exactly the same end value).

This consequently means that we are not dealing with two fundamentally different methods that, with regard to the valuation of the same subject as calculated by the same analyst under the same valuation purpose, should produce two fundamentally different results, but instead that we have two different ways to express exactly the same thing: that the value of the asset in question equals its expected future returns discounted to a present value by a risk-adjusted rate of return. This value may thus be expressed in terms of both an absolute number (i.e. by way of a DCF value) and a key ratio (i.e. by way of a value multiple). *The actual value is, however, still exactly the same.* Hence, the estimated value of the same valuation subject, as calculated by the same analyst under the same valuation purpose, should consequently not allow itself to be influenced by the chosen form of communication.

So if, working with the cash flow approach and the market approach in parallel and for the same valuation subject under the same valuation purpose, you get two fundamentally different outcomes, i.e. two fundamentally different values, it means that you have either made a mistake in the cash flow approach or in the market approach (or in the worst case, you have made a mistake in both).

Explicitly, you have made a mistake (i.e. failed) in the key underlying assumptions for the respective model(s). That is, you have applied alternative assumptions *directly or by implication* for the company in question in the cash flow approach and the market approach, respectively. One must then return to the assumptions and analyze the background of the conflicting results until the values given by the respective models correspond in a satisfactory manner.

Note, however, that this is not the same as there being only one "correct" value for the target company in question. Given that we consider the conditions and assumptions of the subject company to be consistent with reality, and that we have only one well-defined single purpose with the valuation, there is, however, (for us anyway) just one "correct" value. Should we change the conditions and assumptions we have given in any direction (that is, if we for some reason suddenly were to expect a totally different future development or another assessed risk profile than that which forms the basis of our current valuation), then the resulting value will, of course, also change. However, we may *not* apply widely different conditions and assumptions, whether directly or indirectly, for exactly the same valuation subject, if we have the same valuation purpose, depending just upon which model (i.e. the DCF approach or the market approach) we happen to use (i.e. depending upon just what type of spreadsheet we are currently working with), which then is implied by widely different results in the respective models. Or put in other words: *if we believe in our forecasts (i.e. our cash flow projections) and our risk assessment (i.e. our cost of capital assessment), we must believe in them as much in all methods and models.* Correspondingly, if our analysis, on the other hand, has given us reason to doubt our initial conclusions, then we have to apply exactly the same changes to all methods and models and so the values given by the respective multiples and models will, again, converge but at a different level compared with that at the outset, of course.

Correctly applied, the execution of a proper market approach valuation will therefore force us to take a stance on *all* the complex issues of a DCF valuation as these models are each other's exact mirror image. Carried out correctly, the implementation of the market approach will require exactly the same effort and work, and exactly the same complex decisions and assessments with regard to input parameters such as growth, margins, capital requirements, risk exposure, etc., as that of a full-blown cash flow valuation. Some claim that the advantage of the market approach over the discounted cash flow approach is the very fact that it does not require decisions on complex and sensitive variables that are difficult to assess in a forward-looking perspective. This line of reasoning is, however, synonymous with sticking your head in the sand. Complex decisions do not disappear just because we do not care to consider them.

Let us return to the figure initially presented in this book.

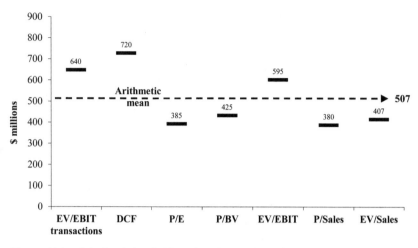

Figure 11.1   Calculated shareholder values (i.e. market value of equity) – ABC Corp

Had XYZ Corporate Finance carried out a correct valuation of ABC Corp, all calculated values as presented in Figure 11.1 would have been set in a relatively straight unbroken line (i.e. all multiples and methods presented in the graph would have generated exactly the same resulting value on the whole). What that value actually should be cannot, however, be understood simply by the information reported above. *All we can say with absolute certainty is that the value spread indicates a perfectly flawed/incomplete analysis.* That the average value happens to be just $507 million is, in this respect, irrelevant. It is just about equally probable that the proper value of ABC is on a par with any of the six individual values given by the respective approaches and multiples above (or pretty much any other value for that matter) as that it is $507 million.

As a final recap, let us delve a little into this matter. Let us first assume (as is usually the case) that the range in Figure 11.1 has been given by the application of average or median peer group multiples. As each of the multiples (let us thus at first focus on the multiples) are associated with different primary value drivers, and that different companies of the exact same earnings capacity can, due to the implementation of different business models, show fundamentally dissimilar patterns with regard to different base metrics and key ratios (remember the case of Company A and Company B at the end of section 8.1), it may be that some average or median multiple in Figure 11.1 may be correct for direct derivation of ABC Corp's value, while another may at the same time be totally wrong. It is then possible that the correct value of ABC Corp is given by only one of the multiples. For example, should the risk profile and the expected growth in EBIT of ABC Corp be exactly in line with the average listed peer as above, all else being equal, the correct value of ABC Corp would then be calculated at $595 million and nothing else (that is, we can then derive the value of ABC Corp using the unadjusted EV/EBIT multiple of the average peer).

That the other value multiples, where the value drivers of the average peer are not in line with that of ABC Corp, give results other than $595 million does not change our opinion about the proper value of ABC Corp. In accordance with the previous reasoning, we will then be forced to adjust these other multiples until they are in line with that justified by the corresponding level of value driver(s) of ABC Corp if we wish to make use of them as well; that is, *if we want to keep them in the chart.* In other words, if we know the multiples in the chart to be flawed/inaccurate, we cannot leave them unattended, as they would then expose us and our shortcomings as analysts fully. They would, in other words, become glorious statements of us:

1. not knowing how to fix the problem; or
2. not being bothered to fix the problem (i.e. not being willing to invest time and effort to derive the real proper/applicable value multiple(s) of the subject company in question).

In other words, it will *not* be good enough to just state they have been disregarded and just leave them there.

When this process is over, the values calculated from the respective multiples will then be on a par with those given by the "correctly" derived multiple, i.e. by the EV/EBIT multiple as in the example above of approximately $595 million (that is, the values given by each and every value multiple, will, when this process is over, converge at a single point estimate as in our Engineering Corp case).

Should that be the case, we can, at the same time, also conclude that we have put too aggressive assumptions or, alternatively, a too low required rate of return (or in the worst case, some combination of both) into our discounted cash flow approach. That is, we have entered data and assumptions into our DCF model that we do not believe in. We must then, as a consequence, return to our DCF model and adjust the input data and assumptions that we find to be inconsistent. When this process is over, i.e. when we have entered exactly the same data and assumptions into our DCF model as we implicitly, using the EV/EBIT multiple applied above, have just said to be true and fair for ABC Corp, the DCF model and the EV/EBIT multiple above, will return exactly the same equity value, i.e. approximately $595 million.

Hence a value distribution in line with that in Figure 11.1 is, in real life, normally (i.e. more or less always) due to the firm or analyst having calculated the value of the target company using unadjusted peer group mean or median multiples. Should this not be the case (i.e. a conclusion in accordance with the above chart is presented even though an analysis has allegedly been carried out), this is still wrong, as one can hardly claim it being logical to receive different values on the same company by no other reason than moving from one valuation spreadsheet to another (or put another way, if it was that easy to increase or decrease the value of a company, why even waste avoidable/unnecessary time and efforts on company improvements/fundamentals).[1]

Hence, company value is driven by company fundamentals, not your choice of valuation multiple/model. Thus, if delivering an opinion in accordance with the above chart, where the valuation subject as well as the valuation purpose are exactly the same, it does not matter whether this is based on unadjusted mean or median values or, alternatively, an extensive analysis; it will still be incorrect.

---

[1] For the avoidance of all doubt: the same type of share of the same company may, as outlined at the beginning of this book, be assigned different values (by way of different valuation models/input data) as a result of control/minority issues, marketability, synergies, etc. Should the same analyst have two fundamentally different assignments at the same time, with two drastically different purposes and prerequisites (although I have to say this is quite unusual), this is preferably handled in two separate valuations. However, this is not the case with the above example (hence XYZ states only one assignment: they have calculated the fair market value of all outstanding shares in ABC on a non-marketable majority interest basis). Notwithstanding the above, to eliminate any possible chances of misunderstandings, were the same analyst to have two radically different assignments at the same time, this does not disqualify the fundamentals as set out above. That is, the calculated value of each assignment may very well differ, but, under the respective assignment, the resulting value should, nonetheless, be the same irrespective of the multiple or methodology applied.

12
Epilog

Although I believe (or hope anyway) that the implementation of a proper market approach valuation has been thoroughly investigated in this book, a common criticism of this kind of theoretical/rational briefing is that they do not apply in the "real world." Hence one may, after reading this book, possibly be tempted to dismiss all examples and relationships as being too perfect or too theoretical. This perception could also be reinforced by the fact that I present all peer group companies of the Engineering Corp case in an anonymous form. One might, if being conspiratorial, suspect that the "anonymization" of "Peer 1" to "Peer 10" has been forced by the simple fact that these relationships do not exist in the "real world."

This is not the case, however. Apart from the fact that in my everyday work (in the "real world") I use exactly the methodologies and relationships set out in this book (specifically, for the simple reason that it is by far the easiest to implement, I prefer methodology no. 2 in the Engineering Corp case, i.e. to calculate implied multiples of the subject company at issue based on the DCF approach and work the market approach, i.e. the scatter charts/the regressions, for verification and reconciliation), I can honestly admit that I began with 10 fictitious peers for this very reason. Punching in all numbers of my own liking, I thought it would be easier as well as clearer to show all relevant relationships and points. Or put another way, I felt that the pedagogical advantage of being able to present clear points and correlations would override the possible interest of being able to present "real" companies. Consequently, as I took the liberty to fabricate all numbers myself, I believed that all multiples, value drivers, and graphs would run smoothly as well as logically.

How wrong I was! The further I went into the calculations, the harder it became to uphold the rigor of the fictitious data. I wanted all multiples, value drivers, and graphs of the Engineering Corp case to logically hang together all through the work, even though the data was itself made up. I did not want to take the easy way and just present individual graphs as per value multiple and value driver without also being able to show clear consistency throughout the complete case study. The first multiples and graphs did work out fine, but as I added more and more multiples and graphs, the relationships and the "main thread" became messier and messier. The data and the conclusions presented in the successive graphs came to collide with the data and the conclusions presented in the preceding graphs (or put another way, when I created a new "perfect" graph, the input data of that failed to logically connect with the input data that I had just outlined in the preceding graphs). One might say that I ended up with the same type of problem that sometimes strikes fantasy authors: the storyline, surroundings, etc., in the follow-up do not (in a credible way anyway) correspond with that outlined in the original. As a consequence, clarity as well as points got lost. This issue brought a *lot* of frustration (and took a *great* amount of time).

Halfway through the work I realized that it would not hold. The fictitious matrix had gotten too messy and too complex to handle. If one end of the "rope" was pulled to dress up a relationship/graph, simultaneously another relationship/graph was ruined. However, the way out was simpler than I had ever imagined. Out of sheer frustration I exchanged the fictitious data for that of ten "real" companies, drawing historical data from their annual reports and forward-looking data from independent equity research analysts (as retrieved from Bloomberg/I/B/E/S). The very second the "real" data was fed into the model, the matrix straightened up. To say that I gave myself a lot of unnecessary trouble is an understatement.

Peers 1 to 10 in the Engineering Corp case are thus derivatives of the Swedish listed engineering companies Alfa Laval, Atlas Copco, Haldex, Sandvik, Seco Tools, SKF, Trelleborg, Cardo, Munters, and KMT.

Like so much else, life is sometimes stranger than fiction. Had I fully trusted the theory from start I would have been spared the whole fictitious data faux pas. Notwithstanding this, the good that came out of this magnificent fiasco was the ultimate reality-based proof that the theories and relationships presented in this book not only try to describe the reality – but *are* in fact reality.

Appendix

Brief Derivation of the Respective Value Multiple's Individual Value Drivers

Definitions:

EV	=	Enterprise value (market value of operating/invested capital)
BEV	=	Book enterprise value (book value of operating/invested capital)
P	=	Price (market value of equity)
BV	=	Book value of equity
Sales	=	Revenues
EBIT	=	Earnings before interest and tax
EBIT%	=	EBIT margin
E	=	Earnings after tax
FCFF	=	Free cash flow to firm
FCFE	=	Free cash flow to equity
WACC	=	Weighted average cost of capital
K_e	=	Cost of equity
g	=	Growth rate
ROIC	=	Return on invested capital (return on operating capital)
ROE	=	Return on equity
T	=	Tax rate
NIR	=	Net investment ratio
RR	=	Retention ratio

(a) EV/Sales

In its most basic form the value of a business enterprise (under a going concern assumption) is given by the discounted cash valuation flow model (i.e. "Gordon's formula"):

$$EV = \frac{FCFF_1}{WACC - g}$$

$FCFF_1$ may be expressed as follows:

$$FCFF_1 = FCFF_0 (1 + g)$$

$FCFF_0$ may also be expressed as:

$$FCFF_0 = Sales \times EBIT\% (1 - T)(1 - NIR)$$

Substituting the term $FCFF_1$ in our cash flow valuation model (in Gordon's formula) with the equivalents above, we reach the following:

$$EV = \frac{Sales \times EBIT\% (1 - T)(1 - NIR)(1 + g)}{WACC - g}$$

Dividing both sides by Sales, we arrive at:

$$\frac{EV}{Sales} = \frac{EBIT\% (1 - T)(1 - NIR)(1 + g)}{WACC - g}$$

From that we can state that the EV/Sales multiple is driven by operating margin (EBIT%), tax rate (T), invested capital net investment ratio (NIR), growth (g), and the required rate of return on invested capital (WACC).

(b) EV/EBIT

In its most basic form the value of a business enterprise (under a going concern assumption) is given by the discounted cash flow valuation model (i.e. "Gordon's formula"):

$$EV = \frac{FCFF_1}{WACC - g}$$

$FCFF_1$ may be expressed as follows:

$$FCFF_1 = FCFF_0 (1 + g)$$

$FCFF_0$ may also be expressed as:

$$FCFF_0 = EBIT (1 - T)(1 - NIR)$$

Substituting the term $FCFF_1$ in our cash flow valuation model (in Gordon's formula) with the equivalents above, we reach the following:

$$EV = \frac{EBIT(1-T)(1-NIR)(1+g)}{WACC-g}$$

Dividing both sides by EBIT, we arrive at:

$$\frac{EV}{EBIT} = \frac{(1-T)(1-NIR)(1+g)}{WACC-g}$$

From that we can state that the EV/EBIT multiple is driven by tax rate (T), invested capital reinvestment ratio (NIR), growth (g), and the required rate of return on invested capital (WACC).

(c) EV/BEV

In its most basic form the value of a business enterprise (under a going concern assumption) is given by the discounted cash flow valuation model (i.e. "Gordon's formula"):

$$EV = \frac{FCFF_1}{WACC-g}$$

$FCFF_1$ may be expressed as follows:

$$FCFF_1 = FCFF_0(1+g)$$

$FCFF_0$ may also be expressed as:

$$FCFF_0 = BEV \times ROIC(1-T)(1-NIR)$$

Substituting the term $FCFF_1$ in our cash flow valuation model (in Gordon's formula) with the equivalents above, we reach the following:

$$EV = \frac{BEV \times ROIC(1-T)(1-NIR)(1+g)}{WACC-g}$$

Dividing both sides by BEV, we arrive at:

$$\frac{EV}{BEV} = \frac{ROIC(1-T)(1-NIR)(1+g)}{WACC-g}$$

From that we can state that the EV/BEV multiple is driven by return on invested capital (ROIC), tax rate (T), invested capital net investment ratio (NIR), growth (g), and the required rate of return on invested capital (WACC).

(d) P/E

In its most basic form the equity value of a company (under a going concern assumption) is given by the discounted cash flow valuation model (i.e. "Gordon's formula"):

$$P = \frac{FCFE_1}{K_e - g}$$

$FCFE_1$ may be expressed as follows:

$$FCFE_1 = FCFE_0 (1 + g)$$

$FCFE_0$ may also be expressed as:

$$FCFE_0 = E(1 - RR)$$

Substituting the term $FCFE_1$ in our cash flow valuation model (in Gordon's formula) with the equivalents above, we reach the following (note: 1 − RR equals dividend payout ratio):

$$P = \frac{E(1 - RR)(1 + g)}{K_e - g}$$

Dividing both sides by E, we arrive at:

$$\frac{P}{E} = \frac{(1 - RR)(1 + g)}{K_e - g}$$

From that we can state that the P/E multiple is driven by equity retention ratio (RR), growth (g), and the required rate of return on equity (K_e).

(e) P/BV

In its most basic form the equity value of a company (under a going concern assumption) is given by the discounted cash flow valuation model (i.e. "Gordon's formula"):

$$P = \frac{FCFE_1}{K_e - g}$$

$FCFE_1$ may be expressed as follows:

$$FCFE_1 = FCFE_0 (1+g)$$

$FCFE_0$ may also be expressed as:

$$FCFE_0 = BV \times ROE(1-RR)$$

Substituting the term $FCFE_1$ in our cash flow valuation model (in Gordon's formula) with the equivalents above, we reach the following (note: $1 - RR$ equals dividend payout ratio):

$$P = \frac{BV \times ROE(1-RR)(1+g)}{K_e - g}$$

Dividing both sides by BV, we arrive at:

$$\frac{P}{BV} = \frac{ROE(1-RR)(1+g)}{K_e - g}$$

From that we can state that the P/BV multiple is driven by return on equity (ROE), equity retention ratio (RR), growth (g), and the required rate of return on equity (K_e).

Index